Taxation, Economy, and Revolt in Ancient Rome, Galilee, and Egypt

This volume introduces new perspectives on taxation policies in the Roman Empire, the Galilee, and Egypt, with unique insights into the economic effects of imperial pacification on local and regional microlevel economies in the Galilee both before and after the First Jewish Revolt against Rome.

Through examining tax documents and other ancient texts in detail, this book offers innovative perspectives on the mechanisms, ideological justifications, and politically hierarchizing functions of taxation and tribute, particularly in the Roman Empire. Moreover, leading archaeologists present important information about the economic effects of the First Jewish Revolt on local economies in the Galilee, based on findings from recent archaeological excavations.

Taxation, Economy, and Revolt in Ancient Rome, Galilee, and Egypt is of interest to students and scholars in Classical, Biblical, and Jewish Studies, as well as economic history and Mediterranean archaeology.

Thomas R. Blanton IV is Associated Fellow at the Max Weber Centre, University of Erfurt (Germany). He is coeditor, with David B. Hollander and John T. Fitzgerald, of *The Extramercantile Economies of Greek and Roman Cities* (Routledge, 2019).

Agnes Choi is Associate Professor of Religion at Pacific Lutheran University, USA.

Jinyu Liu is Professor of Classical Studies at DePauw University, USA, with a guest professorship appointment at Shanghai Normal University, China. She is the author of *Collegia Centonariorum: The Guilds of Textile Dealers in the Roman West* (Brill, 2009).

Routledge Monographs in Classical Studies

Recent titles include:

Married Life in Greco-Roman Antiquity
Edited by Claude-Emmanuelle Centlivres Challet

Future Thinking in Roman Culture
New Approaches to History, Memory, and Cognition
Edited by Maggie L. Popkin and Diana Y. Ng

Aristotle and the Animals
The Logos of Life Itself
Claudia Zatta

The *Aeneid* and the Modern World
Interdisciplinary Perspectives on Vergil's Epic in the 20th and 21st Centuries
Edited by J.R. O'Neill and Adam Rigoni

The Province of Achaea in the 2nd Century CE
The Past Present
Edited by Anna Kouremenos

Making and Unmaking Ancient Memory
Edited by Martine De Marre and Rajiv Bhola

Production, Trade, and Connectivity in Pre-Roman Italy
Edited by Jeremy Armstrong and Sheira Cohen

Taxation, Economy, and Revolt in Ancient Rome, Galilee, and Egypt
Edited by Thomas R. Blanton IV, Agnes Choi, and Jinyu Liu

For more information on this series, visit: https://www.routledge.com/Routledge-Monographs-in-Classical-Studies/book-series/RMCS

Taxation, Economy, and Revolt in Ancient Rome, Galilee, and Egypt

Edited by
Thomas R. Blanton IV,
Agnes Choi, and Jinyu Liu

Routledge
Taylor & Francis Group
LONDON AND NEW YORK

First published 2022
by Routledge
4 Park Square, Milton Park, Abingdon, Oxon OX14 4RN

and by Routledge
605 Third Avenue, New York, NY 10158

Routledge is an imprint of the Taylor & Francis Group, an informa business

British Library Cataloguing-in-Publication Data
A catalogue record for this book is available from the British Library

Library of Congress Cataloging-in-Publication Data
A catalog record has been requested for this book

ISBN: 978-0-367-47220-7 (hbk)
ISBN: 978-1-032-26422-6 (pbk)
ISBN: 978-1-003-04169-6 (ebk)

DOI: 10.4324/9781003041696

Typeset in Times New Roman
by KnowledgeWorks Global Ltd.

Agnes dedicates this work to her parents, Daniel and Winnie

Jinyu dedicates this work to Fuya, Amy, and Allen

Tom dedicates this work to Zach and May May

Contents

Contributors

Mordechai Aviam is an archaeologist at the Department of Land of Israel Studies at Kinneret College, Israel, and serves as the Director of Kinneret Institute for Galilean Archaeology. His recent excavations include the Shiḥin Excavation Project and the El-Araj project, and recent publications include: *The Land of Lost Villages: Survey of Shomera Map* (with D. Shalem; Tzemah, 2021); "In Search of the City of the Apostles" (with S. Notley), *Novum Testamentum* 63 (2021): 143–58; "The Ancient Synagogues in the Galilee," *Early Christianity* 3, no. 10 (2019): 292–314; "A 1st–2nd Century CE Assembly Room (Synagogue?) in a Jewish Estate at Tel Rekhesh, Lower Galilee" (with H. Kuwabara, S. Hasegawa, and Y. Paz), *Tel Aviv* 46, no. 1 (2019): 128–42; and "Excavations of Three Byzantine Churches in the Western Galilee: Two Churches at Horvat Karkara and the Eastern Church at Horvat Eirav, a Preliminary Report" (with A. Cohen-Tavor and J. Ashkenazi), in A. Coniglio and A. Ricco (eds.), *Holy Land: Archaeology on Either Side; Papers Presented to Fr. Eugenio Alliata* (Jerusalem: Franciscan Printing Press, 2020).

Thomas R. Blanton IV is Associated Fellow at the Max Weber Centre for Advanced Social and Cultural Studies, University of Erfurt (Germany). He is the author of *A Spiritual Economy: Gift Exchange in the Letters of Paul of Tarsus* (Yale University Press, 2017) and coeditor (with David B. Hollander and John T. Fitzgerald) of *The Extramercantile Economies of Greek and Roman Cities: New Perspectives on the Economic History of Classical Antiquity* (Routledge, 2019). He is currently writing a monograph entitled *The Circumcision of Abraham: Modeling Ritual from Genesis to the Letters of Paul* for the Anchor Yale Bible Reference Library.

Agnes Choi is Associate Professor of New Testament at Pacific Lutheran University. She is the associate editor of the *Handbook of Women Biblical Interpreters* and is currently working on ancient mobility, the economy of Galilee in the Roman period, and the development of the early Jesus movement in that context.

David A. Fiensy is Emeritus Professor of New Testament at Kentucky Christian University and the author most recently of *The Archaeology of Daily Life: Ordinary Persons in Late Second Temple Israel* (Cascade, 2020).

John T. Fitzgerald is Professor of New Testament and Early Christianity at the University of Notre Dame (USA) and Extraordinary Researcher at North-West University (Potchefstroom, South Africa). One of the founders of the early Christianity and the ancient economy project, he served as a coeditor for *The Extramercantile Economies of Greek and Roman Cities* (Routledge, 2019), to which he also contributed a chapter on early Greek economic thought.

David B. Hollander is Professor of History at Iowa State University. He is the author of *Money in the Late Roman Republic* (Brill, 2007) and *Farmers and Agriculture in the Roman Economy* (Routledge, 2018). He edited *The Extramercantile Economies of Greek and Roman Cities* (with Thomas R. Blanton IV and John T. Fitzgerald; Routledge, 2019) and *A Companion to Ancient Agriculture* (with Timothy Howe, 2020). He also serves as an editor for Wiley's *Encyclopedia of Ancient History.*

G. Anthony (Tony) Keddie is Associate Professor of Early Christian History and Literature at the University of British Columbia in Vancouver, Canada. His recent publications include *Revelations of Ideology: Apocalyptic Class Politics in Early Roman Palestine* (Brill, 2018), *Class and Power in Roman Palestine: The Socioeconomic Setting of Judaism and Christian Origins* (Cambridge, 2019), and *The Struggle over Class: Socioeconomic Analysis of Ancient Christian Texts* (coedited with Steven Friesen and Michael Flexsenhar; SBL, 2021). His current work explores labor practices and occupational identities in the eastern Roman provinces and the New Testament.

Jinyu Liu is Professor of Classical Studies at DePauw University (USA) and has been a Distinguished Guest Professor at Shanghai Normal University (China) since 2014. She is the author of *Collegia Centonariorum: The Guilds of Textile Dealers in the Roman West* (Brill, 2009) and *An Introductory Research Guide to Roman History* (in Chinese; Peking University Press, 1st ed., 2014; repr. 2016; 2nd ed., 2021). Her published articles range from those on Latin inscriptions, the ancient associations, and receptions of Virgil in China, to Chinese translation of and commentary on Ovid.

C. Thomas McCollough is Nelson and Mary McDowell Rodes Professor of Religion Emeritus at Centre College and is the Director of the Osher Lifelong Learning Institute at Coastal Carolina University. He is the Director of the Archaeological Excavations at Khirbet Qana and the Associate Director of the Shiḥin Excavation Project. His books include *Archaeology and the Galilee: Text and Context in the Graeco-Roman and*

Byzantine Periods (with D. Edwards) and *The Archaeology of Difference: Gender, Ethnicity, Class and The Other in Antiquity* (with D. Edwards). His most recent publication is "The Synagogue at Khirbet Qana in Its Village Context" in R. Bonnie, R. Hakola, and U. Tervahaunta, eds., *The Synagogue in Ancient Palestine: Current Issues and Emerging Trends* (Göttingen: Vandenhoeck & Ruprecht, 2021).

James Riley Strange is Charles Jackson Granade and Elizabeth Donald Granade Professor in New Testament at Samford University. He is a coauthor (with Mordechai Aviam) of "Shiḥin Excavation Project: Oil Lamp Production at Ancient Shiḥin" (2017); he is a coeditor (with David Fiensy) of the two-volume set, *Galilee in the Late Second Temple and Mishnaic Periods* (Fortress, 2014 and 2015). He directs the Shiḥin Excavation Project in Israel.

Jürgen K. Zangenberg (PhD, NT Studies; Heidelberg, 1996) is Chair for the History and Culture of Ancient Judaism and Early Christianity at the faculty of Humanities at Leiden University, The Netherlands. His main research interests are in ancient Judaism and early Christian literature and culture in a Mediterranean context, Qumran, Samaritans, Galilee, and the Jesus movement and Gospel traditions. He is Codirector of Kinneret Regional Project and field director of excavations at Horvat Kur/Galilee. His recent publications include, e.g., M. Tiwald and J. K. Zangenberg, eds., *Early Christianity in Town and Countryside: Essays on the Urban and Rural Worlds of Early Christianity* (Göttingen, 2021); and the articles "Will the Real Women Please Sit Down: Interior Space, Seating Arrangements, and Female Presence in the Byzantine Synagogue of Horvat Kur in Galilee," in M. Bauks, K. Galor, and J. Hartenstein, eds., *Gender and Social Norms in Ancient Israel, Early Judaism and Christianity: Texts and Material Culture* (Göttingen, 2019), 91–117; "Anchoring Ancient Galilee at the Lakeshore: Towards Re-conceptionalizing Ancient Galilee as a Mediterranean Environment," *Early Christianity* 19 (2019): 265–91; and "High Noon at Jacob's Well: Jesus Taking a Rest at Sychar in Samaria (John 4:4–6)," in press for P. N. Anderson, ed., *Archaeology, John and Jesus: What Recent Discoveries Show about Jesus from the Gospel of John* (Grand Rapids, 2022).

List of Abbreviations

Ancient Texts

1 Macc	1 Maccabees
1–2 Cor	1–2 Corinthians
Acts	Acts
A.J.	Josephus, *Antiquitates judaicae*
Alc.	Ps.-Andocides, *Against Alcibiades* (*Or.* 4)
Anab.	Arrian, *Anabasis of Alexander*
Ann.	Tacitus, *Annales*
Anton. Pium	Fronto, *Epistulae ad Antoninum Pium*
Apol.	Tertullian, *Apologeticus*
Areop.	Isocrates, *Areopagiticus* (*Or.* 7)
Aug.	Suetonius, *Divus Augustus*
Av.	Aristophanes, *Aves*
Avod. Zar.	Avodah Zarah
b.	Babylonian Talmud
B.J.	Josephus, *Bellum judaicum*
C. Ap.	Josephus, *Contra Apionem*
Cal.	Suetonius, *Gaius Caligula*
Cant. Rab.	Canticles Rabbah
Civ.	Augustine, *De civitate Dei*
Claud.	Suetonius, *Divus Claudius*
Conf.	John Cassian, *Conferences*
Const.	Hyginus, *Constitutio* (*Limitum*)
Diatr.	Epictetus, *Diatribai*
Dig.	Ulpian, *Digesta*
Ep.	Isocrates, *Epistulae*; Pliny the Younger, *Epistulae*; Seneca, *Epistulae morales*
Epig.	Martial, *Epigrams*
Epit.	Florus, *Epitome of Roman History*
Geogr.	Strabo, *Geographica*
Had.	*SHA*, *Hadrian*
Hell.	Xenophon, *Hellenica*

Hist.	Herodotus, *Historiae*; Polybius, *Historiae*; Tacitus, *Historiae*; Thucydides, *Historiae*; Velleius Paterculus, *Historiarum Libri Duo*; Xenophon, *Historiae*
Hist. eccl.	Eusebius, *Historia ecclesiastica*
Hist. rom.	Dio Cassius, *Historiae romanae*
John	John
Ketub.	Ketubbot
Leg. man.	Cicero, *Pro Lege manilia* (*De imperio Cn. Pompeii*)
Lib. spec.	Martial, *Liber spectaculorum*
Luke	Luke
m.	Mishnah
Mark	Mark
Matt	Matthew
Mem.	Valerius Maximus, *Facta et dicta memorabilia*
Natal.	John Chrysostom, *In diem natalem Christi*
Ner.	Suetonius, *Nero*
Off.	Cicero, *De officiis*
Or.	Isocrates, *Orationes*
Pan.	Pliny the Younger, *Panegyricus*
Panath.	Aelius Aristides, *Panathenaicus*; Isocrates, *Panathenaicus* (*Or.* 12)
Paneg.	Isocrates, *Panegyricus* (*Or.* 4)
Pol.	Aristotle, *Politica*
Rom	Romans
Rosh Hash.	Rosh Hashanah
Sat.	Juvenal, *Satirae*
Sem.	Semahot
SHA	*Scriptores Historiae Augustae*
Sheqal.	Sheqalim
Sotah	Sotah
Tib.	Suetonius, *Tiberius*
Verr.	Cicero, *In Verrem*
Vesp.	Suetonius, *Vespasianus*
Vita	Josephus, *Vita*
Vit. phil.	Diogenes Laertius, *Vitae philosophorum*
y.	Jerusalem Talmud
Yad.	Yadayim

Editions of Papyri and Patristic Texts

BGU	*Aegyptische Urkunden aus den Königlichen Staatlichen Museen zu Berlin, Griechische Urkunden*. 15 vols. Berlin: Weidmann, 1895–1937.
CPJ	Tcherikover, Victor, Alexander Fuks, Noah Hacham, and Tal Ilan, eds. *Corpus papyrorum Judaicarum*.

	4 vols. Cambridge: Harvard University Press; Berlin: De Gruyter Oldenbourg, 1957–2020.
P.Berl.Leihg.	Kalén, T. *Berliner Leihgabe griechischer Papyri.* Uppsala: Lundequist, 1932.
P.Col.	Westermann, W. L., et al., eds. *Columbia Papyri.* 11 vols. New York: Columbia University Press, 1929–1998.
PG	Migne, Jacques-Paul, ed. Patrologia Graeca [= *Patrologiae Cursus Completus: Series Graeca*]. 161 vols. Paris: Migne, 1857–1886.
P.Ḥev./Se.	Cotton, Hannah, and Ada Yardeni, eds. *Aramaic, Hebrew, and Greek Documentary Texts from Naḥal Ḥever and Other Sites: With an Appendix Containing Alleged Qumran Texts.* Discoveries in the Judaean Desert 27. Oxford: Clarendon, 1997.
P.Jud.Des.Misc.	Charlesworth, James H., ed. *Miscellaneous Texts from the Judaean Desert.* Discoveries in the Judaean Desert 38. Oxford: Clarendon, 2000.
P.Mich.	*Michigan Papyri.* Ann Arbor: University of Michigan Press, 1931–.
P.Mil.	Calderini, Aristide, and Sergio Daris, eds. *Papiri Milanesi.* Milan: Vita e Pensiero, 1928–1967.
P.Oxy.	Grenfell, Bernard P., et al., eds. *The Oxyrhynchus Papyri.* London: Egypt Exploration Fund, 1898–.
P.Rev.	Grenfell, Bernard P., and J. P. Mahaffy, eds. *Revenue Laws of Ptolemy Philadelphus: Edited from a Greek Papyrus in the Bodleian Library with a Translation, Commentary and Appendices.* Oxford: Clarendon Press, 1896.
P.Tebt.	Grenfell, Bernard P., et al., eds. *The Tebtunis Papyri.* London: Egypt Exploration Society, 1902–.
P.Yad.	Lewis, Naphtali, ed. *The Documents from the Bar Kokhba Period in the Cave of Letters.* Judean Desert Studies. Jerusalem: Israel Exploration Society, 1989.
SB	Preisigke, Friedrich, Friedrich Bilabel, Hans-Albert Rupprecht, and Andrea Jördens, eds. *Sammelbuch griechischer Urkunden aus Ägypten.* Strasbourg: Trubner; Wiesbaden: Harrassowitz, 1915–.

Figures

Tables

Introduction

Thomas R. Blanton IV, Agnes Choi, and Jinyu Liu

The present volume examines two related issues concerning the economies of Rome and two of its provinces, Judea, and, to a lesser extent, Egypt. The volume addresses issues of taxation—how taxes were collected, how they served not only economic but also ideological functions by labeling (and thus constructing) and hierarchizing subject populations, and how they were understood by provincials—as well as the economic effects of imperial pacification in the province of Judea, and more specifically in its northern region, the Galilee. This interdisciplinary volume assesses data provided by well-known Greek and Latin texts (e.g., Thucydides, Aelius Aristides), Egyptian and Arabian census and other taxation documents, and recent archaeological excavations in the Galilee. Recent archaeological work offers an excellent opportunity not only to see how local provincial economies generally fared under Roman rule but also to permit a degree of specificity that is rarely encountered in studies of the Roman economy: Galilean archaeological surveys allow us to compare economic conditions both before and after an unsuccessful revolt against an imperial power. In what follows, we contextualize the present volume both within the ongoing work of the Early Christianity and the Ancient Economy project and within recent studies of Roman taxation; summarize the contexts of the essays collected in the volume; and—to mark the historic circumstances we are living in—offer some brief comments on publishing in a time of pandemic.

Project History

The present volume is the second produced under the auspices of the Early Christianity and the Ancient Economy (ECAE) program unit of the Society of Biblical Literature (SBL).[1] The first volume, *The Extramercantile Economies of Greek and Roman Cities: New Perspectives on the Economic History of Classical Antiquity*, argued that although recent studies of the "ancient economy" influenced by New Institutional Economics (NIE) tend to focus on economic activity directly connected with *markets*, much of the production and transmission of goods and services in antiquity occurred outside of market exchanges; for example, euergetism, personal benefaction,

DOI: 10.4324/9781003041696-1

and activities taking place in associative contexts, such as communal meals.[2] Thus, a robust account of the "ancient economy" must integrate these and other extramercantile aspects into its framework. A programmatic essay by Thomas Blanton and David Hollander (2019) in the *Extramercantile Economies* volume assessed various theoretical frameworks for examining ancient Mediterranean economies, including NIE, economic anthropology, and *régulation* theory, to propose ways in which that goal might be accomplished. Stemming from the same ECAE project, the present volume both presupposes and extends those earlier discussions. In his Epilogue to the present volume, Jürgen Zangenberg correctly points out that the volume does not include a stand-alone contribution on theory and method in the study of ancient economies. The editors note, however, that this volume occurs within the context of a larger project in which pertinent methodological issues have already been addressed. Moreover, in the following section, we briefly situate the current volume both within the broader ECAE project and within recent studies of taxation.

Situating the Present Volume within Discussions of the Roman Economy and Roman Taxation

To add to the methodological issues previously discussed in the *Extramercantile Economies* volume, we briefly indicate how the issue of taxation falls within the broader purview of the study of the Roman economy. Although, as Hollander points out in the present volume, it is difficult to assess the amount of total taxes (and tribute, we may add) collected in the Roman Empire, much less to give a year-by-year account of the value of such contributions; nonetheless, as Peter Bang (2012: 201; see also Bang, 2007) has argued, "Redistribution of wealth and economic resources [through plunder, confiscation of agricultural lands, and taxation] was staggering and must easily have been the single most significant and dynamic factor shaping economic developments." In his study of the "sacred economy" of ancient Israel, Roland Boer (2015) characterizes the economies of Assyria, Babylonia, and Persia as "regimes of plunder," in which military forces directly extracted wealth in the form of booty, and indirectly extracted it in the form of tribute; in the latter case, only the threat of military force, and not its actual implementation, provided the incentive. Regions that were militarily pacified or that simply capitulated were induced to pay taxes to their conquerors. Rome's economy can be characterized along similar lines, as Bang's comment, cited above, already suggests.

Classicists have studied the fiscal impact that Rome's collection of taxes and tributes has had *from the Roman perspective*; that is, by showing how such sources of wealth served to swell imperial coffers. However, the question is less frequently reversed to ask how the provinces themselves fared as the result of Roman economic depredation. We may thus diagnose a strongly Rome-centered perspective in classics. Although this is perhaps to be expected, given that elite literature in Latin (and Greek) forms part of the basis of classical studies, the ECAE project—and indeed the contributions in this volume—holds that the economies of the *provinces themselves* are to be understood as component parts of the Roman imperial economy. Thus, rather than attempting to assess the value of the wealth that the province of Judea contributed *to Rome*, the essays in Part 2 of this volume address economic questions from the provincial perspective: What effect did the destruction and expropriation of resources in the Galilee have on local and regional microlevel economies around the time of the First Jewish Revolt against Rome in 66/67 to 70 CE; for example, in Shikhin, Yodefat, and Khirbet Qana? And how did provincials, both local and regional administrators and the populace at large, perceive and react to Roman demands for the payment of taxes—the question addressed in Part 1 of the present volume?

The essays in the present volume thus contribute to a shift in perspective from one centered on *Rome's benefit* from practices of imperial extraction and expropriation to one that also evaluates the *costs to the provinces* of those same practices. Thus we seek to supplement a Rome-centered perspective with what might be described as a "view from the provinces." The provincial picture that emerges from the essays in this volume is complex: although some Galilean towns (Yodefat and Gamla) were destroyed, resulting in a total loss of their resources and productive capacities, others potentially benefitted from increased possibilities for trade as Roman roads were built in the region (see the contributions of Mordechai Aviam and C. Thomas McCollough herein).

Although Boer's (2015: 187–8) generalization that market activity in antiquity is "a by-product of government needs" (esp., provisioning armies) is overstated, he is certainly correct to point out the close relation between markets and economic predation conducted by states. Philip Kay (2014) has argued convincingly that predation provided Rome with wealth that subsequently stimulated markets. Money and resources expropriated from conquered states provided Rome with a steady income in the form of war indemnities (*phoros* or *stipendium*), *manubiae* ("plunder" or "booty"), and natural resources (e.g., mines). Rome also benefitted from the imposition of taxes in the form of fixed sums (*vectigalia*), agricultural tithes (*decumae*), and *portoria*, or "customs dues" assessed on items transported for sale on the market (see further Agnes Choi's article herein). Mercantile and extramercantile aspects of ancient Mediterranean economies were often intertwined.

"Taxation has always been a central issue in political economy because it is one of the main activities of all states and a necessary condition for everything else states do. It is the core feature of state capacity" (Kiser and Karceski, 2017: 76). Not surprisingly, taxation has featured prominently in the study of the state and economy in premodern states, including the Roman Empire (e.g., Rathbone, 1996; Lo Cascio, 2007; Monson and Scheidel, 2015; Bowman, 2018: 27–52). In terms of the structural and institutional determinants of tax revenue in the Roman Empire, scholars have arrived at different evaluations of the overall tax rates, with some arguing for a relatively low level of taxation (Hopkins, 1980; Scheidel and Friesen, 2009: 61–91; Scheidel, 2015: 229–57), and others insisting on a relatively high level of taxation (Duncan-Jones, 1994; MacMullen, 1987: 737–54; Bowman, 2018; see further the article of Hollander herein). Due to the competition between taxation and rents, the different assessments of tax pressure have resulted in divergent assessments of how many resources were left at the local level, which would have a direct impact on urban prosperity.

The diverse scholarly opinions concerning the tax burden in the Roman Empire can partly be accounted for by the lack of systematic and continuous data, but they are also rooted in the complexity and even the "messiness" of taxation in the Roman Empire. The sources that we have do not give rise to a neat or streamlined picture of Roman taxation (Günther, 2016). Nor do they allow us to say that the purpose of Roman taxation was exclusively about generating revenue. For example, the *fiscus Iudaicus*, imposed in the aftermath of the First Revolt against Rome, seems to have served a penal function by redirecting a tax formerly paid by Judeans to the Jerusalem Temple toward the new purpose of providing funds for the renovation of the Temple of Jupiter Capitolinus in Rome: revenue was thus generated in a manner that humiliated the vanquished party (Josephus, *B.J.* 7.218). Furthermore, while the power disparity between the state and the taxpayers and the predatory nature of taxation have been repeatedly emphasized and elaborated (Bang, 2012 and 2015; similarly, Boer, 2015), the realities of tax collection might have been more tortuous. In the context of studying violence in Roman Egypt, for example, Ari Z. Bryen has documented papyri that have preserved petitions against reckless and abusive behaviors of the tax collectors (e.g., *SB* VI 9458 from Tebtynis, second century CE; Bryen, 2013: 246) as well as petitions from tax collectors complaining about physical violence and/or threats directed at them (Bryen, 2013: 106). In his study of public finance in the Republican period, James Tan has connected taxation with bargaining power on the part of the tax payers, whose bargaining power also became curtailed and compromised when they were exempted from taxation (Tan, 2015; 2017).

All of these insights point to the necessity of more investigation into the realities of taxation on the ground to enable a thorough unfolding of the dynamic interactions between the political, social, financial, and psychological dimensions of taxation. That can to a great extent characterize the direction of the newly published edited volume entitled *Ancient Taxation: The Mechanics of Extraction in Comparative Perspective* (Valk and Soto Marín, 2021), which provides case studies concerning the challenges of taxation, especially with respect to extractive practices from diverse states and societies across the ancient world. The present volume further contributes to enriching our understanding of the complexities and realities of ancient taxation through a series of case studies focusing on various empirical facets of taxation (organization, delivery, compliance, resistance, evasion, its "routinizing" function, and so on) and involving nonmarket aspects of the ancient economies of Rome, Judea, and Egypt.

The essays herein consist of revised and enlarged versions of papers first presented at two sessions of the Early Christianity and the Ancient Economy program unit at the 2018 and 2019 Annual Meetings of the SBL. The sessions included invited papers on taxation in the Roman Empire and the economies of Judea and the Galilee before and after the First Jewish Revolt against Rome by leading archaeologists, classicists, and scholars of early Christianity. Because researchers were invited to address specific topics in the meetings—issues of taxation in the Hellenistic and Roman periods at the 2019 meeting, and the economy of the Galilee before and after the First Jewish Revolt against Rome at the 2018 meeting; represented in Parts 1 and 2 of this volume, respectively—we believe that the essays herein are better integrated than one might otherwise expect in a volume of papers that were first delivered at conferences. Moreover, the two parts of the present volume can clearly be seen as extending the focus on "extramercantile economies" already begun in the project's earlier publication, *The Extramercantile Economies of Greek and Roman Cities*. Whereas the former volume focused on issues of euergetism and associative practices, the present volume moves to consider issues of expropriation and property destruction in the provinces, particularly in the region of the Galilee in Roman Judea, but also in Egypt and Arabia.

Pursuing in greater detail issues raised in the previous volume produced by the Early Christianity and the Ancient Economy program unit, the present volume breaks new ground and aims to reshape current discussions of the economies of Mediterranean antiquity by introducing into the discussion extramercantile factors such as refugeeism, property destruction, and banditry that, although generally overlooked in studies of ancient economies, nonetheless constituted significant factors affecting the production and allocation of resources in ancient Galilee and Judea. Moreover, the volume suggests new approaches to better conceptualize regional economies as interrelated systems that exert mutual, although frequently asymmetric, influence upon each other and upon other regions within the system. Thus, it is not enough simply to study, for example, taxation in relation to the amount of wealth it contributed to imperial coffers; rather, it must be studied from an integrative perspective that takes into account both the revenue generated by those who collected taxes and the concomitant expenditures of those who paid them. That is, the "view from Rome" needs now to be supplemented by a "view from the provinces and on the ground," a process of supplementation to which the present volume contributes.

Overview of Contents

Part I of the present volume concerns taxation, both in Egypt and in the broader Roman Empire. In Chapter 1, John T. Fitzgerald makes an analytical distinction between taxation, imposed upon those who understand themselves to belong within the state that levies the tax; and tribute, imposed upon the inhabitants of external or "foreign" states. Surveying the imposition of tribute by states from third-century BCE Mesopotamia to mid-first century BCE Persia, and subsequently Greece and Rome, Fitzgerald charts a range of responses to the economic practice, ranging from its denunciation by subject states to its wholesale ideological legitimation by Thucydides, for example, who views it as a corollary of what he takes to be a veritable law of nature: the rule of the weak by the powerful. During the Roman period, Aelius Aristides opines that although the imposition of tribute contravenes the principles of equality, fairness, and justice, it is nonetheless justified in practice by a more compelling principle, the "law of superior power." The chapter thus illustrates the ideological mechanisms used to justify a more or less systematically imposed form of extraction that was utilized widely by the "superior powers" of Mediterranean antiquity. As the exponents of both NIE and *régulation* theory point out, ideological factors are not incidental, but structural components of economic systems.[3]

In Chapter 2, Agnes Choi describes the mechanics of tax assessment and tax collection in Ptolemaic and Roman Egypt, based on a close analysis of tax documents from the Tebtynis (and other) papyri that detail the ownership, size, status (as royal, sacred, or cleruchic land), condition, and crop yield of fields such as those in the village of Kerkeosiris in the southwest Fayum circa 120 to 110 BCE, as well as the collection, storage, and delivery of in-kind taxes from those fields, eventually to be delivered to regional centers. Choi points to the interaction of scribal officials representing various regional and local levels, including the nome, district, and village, in a highly organized system of taxation and rent collection that involved significant urban-rural interaction and mobility, at least for those tasked with recording, collecting, storing, and transporting foodstuffs in payment of in-kind taxes.

In Chapter 3, David B. Hollander outlines recent discussions about rates of taxation and GDP in the Roman Empire, noting that numerous elements of the Roman fiscal system are very difficult to quantify, including proceeds derived from rents on public land, liturgies, state-owned mines, and booty. Taxes and tax rates, moreover, were inconsistent; they could be imposed, cancelled, changed, or avoided. In contrast to the problems this variability entails for quantitative studies of taxation in the Roman Empire, Hollander makes three observations of a nonquantitative sort: taxes were "routinely opaque," that is, not easily determined with exactness by the general populace, which facilitated malfeasance on the part of local collectors; they were inconsistent; and they were unfair, sometimes appearing even to serve a penal function (e.g., the *fiscus Iudaicus*). The chapter points to aspects of taxation that are often elided in studies that focus more narrowly on imperial tax revenue that could be used, for example, to provision Rome's massive army.

In Chapter 4, G. Anthony Keddie expands on what Hollander describes as the "unfair" taxation policies of Rome, arguing that Roman censuses collected information that went beyond the minimum needed to facilitate the collection of capitation and land taxes; the information was used to generate lists of persons and groups subject to particular forms of taxation, liturgies, or tax discounts, in practices that normalized the structure of the patriarchal household and constructions of ethnicity, the imposition of the special tax on Judeans after the First Jewish Revolt being a case in point. Moreover, in contrast to a common assumption in New Testament studies, the imposition of Roman taxes in the provinces did not always raise the tax burden; in many cases, it likely remained the same or even decreased relative to previous regimes of taxation, as is evident in Egypt. Keddie's chapter indicates that taxation served both to routinize and to construct sociopolitical differences and to allocate both privileged and marginal status.

Part II of the present volume considers the economies of Judea and the Galilee before and after the First Jewish Revolt, examining the differential effects of Roman imperialism on local economies in a series of case studies. Chapter 5, by Mordechai Aviam, focuses on the economies of Judea and the Galilee. Based on the results of archaeological surveys, some of which he conducted, Aviam compares the evidence for the economic prosperity of four sites in the Galilee before and after the First Revolt: Yodefat, Gamla, Magdala, and Tel Rekhesh. All four sites showed signs of prosperity and economic surplus prior to the First Revolt, including a mansion at Yodefat, a large synagogue at Gamla, an elaborate synagogue with frescoes painted in the Second Pompeian Style at Magdala, and a farmstead, perhaps with its own small synagogue, at Tel Rekhesh. Both Yodefat and Gamla were destroyed by the Roman army and never rebuilt. Magdala's northern quarter, a commercial sector, suffered a rapid decline in the first century CE that Aviam indicates was a result of the war, but otherwise the fishing town continued to exist into the second century. Similarly, the farmstead at Tel Rehkesh survived into the first decades of the second century. The results of the Second Jewish Revolt circa 132 to 136 CE were more severe: "all Judean villages were destroyed and abandoned."

In Chapter 6, C. Thomas McCollough surveys the changes evident in the archaeological record of the village Khirbet Qana (or Cana), some 7 kilometers north-northeast of Sepphoris. In the early first century CE, Cana was a modest village with no public structures, connected to surrounding villages by footpaths, and apparently dominated by subsistence agriculture. In the late first and early second centuries CE, the number and size of houses increased, a synagogue was built, and the conversion of water cisterns for use in grain storage provides evidence for a shift to the marketing of grain. These changes seem to be spurred both by the building of a Roman road in the vicinity and an influx of people and wealth from Judea in the aftermath of the First Revolt. Alongside these changes is some evidence for resistance to Roman cultural influence, including an apparent avoidance of Roman coinage and imported fine wares such as Eastern Terra Sigillata A, and an absence of pig bones. Thus, the presence of roadways, refugeeism (a topic taken up in James Riley Strange's contribution; see below), religio-ethnic identification, and the presence of markets and regional trade were all factors shaping Cana's village economy, which, in stark contrast to Yodefat and Gamla, received a significant stimulus as the result of Roman imperialism.

In Chapter 7, David A. Fiensy takes issue with a prominent strand of New Testament scholarship that views banditry as a product of economic crisis (e.g., oppressive taxation, loss of land, and indebtedness) and social disruption (e.g., through foreign conquest and ineffective government) that resulted in part from the Roman occupation of Judea. (As we have already noted, the essays by Hollander and Keddie deal with the issue of taxation in greater detail, with Keddie suggesting that under Roman imperial rule, taxes in Egypt were assessed at rates that were relatively continuous with or even slightly less than those assessed during the late Ptolemaic period.) Fiensy argues against an idealized view of bandits as Robin Hood figures who robbed from the rich to give to the poor; rather, they robbed indiscriminately, sometimes employing violence, to enrich themselves. Moreover, a 2011 study by economists Olaf de Groot, Anja Shortland, and Matthew Rablen indicates that contemporary piracy (banditry at sea) is not associated with regions where governance is either very efficient or very inefficient, but instead occurs somewhere in between; in a sort of governmental "sweet spot" that is both lax enough for crime to take place and stable enough to allow pirates to transport and sell their stolen goods through the agency of intermediaries. If there was a rise in banditry in first-century Judea, Fiensy argues, this suggests a "weakly effective" government, neither wholly dysfunctional nor highly effective in keeping order. Fiensy's discussion points to an area of the ancient economy that exists *outside* the market in the sense that bandits take by force and without payment, and *on the margins* of the market (i.e., in the "underground economy") in the sense that they sell the goods they acquire to intermediaries who then make their own profits by reselling the same goods *within* other, "legitimate" or quasi-legitimate markets.

Chapter 8, by James Riley Strange, develops a theme that was adumbrated by McCollough's essay, refugeeism. Strange plausibly postulates that as the result of large numbers of casualties, mass enslavement, the destruction of Jerusalem, and Vespasian's confiscation of land in Judea in the aftermath of the First Jewish Revolt against Rome, some Judeans might have moved north to the Galilee in search of a safer and more secure environment, even as others returned to their Judean villages. Strange notes that evidence of refugeeism is difficult to detect archaeologically, particularly when refugees move into a region whose material culture is very similar, as is the case with Judea and the Galilee, and when the number of refugees is not large. Strange notes that lamp-making capacity at Shikhin, a village near Sepphoris, increased during the late first century CE. More importantly, during the same period, craftsmen at Shikhin began producing the so-called Northern Darom lamp, itself based on the Darom ("Southern")-type lamp that Varda Sussman proposes originated in Judea. Strange posits that the apparent spread of the lamp form from south to north could be explained by the movement of refugees who took their craft with them as they migrated northward in the wake of the First Revolt, noting, however, that the hypothesis is tentative and needs to be corroborated by additional lines of evidence.

Finally, the volume is rounded out by an Epilogue in which Jürgen K. Zangenberg critically assesses the collected essays and raises issues for further research.

Brief Comments on Working in a Time of Multiple Global Crises

On March 24, 2020, the editors of the present volume received an email from Amy Davis-Poynter, Commissioning Editor in Classics, Archaeology, and Biblical Studies at Routledge. The email, labeled with the heading, "COVID-19 update for Routledge contracted authors," noted that many authors worldwide were experiencing "difficulties … with library closures, childcare issues, switching to online teaching, and the whole host of other issues that have arisen from the pandemic." Although it is nothing new to publishers to receive manuscripts after the contracted due date, it is highly unusual for publishers to send out mass emails to their authors offering to extend publication deadlines. But unusual times call for unusual measures; and indeed, the present volume was itself submitted approximately eighteen months after the initial due date. Thus, the editors agree that some brief comments ought to be included concerning the unusual circumstances under which the present volume was produced. COVID-19 constitutes a pandemic of historic proportions, and this, we feel, should be marked here. As of November 9, 2021, the COVID-19 Dashboard published online by the Center for Systems Science and Engineering at Johns Hopkins University registered a total of 250,640,822 cases and 5,060,994 deaths globally from the pandemic.[4] This is likely to be an undercount since it relies on diagnosed cases; many cases, particularly those that do not require hospitalization, go unreported. Fortunately, several highly effective vaccines have been developed against the disease, although global distribution is highly uneven, and political polarization and misinformation hamper the implementation of vaccination policies.[5]

The pandemic brought library closures and the concomitant need to access academic resources online, parents' difficulties in obtaining childcare, school closures and "work from home" policies, and a sudden, massive shift toward online teaching. All of these changes made academic research more difficult. Researchers, however, were in many cases able to devise work-arounds to facilitate their projects, including resorting increasingly to online databases and repositories of texts, writing to other researchers working on similar topics to request copies of their most pertinent published articles in portable document format (PDF), the sharing of available resources among close colleagues, and purchasing books in lieu of borrowing the physical copies from university libraries. Scholars have strived to continue with their work, develop new skills in accessing resources online, and maintain collaboration. Yet, due to the disparity of access to resources and technology, the impact of the pandemic on different institutions or individuals as well as different regions of the world has also been unequal.

But COVID-19 was not the only notable global issue as this volume was in preparation: climate change brought unprecedented flooding to many parts of the globe, fueled wetter and slower-moving hurricanes, and contributed to hotter- and longer-burning wildfires.[6] Moreover, the killing of George Floyd by a white police officer on May 25, 2020, an incident that was video-recorded on a witness's cellphone and subsequently widely viewed on YouTube, sparked marches in protest against structural racial inequality in the United States, with participants united under the motto "Black lives matter."[7] An estimated 15 million to 26 million people participated in marches across the United States in June 2020, making Black Lives Matter perhaps the largest movement in US history (Buchanan, Bui, and Patel, 2020). Sympathetic marches were held internationally in Kyoto, Mexico City, Bogota, Berlin, Rome, and Helsinki, to name only a few of the locations.[8] Although the conviction of the officer who killed Floyd on counts of murder and manslaughter was widely viewed as a positive step toward racial justice, many of the structural issues of which the murder was a symptom remain firmly in place in the United States (Eligon et al., 2021; O'Grady, Pannett, and Hassan, 2021).

It is perhaps fitting, then, that this volume, which foregrounds the mechanisms of power and resistance in the area of political economy, has emerged at this time. Its value also lies in the fact that it compels us to consider the macro with the micro. Just as the global pandemic (macro) is related to local vaccine availability (micro), and global warming (macro) is related to hurricanes in one city or a heat dome in another (micro), so too, the Roman Empire's taxation policy (macro) was related to the microlevel economy of a particular location, whether that be Kerkeosiris, Gamla, or Khirbet Qana, for instance.[9]

Although the business of producing academic monographs was carried on successfully during the years of 2019 to 2022, when the present volume was in preparation, it was hardly "business as usual." Thus, the editors are grateful to the contributors for their labor and perseverance during these extraordinary times, and to Amy Davis-Poynter and the staff at Routledge for working with us with great patience. Lastly, we invite the reader to reap the fruits of our contributors' collective labors.

Notes

1. At the time of writing this Introduction, Thomas Blanton and Agnes Choi are the co-chairs of this unit; and Jinyu Liu also serves on the steering committee, as do Michelle Christian, John Fitzgerald, and David Hollander. Liu is also chair of the corresponding SBL international program unit.
2. Hollander, Blanton, and Fitzgerald, 2019. For a brief account of the activities of the SBL's Early Christianity and the Ancient Economy program unit, see the Introduction to that volume.
3. See, e.g., Blanton and Hollander, 2019.
4. COVID-19 Dashboard, Coronavirus Resource Center, Center for Systems Science and Engineering at Johns Hopkins University, https://coronavirus.jhu.edu/map.html, last accessed Nov. 9, 2021.
5. "COVID Vaccines: Widening Inequality and Millions Vulnerable," UN News: Global Perspective Human Stories, Sept. 19, 2021, https://news.un.org/en/story/2021/09/1100192.
6. On flooding: Eddy et al., 2021; on wildfires: Borunda, 2020; on hurricanes: Welch, 2018.
7. On Floyd's murder: Arango et al., 2021; on the marches in protest: Anon., 2020; on the Black Lives Matter movement: Black Lives Matter, Black Lives Matter Global Network Foundation, Inc., https://blacklivesmatter.com/, last accessed Oct. 28, 2021; Buchanan, Bui, and Patel, 2020.
8. "List of George Floyd Protests outside the United States," Wikipedia: The Free Encyclopedia, https://en.wikipedia.org/wiki/List_of_George_Floyd_protests_outside_the_United_States, last accessed Oct. 28, 2021.
9. On the recent heat domes in the US, see Gibbens, 2021.

Bibliography

Anon. 2020. "In Photos: Protesters March in Cities across America." *The New York Times*. June 1.

Arango, Tim, et al. 2021. "How George Floyd Died, and What Happened Next." *The New York Times*. Oct. 5.

Bang, Peter Fibiger. 2007. "Trade and Empire: In Search of Organizing Concepts for the Roman Economy." *Past and Present* 195: 3–54.

Bang, Peter Fibiger. 2012. "Predation." Pages 197–217 in *The Cambridge Companion to the Roman Economy*. Edited by Walter Scheidel. Cambridge: Cambridge University Press.

Bang, Peter Fibiger. 2015. "Tributary Empires and the New Fiscal Sociology: Some Comparative Reflections." Pages 537–56 in *Fiscal Regimes and the Political Economy of Premodern States*. Edited by Andrew Monson and Walter Scheidel. Cambridge: Cambridge University Press.

Blanton, Thomas R., IV, and David B. Hollander. 2019. "The Extramercantile Economy: An Assessment of the New Institutional Economics Paradigm in Relation to Recent Studies of Ancient Greece and Rome." Pages 8–28 in *The Extramercantile Economies of Greek and Roman Cities: New Perspectives on the Economic History of Classical Antiquity*. Edited by David B. Hollander, Thomas R. Blanton IV, and John T. Fitzgerald. London: Routledge.

Boer, Roland. 2015. *The Sacred Economy of Ancient Israel*. Library of Ancient Israel. Louisville: Westminster John Knox.

Borunda, Alejandra. 2020. "The Science Connecting Wildfires to Climate Change." *National Geographic*. September 17. https://www.nationalgeographic.com/science/article/climate-change-increases-risk-fires-western-us.

Bowman, Alan K. 2018. "The State and the Economy: Fiscality and Taxation." Pages 27–52 in *Trade, Commerce, and the State in the Roman World*. Edited by Andrew Wilson and Alan K. Bowman. Oxford: Oxford University Press.

Bryen, Ari Z. 2013. *Violence in Roman Egypt: A Study in Legal Interpretation*. Philadelphia: University of Pennsylvania Press.

Buchanan, Larry, Quoctrung Bui, and Jugal K. Patel. 2020. "Black Lives Matter May Be the Largest Movement in U.S. History." *The New York Times*. July 3.

Duncan-Jones, Richard. 1994. *Money and Government in the Roman Empire*. Cambridge: Cambridge University Press.

Eddy, Melissa, Jack Ewing, Megan Specia, and Steven Erlanger. 2021. "European Floods Are Latest Sign of a Global Warming Crisis." *The New York Times*. July 16.

Eligon, John, Tim Arango, Shaila Dewan, and Nicholas Bogel-Burroughs. 2021. "Derek Chauvin Verdict Brings a Rare Rebuke of Police Misconduct." *The New York Times*. April 20.

Gibbens, Sarah. 2021. "What Is a Heat Dome? Pacific Northwest Swelters in Record Temperatures." *National Geographic*. June 29. https://www.nationalgeographic.com/environment/article/heat-dome-deadly-hot-weather-descends-on-pacific-northwest.

Günther, Sven. 2016. "Taxation in the Greco-Roman World: The Roman Principate." In *Oxford Handbooks Online: Scholarly Research Reviews*. DOI: 10.1093/oxfordhb/9780199935390.013.38. Last accessed 2 August 2021.

Hollander, David B., Thomas R. Blanton IV, and John T. Fitzgerald, eds. 2019. *The Extramercantile Economies of Greek and Roman Cities: New Perspectives on the Economic History of Classical Antiquity*. Routledge Monographs in Classical Studies. London: Routledge.

Hopkins, Keith. 1980. "Taxes and Trade in the Roman Empire (200 B.C.–A.D. 400)." *Journal of Roman Studies* 70: 101–25.

Kay, Philip. 2014. *Rome's Economic Revolution*. Oxford: Oxford University Press.

Kiser, Edgar, and Steven M. Karceski. 2017. "Political Economy of Taxation." *Annual Review of Political Science* 20, no. 1: 75–92.

Lo Cascio, Elio. 2007. "The Early Roman Empire: The State and the Economy." Pages 619–48 in *The Cambridge Economic History of the Greco-Roman World*. Edited by Walter Scheidel, Ian Morris, and Richard P. Saller. Cambridge: Cambridge University Press.

MacMullen, Ramsay. 1987. "Tax-Pressure in the Roman Empire." *Latomus* 46: 737–54.

Monson, Andrew, and Walter Scheidel, eds. 2015. *Fiscal Regimes and the Political Economy of Premodern States*. Cambridge: Cambridge University Press.

O'Grady, Siobhán, Rachel Pannett, and Jennifer Hassan. 2021. "Verdict Heard around the World: Global Reactions to the George Floyd Case." *The Washington Post*. April 21.

Rathbone, Dominic. 1996. "The Imperial Finances." Pages 309–23 in *The Augustan Empire, 43 B.C.–A.D. 69*. Vol. 10 of *The Cambridge Ancient History*. Edited by Alan K. Bowman, Edward Champlin, and Andrew Lintott. Cambridge: Cambridge University Press.

Scheidel, Walter. 2015. "The Early Roman Monarchy." Pages 229–57 in *Fiscal Regimes and the Political Economy of Premodern States.* Edited by Andrew Monson and Walter Scheidel. Cambridge: Cambridge University Press.

Scheidel, Walter, and Steven J. Friesen. 2009. "The Size of the Economy and the Distribution of Income in the Roman Empire." *Journal of Roman Studies* 99: 61–91.

Tan, James. 2015. "The Roman Republic." Pages 208–28 in *Fiscal Regimes and the Political Economy of Premodern States.* Edited by Andrew Monson and Walter Scheidel. Cambridge: Cambridge University Press.

Tan, James. 2017. *Power and Public Finance at Rome (264–49 BCE).* New York: Oxford University Press.

Valk, Jonathan, and Irene Soto Marín, eds. 2021. *Ancient Taxation: The Mechanics of Extraction in Comparative Perspective.* Institute for the Study of the Ancient World Monographs 11. New York: New York University Press.

Welch, Craig. 2018. "Hurricanes Are Moving Slower—And That's a Huge Problem." *National Geographic.* June 6. https://www.nationalgeographic.com/science/article/hurricanes-cyclones-move-slower-drop-more-rain-climate-change-science.

Part I

Taxation in Egypt and the Roman Empire

1 Taxation and Tribute in Early State Thought and Practice

John T. Fitzgerald

There were originally two chief financial centers in the ancient Levantine and Mediterranean world. These were the temple and the palace, and their coexistence as financial institutions occurred at a time when the separation of "church" and "state" was nonexistent. There were important overlaps between these two institutions, and one of these overlaps involved taxation. As Leo Oppenheim (1947: 118) argued long ago in regard to Mesopotamia, "the secular authorities collected tax payments, dues, etc., in the same way as did the temple organization."[1] Furthermore, both institutions received mandatory payments as well as offerings that were more or less voluntary. This overlap between temple and palace was especially conspicuous in the ancient Near East, where tithes and taxes were often paid in "silver, commodity staples (barley, dates, sesame), sheep, or other animals" (Stevens, 2006: 99), and where state and temple revenues could also include conscripted labor. Many of the same overlaps between the state and its religious groups also existed in both Greece and Rome, with public and sacred finances often intertwined in various ways (Migeotte, 1998; 2006; Dignas, 2002), and with temples on occasion even extending loans to the state (Pritchard, 2012).

Taxation and Tribute

Given these facts, it is not surprising that there was also a terminological overlap. Today, we routinely use different terms to distinguish between the assets directed to these two institutions. We tend to call the mandatory payments made to the temple a "tithe" and the compulsory payments to the palace a "tax." Voluntary offerings directed to the temple and palace are both called "gifts." Ancient nomenclature, however, was often far messier and not clearly differentiated. As Marty Stevens has correctly noted (2006: 7), in ancient texts "taxes were due to the temple, tithes were presented to the palace, gifts were owed to the king, predetermined amounts of tribute were paid annually, the state appropriated gifts to the temple, and the temple made use of gifts destined for the crown."[2] Furthermore, socioeconomic considerations were sometimes operative in the terminology employed. "Peasants paid 'taxes' and the nobility gave 'gifts,'" with commodities given

DOI: 10.4324/9781003041696-3

as taxes and prestige goods accepted as gifts (Stevens, 2006: 100).[3] In this kind of institutional context, "gifts were calculated and obligatory, [and] … were, in fact, forms of taxation or remuneration" (Claessen, 1989: 48).

The practices of levying taxes and exacting tribute were well established in the ancient world long before the time of classical antiquity. Indeed, cultural anthropologist Henri J. M. Claessen (1989: 55) argues not only that taxation and tribute were characteristic of early states, but also that they were historically the two most important sources for early state economics.[4] For example, both tribute and taxes were already a firm reality in Mesopotamia as early as the third millennium BCE. As Steven Garfinkle (2012: 6920) notes with regard to the third dynasty at Ur in southern Mesopotamia, "Support for the various activities of the kings came largely from tribute, the result of raids and conquest east of the Tigris, and from taxing the wealthy provinces at the center of the state." The taxation system at Ur was remarkably developed and complex, with particular and specialized resources extracted from the various provinces and with new cities built to serve as administrative processing centers (Garfinkle, 2012: 6920).[5]

Taxes played a key role in early state ideology, which was ostensibly based on the principle of reciprocity.[6] As Claessen and Skalník (1978: 638) observe, "all categories of subjects provide the sovereign with goods and services (tribute and tax), while the sovereign for his part is responsible for his subjects' protection, law and order, and the bestowal of benevolence." Viewed in this way, taxes were seen as part of a redistributive economy and were politically justified on that basis. Yet there are at least two problems involved with this formulation. First, there is a growing debate as to whether "redistribution" is an appropriate and useful term to understand ancient palatial societies and economies (Halstead, 2011). Second, even granted a qualified use of the term "redistribution" as an economic concept, actual palatial economies "were not 'redistributive' but distributive" (Manning, 2018: 43). That is, the actual reciprocation involved in early states was often imbalanced and unequal, resulting in redistributive exploitation and enhanced social inequality (Claessen and Skalník, 1978: 614, 638–9, 644) rather than distributive justice. In such cases, the rhetoric of reciprocity functioned to justify the exploitation and served to mask the reality that reciprocation as practiced was more fictive than real.[7]

In the remaining portion of this essay, I shall focus on tribute, distinguishing it conceptually from taxes. In distinguishing between taxes and tribute, I treat taxes as contributions made by those who understand themselves to be part of the state to which their contributions are made, and tribute as contributions made to other (foreign) states.[8] If the tribute is to be given on a regular basis, "tribute relations" between the receiving state and the contributing state are created. Tribute relations are thus "a form of economic exploitation which consists of the regular appropriation of products from the conquered population which for the most part retains its former economic and social structure" (Pershits, 1979: 150).

Claessen (1989: 51) also distinguishes between taxes and tribute, but he uses redistribution as the key difference: "Taxation is found when the contributing group falls within the redistribution system, and tribute when the contributing group falls outside the redistribution." For him, "Taxation is based in [the] last analysis on some form of redistribution—tribute never" (Claessen, 1989: 51). While this is an important distinction, it remains unclear whether it is valid for large early empires, which, like Ur III, treated core provinces differently from the way it did its more distant territories.[9] Even in a league of ancient, allied states, not all allies were equal. Some states in the league were strong and remained independent, with the terms of their alliance and the amount of their financial contribution a matter of negotiation with the league's leader. Other allied states had been previously defeated in war and were clearly subservient; their obligations to the league leader were typically defined by treaty.[10] In the case of certain empires (such as Rome), some cities and states began giving tribute after being conquered or after accepting foreign rule without active resistance; at a later time, they were formally incorporated into the empire. Some benefits (such as political stability promised by the vaunted Pax Romana) were claimed as flowing to the conquered states, especially those that were administratively incorporated within a burgeoning empire. To the extent that such benefits were part of the terms agreed upon by the conqueror and the conquered for the tribute, groups paying the tribute had every right to expect the promised redistribution. The reciprocity involved was, to be sure, starkly asymmetrical, but the notion was still present.[11] This stands in stark contrast to booty and plunder, where confiscation of goods belongs ideologically to the spoils of war.[12]

The Significance of Tribute

The importance of tribute was linked to the significance of warfare for early states and empires, especially in the first millennium BCE. As Joseph Manning (2018: 189) has noted, states' war-making capacity had significant implications for "their size and endurance as well as their extractive power, and war was a critical driver in economic change and in imperial performance." War was a key aspect of fiscal policy for Assyria, Babylon, Egypt, Persia, Athens, the Hellenistic kingdoms, and Rome, as well as other states and empires. As Manning (2018: 189) puts it,

> War was a "mode of acquisition"; it was a "structural" part of premodern economies more broadly, a method of revenue extraction, a style of governance (rulers as war leaders); and the acquisitive aspect of war was something that Rome … benefitted enormously from.

Early states and empires uniformly required their subjugated enemies to pay tribute and often expected even their allies to do the same as the price they paid for the greater power's leadership and their own security.[13] In the world of Realpolitik, payment of tribute was the universal norm, with the amount due usually based on the stronger power's assessment of the subdued state's ability to pay or determined by negotiations between the parties involved. Exemption from tribute or taxes was typically a reward for loyalty and meritorious actions, a measure to facilitate the integration of a city and its citizens into the new state or empire, a means of providing relief in difficult times, or an incentive for good behavior. Such exemptions were usually temporary or dependent upon a variety of other factors, such as continuing good relations between the two states or the financial needs of the state granting the exemption.[14]

Persia

The practice of levying of tribute appears only seldom, if ever, to have been ethically questioned in the ancient world. Anyone who seriously questioned it might well have been thought to be utterly ignorant of sovereignty and the nature of things, "living, as one might say, on a different planet" (Aelius Aristides, *Panath.* 306).[15] The taking of spoils and the exaction of tribute from a conquered foe were not viewed as actions requiring any defense whatsoever.[16] Indeed, as the depiction of the tribute-bearers from twenty-three subject nations found on the monumental stairways of the Apadana building at Persepolis indicates, the influx of tribute was a cause for celebration, boasting, and propaganda.[17] States that paid tribute, by contrast, almost always viewed it as extortion, as the necessary cost of self-preservation that they were forced to pay in order to survive. At the same time, there was also an acute realization that conquering states differed in how they extracted tribute, with some rulers and/or states regarded as being more ruthless and demanding than others. In this sense, tribute extraction was viewed in the same way as slavery, where it was commonly recognized that some enslavers were harsher toward their enslaved persons than were others who claimed people as property (Fitzgerald, 2010). Herodotus, for example, distinguishes between three different Persian rulers: Cyrus the Great, Cambyses, and Darius. Cyrus (the true creator of the Achaemenid Empire) and his son Cambyses had conquered Asia (*Hist.* 3.88), and Cambyses also enlarged the empire by conquering Egypt, but it was Darius who organized and consolidated it. He established twenty provinces (satrapies), appointed governors for each province, and determined how much tribute (*phorous*) each should pay (*Hist.* 3.89.1).[18] Herodotus then says the following:

> In the reigns of Cyrus and Cambyses there had been no regular fixed tribute [*phorou*], only collection of gifts [*dōra*]. Because of his fixing of the tribute assessment, and other things of the same kind, the Persians have a saying that Darius was a shopkeeper [*kapēlos*], Cambyses a master of slaves [*despotēs*], and Cyrus a father [*patēr*]. What they mean is

> that Darius kept petty accounts for everything, that Cambyses was hard and contemptuous, and that Cyrus was gentle and contrived everything for their good.
>
> (*Hist.* 3.89.3)[19]

When a city was confronted by a demand for tribute, it was forced to decide whether to pay or to refuse to pay. The risk of refusing to pay or in ceasing to pay the tribute assessment was war, which often entailed the destruction of the city and either death or slavery for its inhabitants. In a pseudonymous letter, the presocratic philosopher Anaximenes of Miletus (sixth century BCE) is depicted as writing to his contemporary, Pythagoras, who had left his native city of Samos in the eastern Aegean for Croton in southern Italy in circa 530 BCE. Anaximenes tells Pythagoras that his move was well advised, whereas he and his fellow Milesians have a precarious situation:

> You were the best advised of us all: for now that you have moved away from Samos to Croton, you live in peace there. Aeaces's sons [i.e., the tyrant Polycrates and his brothers] commit dreadful evils, and tyrants continue to rule the Milesians. The king of the Medes too is terrifying [*deinos*] for us, unless indeed we are willing to pay him tribute. But the Ionians are about to start a war against the Medes for the sake of everyone's freedom. But if this happens, we shall lose any hope of being saved. How then could Anaximenes still think to study the heavens, living as he does in fear of death or slavery? But you find favor with the Crotonians and also the other Greeks in southern Italy; and pupils come to you even from Sicily.
> (Diogenes Laertius, *Vit. phil.* 2.5 [trans. Laks and Most, 2016: 375, 377])

In short, Ps.-Anaximenes refers here to the looming Ionian Revolt of 499–493 BCE. The Persian (Medes's) demand for tribute is depicted as so onerous that the Ionians are about to revolt, but Ps.-Anaximenes is rightly worried. The revolt proved disastrous for Miletus, which was sacked by the Persians in 494 BCE.

Greece

The Persian Wars

I begin this section by briefly rehearsing the Persian Wars so as to provide a historical background for the subsequent discussion of tribute. In the early fifth century BCE, Persia made two attempts to conquer Greece, the first by Darius and the second by Xerxes. Its first invasion, in 490 BCE, was thwarted at the Battle of Marathon that same year (Thucydides, *Hist.* 1.18.1).

A second invasion occurred a decade later in 480 BCE (Thucydides, *Hist.* 1.18.2) and was slowed but not stopped by the Spartans at Thermopylae. Next, Xerxes took Athens, with the Persians first plundering the acropolis temple and then burning the entire acropolis (Herodotus, *Hist.* 8.53). That triumph, however, marked the beginning of the end of the Persians' occupation of parts of Greece. They were decisively defeated at the naval Battle of Salamis in 479 BCE, and the invasion itself ended with their defeat at the land Battle of Plataea in 479 BCE. At the same time that one coalition of Greeks was defeating the Persians at Plataea, another Greek coalition was defeating the Persians in Ionia at the Battle of Mycale (Herodotus, *Hist.* 9.96–101). Herodotus says that the two battles took place on the same day of the same month and year. For the Greeks, the simultaneity of the two victories was no mere coincidence, but a sign of the divine ordering of events (*Hist.* 9.100–101), or, as Herodotus says elsewhere, "by coincidence of chance, God doing it" (*Hist.* 9.91); that is, "God's contrivance of a coincidence" (Grene 1987: 651). Fighting together in a common effort (*koinē*), the Greeks, led by both Athens and Sparta, had foiled Persian ambitions for mainland Greece (Thucydides, *Hist.* 5.18.2).

The Athenian Empire and the Delian League

As frequently happens following a great victory, the coordinated effort that had made possible the success against Persia ceased as soon as the imminent threat vanished. Athens and Sparta had irreconcilable differences, making their joint leadership of the alliance in the post-war period impossible (Thucydides, *Hist.* 1.18.2–3; 95.7–97.1). Their antagonism fractured the coalition of other Greek city-states, with some of them aligning themselves with Athens and others with Sparta (*Hist.* 1.18.2). The Delian League was formed in 478/477 BCE on the sacred island of Delos, with the putative purpose of continuing the war against Persia.[20] It consisted of Athens and its allies—more than 300 of them—with Athens's rule over its allies from 478 to 404 BCE often called the "Athenian Empire."[21] The exact date when the Peloponnesian League was formed is unknown and debated; it may have been formed by Sparta as early as the sixth century BCE, but it certainly existed by the time that the Delian League was formed. The two leagues differed in many ways, but the key difference for our purposes involved tribute. Sparta did not make its allies pay tribute (*phoros*), whereas Athens did. Instead of tribute, Sparta ensured that their allies had oligarchies that governed their cities in a manner that was amenable to Spartan interests (*Hist.* 1.19.1; 76.1). Athens, by contrast, did two things. First, it took over the ships of almost all of its allies, giving it a massive naval fleet. Second, it imposed tribute on its allies in the form of contributions of money (*chrēmata*: *Hist.* 1.19.1). In short, Athens "assessed the various contributions to be made for the war against Persia, and decided which states should furnish money, and which states should send ships" (*Hist.* 1.96.1).[22]

As Sarah Bolmarcich (2005) has demonstrated, Thucydides understood that the Spartans and the Athenians adopted two quite different methods for controlling its allies. Sparta did so by dictating its allies' form of government (oligarchy) and insisting that it pursue a domestic policy that was congenial to Sparta's interests. Athens, by contrast, controlled its allies' foreign policy by appropriating their naval forces and exacting tribute. "The Athenian Empire was built on the visible manifestation of Athenian power, her navy, and her money; the Peloponnesian League was built on Spartan politicking" (Bolmarcich, 2005: 32).

In requiring members of the Delian League to pay tribute, Athens partly followed Persia, using it as a model and treating tribute as an instrument of empire (Raaflaub, 2009: 98–101).[23] The tribute that Athens received from its allies enriched Athens, enhancing not only its wealth but its capacity for war. As King Archidamus of Sparta recognized, money matters, and war is not so much a matter of arms as it is of money; it is money that makes arms and their use effective (Thucydides, *Hist.* 1.88.2). Because tribute was a central aspect of Athenian foreign policy, it necessarily had to create a mechanism for administering the tribute. Thucydides writes,

> At this time [476 BCE] the officials known as "Hellenic Treasurers" were first appointed by the Athenians. These officials received the tribute [*phoron*], which was the name given to the contributions in money [*tōn chrēmatōn hē phora*]. The original sum fixed for the tribute was 460 talents. The treasury of the League was at Delos, and representative meetings were held in the temple there.
>
> (*Hist.* 1.96.2)[24]

From this point on, conflicts between Athens and its allies over the tribute were inevitable. This was especially true because "the Athenians throughout the mid-fifth century channeled the tribute to solidify and enlarge their own democratic culture at home while seeking tyrannical aggrandizement abroad."[25] Furthermore, the Athenians justified their policy politically. According to Hanson (2008: xviii),

> In the process, Thucydides says, Pericles and the Athenian intelligentsia craft a policy for their oppression. It becomes a determinist, Hobbesian doctrine which explains that power—and hence justice—always and rightly accrues to the strong (2.64; 5.97).

Indeed, even before war was officially declared, the Athenians present at a meeting of the Peloponnesian League at Sparta admitted that its own allies thought that Athens's rule was oppressive (*chalepē*) because it forced them to bear a heavy (*bary*) yoke (*Hist.* 1.77.5). They adamantly defended their state's use of its power by saying, "It has always been a rule that the weak should be subject to the strong" (*Hist.* 1.76.2). Furthermore, they believed that they merited (*axioi*) their rule and considered their use of their power as moderate (*Hist.* 1.76.3–4; 77.2). In their view, the proper reaction of their allies should have been gratitude (*charis*) rather than indignant vexation (*chalepōteron*):

> Our subjects … are used to being treated as equals [*isou*]; consequently, when they are disappointed in what they think right and suffer even the smallest disadvantage … because of the power [*dynamei*] that our empire gives us, they cease to feel grateful [*charin*] to us for all of the advantages which we have left to them.
>
> (Thucydides, *Hist.* 1.77.3)

Melos and the Melian Dialogue

As an example of Athenian conflict with its allies over tribute, I shall focus on Melos and do so by briefly discussing the Melian Dialogue of Thucydides (*Hist.* 5.84–116). I have chosen it because it is a famous early Greek example of negotiations between emissaries of an imperial force and the leaders of a threatened city.[26] Thucydides himself was not present to hear what was actually said, so the dialogue represents what he believed would have been appropriate for both groups to say on the occasion. Although he has tailored the dialogue to fit the historical situation of Athens and Melos, he is almost certainly drawing upon a longstanding tradition of interstate negotiations and the kinds of remarks that were typically made on both sides of a confrontation. The Melian Dialogue is thus a dramatic representation of arguments typically made on such occasions.

The context of this dialogue is the Second Peloponnesian War (441–404 BCE) between Athens and its allies (the Delian League) and Sparta and its allies (the Peloponnesian League). Melos, an island in the Aegean, was a Spartan colony with a strong Doric identity (*Hist.* 5.84.2, 89, 106, 112.2), but when the war broke out, it sought to remain neutral (*Hist.* 5.84.2; Bauslaugh, 1991: 113–7). In 426 BCE, Athens had attempted unsuccessfully to force Melos to join the Delian League (*Hist.* 3.91.1–2)—or at least contribute financially to it—possibly after the Melians had made a contribution to the Spartan war fund (Loomis, 1992). They made a second attempt in 416 BCE, and this is the setting for the dialogue.

A full analysis of the dialogue is beyond the scope of this essay, but three things stand out. First, the Athenian emissaries argue that appeals to justice are irrelevant in situations involving unequal powers: "In human negotiations justice is taken into account [only] when there is equal power to compel" (*Hist.* 5.89).[27] When a greater military power (Athens) confronts a lesser one (Melos), "the powerful exact what they can and the weak suffer what they must" (5.89). Second, the Melians refuse to concede the Athenian claim that justice is irrelevant to those who are militarily weaker. They declare that their cause is just (5.86) and that the Athenians are ignoring justice (5.90); they even assert that the Athenians are unjust, whereas they are pious (5.104). Because of this, they contend that the gods will help them to resist the Athenians: "We trust that, so far as fortune is concerned, we shall through divine favor be at no disadvantage because we are god-fearing men standing our ground against unjust men" (5.104). Third, the Athenians reject the Melians' theological argument: "Our opinion of the gods and our knowledge of humans lead us to conclude that it is a general and necessary law of nature to rule whatever one can" (5.105.2). The gods rule by virtue of their power, and powerful humans do the same. This is a law (*nomos*) that corresponds to both divine and human nature (*physis*). Therefore, inasmuch as it is the divinely ordained nature of reality for the strong to rule over the weak, the Athenians can be confident of divine favor if negotiations fail and war ensues. In short, in support of the Melians' case for remaining neutral and not paying tribute to Athens, Thucydides has their leaders make a number of arguments. The latter include both moral and theological arguments, but neither proves persuasive. The Athenians thus began taking steps against the Melians and felt morally and theologically justified in doing so. The result was a horrific siege that ended with the execution of all the men of military age and the sale of the women and children into slavery (5.116.4).

The point is that both sides in this confrontation had arguments in support of their actions. The same was doubtless true in many similar situations. Those cities and states that paid tribute usually felt that they were being extorted, and they did so ultimately because they thought acquiescence to the demands of a stronger force was more prudent than resistance. There appears to be little evidence that the stronger party ever felt any remorse about making their financial demands. What did prompt criticism and debate were the kinds of actions taken by the conquering army when a city or state refused to give the demanded tribute and offered military resistance. When conquering powers were deemed to have used excessive force to punish the conquered city or state, some individuals and states condemned their extreme brutality. This is exactly what happened following the Athenian atrocities at Melos, which had been preceded by the same atrocities at Scione in 421 BCE, five years earlier (*Hist.* 4.122.6; 5.32.1).[28] Because the men of military age had been massacred and the women and children sold into slavery at both Melos and Scione, the Athenian actions at these two places were often remembered together.

Responses to the Melian Siege, Massacre, and Enslavement

The first surviving comment on the atrocity at Melos was made by Aristophanes in his comedy *Birds*, which was produced in 414 BCE, two years after the siege and subsequent massacre. He refers to the "Melian famine" in a line (*Av.* 186) often taken as a casual joke (so Henderson 2000: 8), though it may well have a serious political and religious underlying point.[29]

Romer (1994) argues that Aristophanes is also alluding here and elsewhere in the *Birds* to Diagoras of Miletus, the famous atheist:

> In 416 it was the Athenian demos who (like Peisetairos) had been both *atheos* and *turannikos*, for, in that year the Athenians' *Realpolitik* had defeated not only the Melians' trust in the Spartans but also their trust in the gods (Thuc[ydides, *Hist.*] 5.104). Peisetairos' *limos* is *atheos* precisely because it is an assault on the established gods by those who no longer credit the gods.
>
> (Romer, 1994: 358)

The first substantial response to Melos was given by Isocrates in two of his orations. Both orations reveal how adverse the reaction to the notorious incident was in some circles. The first is his *Panegyricus* (*Or.* 4), a speech that was written over some ten to fifteen years and was finished circa 380 BCE, thus some thirty-five to forty years after the atrocities had occurred. In the intervening years, the Second Peloponnesian War had ended (404 BCE), with Sparta victorious over Athens and the Delian League dissolved. Sparta's victory, which had been made possible by the financial support of Persia, meant that it was now totally free to pursue its hegemonic ambitions, which it did by embracing an expansionist policy. From 404 to 371 BCE, Sparta thus "dominated the lives of the Greeks" (Fine, 1983: 578).[30] Resistance by other Greek cities was inevitable. Widespread fear of Spartan expansionism in Asia Minor and Greece led to the Corinthian War (395–386 BCE), which pitted Sparta against not only Athens, but also its former allies Corinth and Thebes, as well as Persia (Hornblower, 2012).

The hostilities ended with the King's Peace of 387/386 BCE, a royal edict issued by the Persian king Artaxerxes II. The edict appears to have been the result of an agreement worked out between Artaxerxes and Antalcidas of Sparta (and thus the agreement is also known as the Peace of Antalcidas). Both Sparta and Persia gained significantly from the accord. Persia gained politically by having its longstanding claims for the cities of Asia Minor acknowledged, along with its wish for sovereignty over Clazomenae and Cyprus granted (Xenophon, *Hell.* 5.1.31). This arrangement enabled it to include the Greek Asiatic cities within the Achaemenid Empire and begin to administer them. Sparta's position was also vastly improved (Xenophon, *Hell.* 5.1.36). The autonomy of the mainland Greek cities (with a few exceptions) was recognized by the King's Peace, which enabled Sparta to continue its hegemonic ambitions for the control of Greece without fear of Persian intervention. In short, by 380 BCE, the date when the *Panegyricus* was published, "most Greek states saw Sparta, not Persia, as the chief menace to their autonomy" (Usher, 1990: 10).

Isocrates's *Panegyricus* is an appeal for a resumption of Athenian hegemony and reflects the conviction that Persia remained the most dangerous enemy. Following the prooemium (*Paneg.* 1–14) and statement of the main proposition (15–20), the speech has two major sections—the first largely epideictic (23–128, followed by 129–32) and the second deliberative (133–69)—and concludes with an epilogue (170–89). In keeping with epideictic speech in general, the first section is an effusive glorification of Athens. Using both mythical and historical arguments, Isocrates presents "Athens' claim to the moral and cultural leadership of the Greek world," and he "demonstrates [its] Panhellenic sympathies by enumerating the cultural benefits in which Athens allows the other Greek cities to participate" (Usher, 1990: 19). He next extols Athens's military record in the Persian Wars (up to the victory at Salamis in 480 BCE) by rehearsing its various victories and achievements in war, thus demonstrating its prowess. In short, since Athens is a proven leader, the other Greek cities should unite under its leadership and conduct a national, Panhellenic war against Persia, its common enemy (Fine, 1983: 566). Indeed, he even says that "all would agree that our city has been the source of the most benefits, and that the leadership should be hers by right" (*Paneg.* 100).[31]

It is precisely here, where he claims that it is "just" (*dikaiōs*: *Paneg.* 100; see also 18, 20) for Athens to lead the coalition, that he is forced to address a problem that he previously had glossed over in patriotically lavishing praise on Athens; namely, the Athenians' atrocities at Melos and Scione:

> But regarding subsequent history there are some who accuse us of being responsible for many evils [*kakōn*] against the Greeks after we took over command of the sea. They cite against us the enslavement [*andrapodismon*] of the Melians and the annihilation [*olethron*] of the Scionians.
>
> (*Paneg.* 100)

As we have seen, the conclusion of the Persian Wars had led to the formation of the Delian League in 478/477, and it existed until 404 BCE, when the League was dissolved following Sparta's victory. So, the key question left unanswered by Isocrates in his glowing encomium on Athenian leadership was, quite simply, what kind of record had it compiled as leader of the Delian League? The critics mentioned by Isocrates certainly included Sparta and undoubtedly some Athenians as well, especially those whose political viewpoint differed from that of Pericles and his supporters. Even before the Second Peloponnesian War formally began, Sparta and its allies had a long list of grievances against Athens and members of the Delian League (Thucydides, *Hist.* 1.67.1, 3–4; 68.2; 69.2, 6; 79.2; 82.1; 86.1–2; etc.), and Athens already had crushed the revolts of some of its own disenchanted allies (*Hist.* 1.75.4).[32] In his speech to the Peloponnesian League, the Spartan ephor Sthenelaidas argues that the Athenians had a good track record regarding Persia, but a bad record against Sparta and their allies. In short, "they once were good [*agathōn*], but now have become bad [*kakoi*]" (*Hist.* 1.86.1).

The harsh truth is that Melos and Scione were not completely isolated events, exceptions to an otherwise spotless record. The reality was that, as Xenophon acknowledges, the Athenians had treated "many other of the

Greeks" harshly, including the Histiaeans, the Toronaeans, and the Aeginetans (*Hell.* 2.2.3). It was the Athenians' knowledge of what they had done to other Greeks that made them fear, following their disastrous defeat at the Battle of Aegospotami—the last and decisive battle of the Second Peloponnesian War—that they would suffer the same horrible fate that they had "unjustly" (*ēdikoun*) inflicted on others in "wanton violence" (*hybrin*: *Hell.* 2.2.10).

Isocrates offers two responses to the critics of Athenian actions. The first is as follows:

> It is my view, however, firstly, that it is no proof that we ruled badly [*kakōs*] if some who waged war against us were severely punished [*spodra … kolasthentes*], but a much more convincing indication that we administered the alliance's affairs fairly [*kalōs*] is to be found in the fact that none of the cities that stayed under our control suffered these hardships.
>
> (*Paneg.* 101)

Here, Isocrates minimizes the atrocities, calling them "severe punishment" and "hardships" or "misfortunes" (*symphorais*). He describes the actions of Melos and Scione as "waging war" (*polemēsantōn*), using the active participle so as to emphasize their agency, but switches to the passive participle *kolasthentes* ("being punished") in order to obscure the historical facts and to minimize Athenian agency (Usher, 1990: 174; Seaman, 1997: 414, n. 105). In short, he argues that it was the disobedience of Melos and Scione that led to their punishment; the fact that the Athenians did not treat obedient allies in this same way is offered as proof that they had led the league properly. In his *Aeropagiticus*, Isocrates mentions the allies making their financial contributions (*syntaxeis*) in conjunction with them obeying Athenian commands (*to prostattomenon poiountas*: *Areop.* 2). For him, paying tribute is a matter of following orders, and not paying it is disobedience, which cannot be permitted.

Isocrates's second response is:

> In the second place, if others had dealt more mildly [*praoteron*] with the same situations, they might reasonably criticise [*epitimōen*] us; but since this has not been the case, and it is impossible to govern [*kratein*] such a large number of states if one does not punish [*kolazē*] offenders [*examartanontas*], how are we not actually deserving of praise [*epainein*], when we were able to hold on to our empire for the longest time, while dealing harshly [*chalepēnantes*] with the smallest [*elachistois*] number of our subjects?
>
> (*Paneg.* 102)

In this second part of Isocrates's *apologia* for Athenian rule during most of the fifth century BCE, he repeats his assertion that Athens's actions constituted punishment, this time making explicit that the real "offenders" (*examartanontas*) were the Melians and Scionians. It is impossible to govern either well or for any long period of time—in the case of Athens some sixty-five (*Panath.* 56) or seventy years (*Paneg.* 106)—without punishing offenders, and it is only in a "very small" (*elachistois*) number of cases that Athens has resorted to harsh punishment. On the whole, they have governed with moderation and mildness—no state has been "milder" (*praoteron*). In short, Athenian rule has resulted in its empire enjoying "the greatest number of benefits" (*pleistōn agathōn*) with "the smallest number" (*elachistois*) of severe actions, with Isocrates using the two superlatives to bracket his entire discussion (Usher, 1990: 174). It is therefore "just" (*dikaion*) to give the Athenians praise rather than censure.

The last time that Isocrates mentions the Melians is in his *Panathenaicus*, his last oration, which he finished writing and published in 339 BCE, at the age of 97. Like the *Panegyricus*, it is a glorification of Athens, but it differs from it in many respects. One of these differences involves Melos. Here he mentions them twice. The first time is in *Panath.* 63 in the midst of a comparison (*synkrisis*) of the Athenians and Spartans, where he complains that Athens's critics "always" (*aei*) denounce it by recounting the "most offensive" (*dyscherestatas*) acts that occurred during the heyday of the Athenian Empire, by misrepresenting the way that lawsuits involving the allies were adjudicated in Athens, and, above all, by dwelling "on the cruelties [*pathē*] suffered at her hands by the Melians and the Scionians and the Toronians."[33] The second time is at *Panath.* 89, where he returns, after a digression, to the task of responding to "those who reproach [*oneidizousin*] us with the misfortunes [*symphoras*] of the Melians and of villages with like populations."

Here in the *Panathenaicus*, in stark contrast to the *Panegyricus*, he is willing to concede wrongdoing on Athens's part, not seeking to conceal it through minimization. Indeed, he says he will make no effort to refute any of the criticisms that could "justly" (*dikaiōs*) be made against Athens (*Panath.* 63). Furthermore, instead of referring to the Melians as among those who "erred" (*examartanontas*) as he did in the *Panegyricus* (102), he now freely admits that Athens had "erred" (*examartein*: *Panath.* 70; *ēmartēmenōn*: *Panath.* 89) and disavows any attempt "to persuade you that our commonwealth has never erred [*peplēmmelēken*] in any instance whatsoever" (*Panath.* 64). He says that he would be "ashamed" (*aischynoimēn*) even to make such a claim. After all, no one is without error; indeed, as is generally recognized, even the gods are "not free from error" (*anamartētous*: *Panath.* 64).[34] His defense regarding Athenian atrocities thus consists not in asserting Athens's innocence but in contending that the Spartans were far, far worse and much more reprehensible in how they abused and mistreated other cities than Athens ever was (*Panath.* 66, 89). Not only had Sparta abused more cities than Athens, but greater ones (*Panath.* 70, 89); places like Melos were, by contrast, "tiny islands" (*nēsydria*), towns "so small and insignificant that many of the Hellenes do not even know of their existence" (*Panath.* 70).

As far as the tribute itself is concerned, his defense is threefold: (1) their allies had voluntarily agreed to pay it when they conferred the leadership of the Delian League; (2) they did so, not for Athens's security, but to preserve their freedom and form of government; and (3) they paid the tribute out of resources that they possessed on account of Athens, not their own savings (*Panath.* 68). That is, Athenian aid had enabled them to become so prosperous that their contributions were only a small percentage of their total wealth, and even after paying the tribute, they were just as prosperous as cities in the Peloponnesian League that paid no tribute (*Panath.* 69). In short, Isocrates argues that the proper and "just" (*dikaiōs*) attitude of the allies toward Athens should have been "gratitude" (*charis*: *Panath.* 69), which was exactly the same viewpoint that the Athenians had before the war began (Thucydides, *Hist.* 1.77.3).

The Athenian atrocities at Melos and elsewhere were long remembered, not simply because of the prominence given to the preceding negotiations by Thucydides in his Melian Dialogue (Andrewes, 1992: 446), but also because of the magnitude of the injustice (Seaman, 1997: 414, n. 105). Later responses tend to fall into four categories. The first is simple remembrance of the atrocity, with Strabo serving as an example of this response. In discussing the islands in the Aegean, he mentions Melos and says without elaboration that an Athenian expedition to the island "had slaughtered [*katesphaxan*] most of the inhabitants from youth upwards" (*Geogr.* 10.5.1 [trans. Jones, 1928: 163]).

The second kind of response is represented by Aelius Aristides in his own glorification of Athens, the *Panathenaicus.* Aristides outdoes even the *Panegyricus* of Isocrates in his defense of Athens's actions. As Trapp (2017: 6–7) notes, Aristides (*Panath.* 302–312) defends the atrocities at Melos and Scione in two ways: by exhorting critics "to look at the Athenian record overall, rather than at particular episodes," and by insisting "on the brutal realities of imperialism."

The third kind of response was to acknowledge Athenian fault, but to place most of the blame on Alcibiades, the controversial Athenian general, thus making him the scapegoat for the state's inhumane actions. This tradition is represented by the *Against Alcibiades* (*Or.* 4) of Ps.-Andocides, who accuses him of not only recommending the sale of the Melian survivors into slavery, but also purchasing one of the Melian women and fathering a son by her. He regards these actions as odious and beyond the pale of acceptable conduct, going to "the extreme limits of errors" (*tōn hamartēmatōn hyperbolas*: *Alc.* 22–23) and being conspicuous among the many egregious actions that warranted Alcibiades's ostracism (*Alc.* 2, 40).[35] Plutarch in his *Life of Alcibiades* follows this tradition, repeating the story that he took one of the Melian women to be his mistress and later fathered a son by her. Yet he differs from Ps.-Andocides by viewing Alcibiades's actions toward the woman and her son as "humane" (*philanthrōpon*) rather than reprehensible, and he makes the cutting of the Melians' throats (*aposphagēnai*) mostly Alcibiades's responsibility (*tēn pleistēn aitian*) because he had supported the decree calling for the men's execution (*Alc.* 16.4–5).

The fourth kind of response is represented by Arrian, who did not hesitate to castigate the Athenians for what they had done. He called the Athenians' actions at Melos "shameful" (*aischynē*) and "shocking" (*paralogon*). Yet the former outweighed the latter, for the capture of Melos "brought more shame to the perpetrators than any great shock to the whole Greek world" (*Anab.* 1.9.5 [trans. Brunt, 1976: 41]).

Conclusion, with Comments on Rome

Both the levying of taxes and the extraction of tribute played an important role in the formation of early states and even more so in the strategies of early empires. This essay has focused on tribute, treating Persia briefly and concentrating on the Athenian Empire and its imposition of tribute on its allies during the fifth century BCE. Tribute was assessed according to a state's size and ability to pay, with some states contributing ships and others money. Both of these forms of tribute added to Athens's wealth and strengthened its military capacity, especially at sea. Athens responded aggressively to quell revolts of allied cities and to punish any state that refused to pay tribute. That included even city-states such as Melos that wished to remain neutral in the conflict between Athens and Sparta. Forcing other states to pay tribute was by no means an unusual practice, but the severity of its treatment of Melos sparked intense debate and was remembered for centuries as a serious blight on Athens's record.

Rome, too, was imperialistic, with not only its powerful generals but especially its senators taking "the lead in imperialism in both its principal senses: in exploitation and in aggression" (Badian, 1968: 79).[36] Cicero, who was fully capable of using imperialist rhetoric when it served his purposes (Rose, 1995), spoke for many Romans when he exclaimed, "What a splendid thing it is to rule over foreign nations" (*praeclarum esset exteris gentibus imperare*: *Verr.* 2.2.1.2). Peter A. Brunt (1978: 160) states the Roman view of their burgeoning empire by saying:

> The Romans themselves liked to believe that they had acquired their dominions justly, by fighting for their own security or for the protection of their allies. Victory had conferred on them the right to rule over the conquered, and they were naturally conscious that this right was profitable to them, nor were they ashamed of the booty and tribute they exacted. However, they preferred to dwell on the sheer glory of empire, which made Rome specially worthy of the devotion of her citizens.... This dominion was ordained by the gods, whose favor Rome had deserved by piety and justice, and it was exercised in the interest of the subjects.

In Cicero's view, "revenues are the sinews of the republic" (*vectigalia nervos esse rei publicae*: *Leg. man.* 17), which meant that Rome had a vested interest in levying taxes, exacting tribute, and taking spoils from the lands they conquered. Taxes, tribute, and other indemnities were "the reward for victory" (*victoriae praemium*) that Rome reaped and "the penalty of war" (*poena belli*) that defeated foes necessarily paid (Cicero, *Verr.* 2.3.6.12). Without tribute, there could be no Roman empire. As Q. Petillius Cerialis says to an assembly of the Treviri and Lingones during the Batavian revolt of 69–70 CE,

> There were always kings and wars throughout Gaul until you submitted to our laws. Although often provoked by you, the only use we have made of our rights as victors [*iure victoriae*] has been to impose on you the necessary costs of maintaining peace [*pacem*]; for you cannot secure tranquility among nations without armies, nor maintain armies without pay, nor provide pay without tribute [*tributis*].
>
> (Tacitus, *Hist.* 4.74 [trans. Moore 1931: 145, 147, slightly modified])

In addition to using tribute money to support its military, Rome used these revenues to augment its strength and wealth and thereby to lessen the tax burden of its own citizens. One of the most financially profitable victories was that of the consul L. Aemelius Paullus over King Perseus of Macedonia at Pydna in 168 BCE, which ended the Third Macedonian War (171–168 BCE). As Valerius Maximus in his *Memorable Doings and Sayings* remarks, Paullus "satiated" Rome's "hereditary poverty" with "the wealth of Macedonia," thus relieving Roman citizens of "the burden of war tax" (*Mem.* 4.3.8 [trans. Shackleton-Bailey, 2000: 375]). Indeed, Cicero (*Off.* 2.760) says, "When Paullus got possession of all the wealth of Macedon—and it was enormous—he brought into our treasury so much money that the spoils of a single general did away with the need for a tax on property in Rome for all time to come" (trans. Miller, 1913: 253; see also Polybius, *Hist.* 18.35.4–9).

As for those countries and people compelled to pay tribute, they typically viewed it, at the very least, as a burden to be tolerated (*tributa toleravere*) (Tacitus, *Hist.* 4.71). Many, however, viewed it as so onerous a financial obligation that it was tantamount to slavery. Thucydides already links the paying of tribute to slavery in book 1 of his *History of the Peloponnesian War*. In their speech to the Spartan allies prior to the declaration of war, the Corinthian representatives remark that Athens's "allies will not fail to pay tribute for their own enslavement" (*douleia*) (Thucydides, *Hist.* 1.121.5 [trans. Smyth, 1956: 611, 2968e]). They argue that Athens's opponents, by contrast, should be willing to make financial contributions to secure safety and liberty for themselves (1.121.5; 122.3). They must not only wage war but must do so successfully, for defeat would mean "downright slavery" (*antikrys douleia*: 1.122.2).

It was precisely that statement by Thucydides that Josephus used to express the viewpoint of Judas the Galilean and his supporters at the time of the Roman census and property assessment in 6 CE. "They said that the assessment carried with it a status amounting to downright slavery [*antikrys douleian*], and appealed to the nation to make a bid for independence" (*eleutherias*) (Josephus, *A.J.* 18.4 [trans. Feldman 1965: 5, 7]).[37] In short, Josephus depicts the initial Jewish resistance to Rome and its demands for tribute in terms reminiscent of the Corinthian war hawks prior to the outbreak of the Peloponnesian War.

On occasion, the Romans could acknowledge that paying tribute constituted slavery (Tacitus, *Hist.* 4.59: *servitium*), but they tended to view complaints about tribute as just the carping of the conquered, as being among "all the charges that are conventionally brought up against mighty empires" (*Hist.* 4.68.5), and particularly against Rome.[38] Rome's ultimate justification for the extraction of tribute was the "might makes right" argument, which is what Finley (1978: 59) meant when he identified hierarchy as one of the "unchallenged concepts" of antiquity: "domination was 'natural.'" Although Aelius Aristides was primarily justifying Athens's use of its power to demand tribute, he may also (as Trapp 2017: 257, n. 219, suggests) be thinking of Rome when he offers his apology for tribute. I conclude by quoting his *apologia:*

> All sovereignty [*archē*] of course belongs to the more powerful and directly contravenes the principle of equality [*isotētos*]. Otherwise, how ever is it fair [*ison*] or just [*dikaion*] to extract tribute [*phorous*] from foreign lands, or make laws for people who do not ask for them, or arbitrate over their disputes, or give them orders, or wage war, or appropriate what does not belong to you? Quite in general, none of this happens as a matter of fairness [*isou*]. Therefore anyone who quibbles about justification and prefers clever argument to acceptance of the real nature of things ought simply to strike out all forms of sovereignty and rule straight away, because all of them are covered by the law of superior power [*tō thesmō tou kreittonos*].
>
> (*Panath.* 306)

Notes

1. Hudson (2000: 3) points out that ancient communities "set aside designated lands" for both the temple and the palace "to produce an economic surplus or usufruct to support their public activities." Inasmuch as ancient societies were largely agrarian, it was "natural for the land to provide the basis for public revenue" (Hudson, 2000: 3). In addition to lands, herds of animals could also be dedicated to support the activities of the palace and temple. Furthermore, some of these lands were leased to farmers, who paid rent to both palace and temple (Hudson, 2000: 5).

2. On this terminological overlap, see also Stevens, 2006: 96, 98.
3. In early Greece, the term "gift" was applied to a wide variety of financial transactions. Homer, for example, uses the word "gift" for what would later be called "taxes and other dues to lords and kings" (Finley, 2002: 63).
4. For the groundbreaking work of Henri J. M. Claessen and Peter Skalník (1978) on the formation of early states, see Grinin (2008: 67), who calls their theory the last of "the great epoch-making political-anthropological theories" of the 1960s and 1970s. Their theory was based on the study of twenty-one early states, and they found that taxation, though administratively primitive and often ad hoc, was a frequent feature of even inchoate early states (Claessen and Skalník, 1978: 23, 641). By the time of the transitional phase of the early state, when it was nearing the next (second) stage of development (the developed state), "taxation had developed into a well-defined system, with a complex apparatus to ensure its regular flow" (Claessen and Skalník, 1978: 641). In the second stage proper, "taxation became more regular and ordered" (Claessen and Skalník, 1978: 641), and it became even more so once the third stage of development (the mature state) was reached (Grinin, 2008: 72). In sum, taxation tends to become more regular, systematic, and efficient as states evolve. For a discussion (with mixed results) of early Greece and Rome using the early state theory of Claessen and Skalník, see van der Vliet, 1990, 2008.
5. Ur III was quite extensive geographically and had different kinds of taxes, including the *măsdaria* (apparently a tax paid by provincial governors, temple administrators, and others), the *gún* (*gún-mada*), and the *bala* (Sharlach, 2004: 162–3). According to Sharlach (2008: 79), "One of the fundamental distinctions between the core territories and the other regions was their means of government. Provinces had governors, whereas outlying areas had only generals; provinces had a system of taxation known as *bala*, 'turn, rotation,' whereas external regions paid a tax called *gún-mada*, 'tax of the land.'" For studies of the *bala* system used at Ur III, see Hallo, 1960; Steinkeller, 1987; Sallaberger, 1993: 32–4; Maeda, 1994, 1995; Sharlach, 2004, 2008; and Dahl, 2006.
6. Claessen and Skalník, 1978: 23, 633–4. In their view, reciprocity began to wane during the later stages of the early state (Claessen and Skalník, 1978: 610), and the developed state was no longer founded on the principles of reciprocity and genealogical separation from the sovereign. Therefore, they "consider the period of the early state as having terminated as soon as the ideological foundation of the state no longer is based upon *these* [two] concepts [reciprocity and genealogical separation]" (Claessen and Skalník, 1978: 633). In their view, reciprocity does not necessarily disappear in the developed state; traces of it may remain, but it no longer serves as the ideological foundation of the state. The mature state is regarded as non-reciprocal (Claessen and Skalník, 1978: 610, 646).
7. According to Claessen and Skalník (1978: 644), "the development of the early state correlated with a considerable elaboration of social inequality, leading to a division of the society in question into at least two social categories (emergent social classes, superstrata), which division was at the same time concealed behind the notions of a 'social contract' ideology of which the idea of reciprocity was the key feature. The effort to overcome the problems posed by the growing cleavage of society resulted, under specific circumstances, in the development of the socio-political organization of the early state."
8. The distinction made here between taxes is conceptual rather than linguistic. The English word "tribute" derives from the Latin word *tributum*, which originally designated the war tax that Roman citizens occasionally paid through the tribes (*tribus*). For the purposes of this paper, that was a tax. For a brief treatment of Roman taxation, see Hollander, 2012.

9. See note 5 above. For a cultural anthropological discussion of the concept of empire, see Thapar, 1981, who argues against attempts to see early empires as seeking to impose uniformity upon the often vastly different kinds of states and political structures they conquered and controlled. "It need not mean the imposition of a uniform, monolithic administration, evenly in every part of the empire, but can be limited to the controlling of revenue through a series of apparently flexible relationships between the metropolitan state and the periphery" (Thapar, 1981: 425).
10. See Bolmarcich, 2005, on the vastly different states that comprised the Peloponnesian League.
11. For discussion and debate on the concept of asymmetrical reciprocity, see Orenstein, 1980.
12. Finley (1978: 59) identifies the victor's rights to the spoils of war as one of the universal rules and uncontested concepts of the ancient world. The key difference between booty and tribute is that the former is usually understood as goods forcibly acquired by the victor in the context of war and other military actions. The latter term is usually used in regard to goods given or acquired after military actions have ceased or after negotiations have ended. In her study of Sennacherib's campaign against Jerusalem and Judah, Matty (2016: 47–58) discusses both booty and tribute under the general rubric of economic exploitation. She helpfully distinguishes four different occasions for Sennacherib's taking of booty, with the two most frequent being after the conquest of a city and following an open field battle. People, domestic animals, and war equipment were the most frequent kinds of booty taken. Following Yamada (2000: 236–41), she distinguishes between "spot tributes" that are given "on the spot" following the surrender by a city or state, and "annual tributes" that are given yearly or on a regular basis. Similarly, Elat (1982) distinguishes between "tributes of surrender" and "annual tributes." Liverani (1992: 155–6) uses three categories: spot tributes, annual tributes, and tributes from afar.
13. Finley (1978: 60) includes the exaction of tribute as one of the typical characteristics of an empire, and Carusi (2012: 3424) mentions tribute as one of the principal instruments of imperialism.
14. On exemptions from taxes and tribute, see Migeotte, 2012. For examples of Jewish exemptions from tribute, taxes, and other levies, see 1 Macc 10:29–31, 33, 42; 11:28, 34; Josephus, *C. Ap.* 2.43–44 (citing Hecataeus of Abdera).
15. See also Aelius Aristides, *Panath.* 302: "Where on earth are they on land or sea that they can bring such charges?" Translations of Aelius Aristides are those of Trapp, 2017, sometimes slightly modified.
16. At Rome, spoils (especially captured arms) were conspicuously paraded in triumphal processions and even displayed on the doors and walls of private residences. See esp. Rawson, 1990.
17. See Root, 1979: 86–95, 227–84; 1985; Nylander, 1979; Jamzadeh, 1992; Boardman, 2000; and, for Persian propaganda in general, Kelly, 2003.
18. See esp. Descat, 1989; and Briant, 2002: 388–471.
19. The translation is that of Grene (1987: 252), slightly modified. For a discussion of this passage, see Scott, 2005: 47–8; and Asheri, Lloyd, and Carcella, 2007: 481–2.
20. For a brief overview of the Delian League and its history, see Papazarkadas, 2012a.
21. See, for example, Low, 2008.
22. Unless otherwise indicated, translations of Thucydides are those of Warner (1972). See note 27 below.
23. When Alexander and the other Macedonian conquerors subsequently defeated Persia in the fourth century BCE, they largely "inherited its tributary system" (Fantasia, 2012: 6857) and adapted it for their purposes, which in some cases included exemption from tribute (see Faraguna, 2003: 109–13).

24. On the league's treasurers, see Baron, 2012. In 454/453 BCE, the treasury was moved from Delos to Athens, which kept records of the tribute. On these records, known as the Athenian tribute lists, see the overview by Papazarkadas, 2012b. The amount of the first assessment and the role played in it by the Athenian general Aristides has been much debated; see, for example, Chambers, 1958; Hammond, 1967; and Finley, 2008: 21–5.
25. So Hanson, 2008: xviii, citing Thucydides, *Hist.* 1.89.1–177.3.
26. Scholarly treatments of the Melian Dialogue are extensive; see, for example, Wassermann, 1947; Hudson-Williams, 1950; Amit, 1968; Liebeschuetz, 1968; Volk, 1970; Macleod, 1974; Alker, 1988; Gómez-Lobo, 1989; Bosworth, 1993; and Seaman, 1997.
27. I have used the translations of Seaman (1997: 393) for Thucydides, *Hist.* 5.89 and 5.104, and have modified the rendering of Warner (1972) for *Hist.* 5.101. The translation of *Hist.* 5.89 combines the renderings of Jowett (1881) and Crawley (1950).
28. According to Thucydides, Scione was a Peloponnesian settlement in Pellene in northern Greece that defected from Athens and embraced the Spartan cause (*Hist.* 4.120.1; see also 2.9.2). Their defection as well as their public honoring of the Spartan commander Brasidas with a golden crown as the liberator of Hellas (*Hist.* 4.121.3) prompted harsh reprisals by Athens.
29. The *Suda* explain the phrase "Melian famine" by saying that the Melians "perished by famine" as a result of the Athenian siege. See Seaman, 1997: 405.
30. This Spartan dominance ended in 371 BCE at the Battle of Leuctra, when a coalition led by Thebes defeated Sparta and its allies.
31. Translations of the *Panegyricus* are those of Usher (1990).
32. The revolts mentioned by Thucydides included those by Naxos (*Hist.* 1.98.4) and Thasos (*Hist.* 1.100.2–101.3).
33. Translations of the *Panathenaicus* by Isocrates are those of Norlin (1929). On the revolt of Torone, see Thucydides, *Hist.* 5.2.2–3.6. The surviving men were sent to Athens, and the women and children enslaved (*Hist.* 5.3.4).
34. Earlier, in *Ep.* 2.16, Isocrates had adopted a middle position between Athenian critics and its staunch defenders: "To the bitter accusers of our city I think I should place in contrast those who say that the very opposite is true, that is, those who assert that she has done no wrong at all, whether great or small. For my part, I would not make any such claim; for I should be ashamed if, while men in general do not regard even the gods as blameless, I should dare to affirm that our city had never transgressed at all." The translation is that of Van Hook (1945: 393).
35. On the speech, see Gribble, 1997; and on Alcibiades and Melos, see esp. Vickers, 1999.
36. One of the key debates is when imperialism emerged as a conscious concept in Roman thought. Gruen (1984: 286) argues that it was late and largely retrospective: "Overseas empire as an articulated concept gained formulation only after Rome had achieved it as a fact."
37. The influence of Thucydides on Josephus has long been noted; see, for example, Feldman 1965: 6–7, n. a, and Schwartz 2002: 67, n. 7, 68, n. 11.
38. On anti-Roman rhetoric, see Städele, 1981; and esp. Rutherford, 2010. The translation of Tacitus, *Hist.* 4.68.5, is that of Rutherford (2010: 330, n. 1). For Q. Petillius Cerialis, the call for liberty was simply one of several specious pretexts for a revolt (Tacitus, *Hist.* 4.73).

Bibliography

Alker, Hayward R., Jr. 1988. "The Dialectical Logic of Thucydides' Melian Dialogue." *American Political Science Review* 82: 805–20.

Amit, M. 1968. "The Melian Dialogue and History." *Athenaeum* 46: 216–35.

Andrewes, A. 1992. "The Peace of Nicias and the Sicilian Expedition." Pages 433–63 in *The Fifth Century B.C.* Vol. 5 of *The Cambridge Ancient History*. 2nd ed. Edited by David M. Lewis, John Boardman, J. K. Davies, and M. Ostwald. Cambridge: Cambridge University Press.

Asheri, David, Alan Lloyd, and Aldo Carcella. 2007. *A Commentary on Herodotus, Books I–IV*. Edited by Oswyn Murray and Alfonso Moreno. Translated by B. Graziosi. Oxford: Oxford University Press.

Badian, Ernst. 1968. *Roman Imperialism in the Late Republic*. 2nd ed. Ithaca: Cornell University Press.

Baron, Christopher. 2012. "Hellenotamiai." Pages 3125–6 in *The Encyclopedia of Ancient History*. Edited by Roger S. Bagnall, Kai Brodersen, Craige B. Champion, Andrew Erskine, and Sabine R. Huebner. Malden, MA: Wiley-Blackwell.

Bauslaugh, R. A. 1991. *The Concept of Neutrality in Classical Greece*. Berkeley: University of California Press.

Boardman, John. 2000. *Persia and the West: An Archaeological Investigation of the Genesis of Achaemenid Persian Art*. London: Thames & Hudson.

Bolmarcich, Sarah. 2005. "Thucydides 1.19.1 and the Peloponnesian League." *Greek, Roman, and Byzantine Studies* 45: 5–34.

Bosworth, A. B. 1993. "The Humanitarian Aspect of the Melian Dialogue." *Journal of Hellenic Studies* 113: 30–44.

Briant, Pierre. 2002. *From Cyrus to Alexander: A History of the Persian Empire*. Translated by Peter T. Daniels. Winona Lakes, IN: Eisenbrauns.

Brunt, Peter A., trans. 1976. *Arrian: Anabasis of Alexander, Books 1–4*. Loeb Classical Library. Cambridge: Harvard University Press.

Brunt, Peter A. 1978. "*Laus Imperii*." Pages 159–91 in *Imperialism in the Ancient World*. Edited by P. D. A. Garnsey and C. R. Whittaker. Cambridge Classical Studies. Cambridge: Cambridge University Press.

Carusi, Cristina. 2012. "Imperialism, Greek (Classical and Hellenistic)." Pages 3424–6 in *The Encyclopedia of Ancient History*. Edited by Roger S. Bagnall, Kai Brodersen, Craige B. Champion, Andrew Erskine, and Sabine R. Huebner. Malden, MA: Wiley-Blackwell.

Chambers, Mortimer. 1958. "Four Hundred Sixty Talents." *Classical Philology* 53: 26–32.

Claessen, Henri J. M. 1989. "Tribute and Taxation—Or How to Finance Early States and Empires." Pages 45–59 in *Le tribute dans l'Empire perse: Actes de la Table ronde de Paris, 12–13 Décembre 1986*. Edited by Pierre Briant and Clarisee Herrenschmidt. Travaux de l'Institut d'études iraniennes de l'Université de la Sorbonne nouvelle 13. Paris: Peeters.

Claessen, Henri J. M., and Peter Skalník, eds. 1978. *The Early State*. New Babylon 32. Berlin: De Gruyter Mouton.

Crawley, Richard, trans. 1950. *The History of the Peloponnesian War*. Everyman's Library 455A. New York: Dutton.

Dahl, Jacob L. 2006. "Revisiting Bala." *Journal of the American Oriental Society* 126: 77–88.

Descat, Raymond. 1989. "Notes sur la politique tributaire de Darius Ier." Pages 77–93 in *Le tribute dans l'Empire perse: Actes de la Table ronde de Paris, 12–13 Décembre 1986*. Edited by Pierre Briant and Clarisee Herrenschmidt. Travaux de l'Institut d'études iraniennes de l'Université de la Sorbonne nouvelle 13. Paris: Peeters.

Dignas, Beate. 2002. *Economy of the Sacred in Hellenistic and Roman Asia Minor.* Oxford Classical Monographs. Oxford: Clarendon.

Elat, M. 1982. "The Impact of Tribute and Booty on Countries and People within the Assyrian Empire." *Archiv für Orientforschung* 19: 244–51.

Fantasia, Ugo. 2012. "Tribute." Pages 6857–8 in *The Encyclopedia of Ancient History.* Edited by Roger S. Bagnall, Kai Brodersen, Craige B. Champion, Andrew Erskine, and Sabine R. Huebner. Malden, MA: Wiley-Blackwell.

Faraguna, Michele. 2003. "Alexander and the Greeks." Pages 99–130 in *Brill's Companion to Alexander the Great.* Edited by Joseph Roisman. Leiden: Brill.

Feldman, Louis H., trans. *Josephus: Jewish Antiquities, Books XVIII–XX.* Vol. 9 of *Josephus.* Loeb Classical Library 433. Cambridge: Harvard University Press, 1965.

Fine, John V. A. 1983. *The Ancient Greeks: A Critical History.* Cambridge: Belknap.

Finley, Moses I. 1978. "Empire in the Graeco-Roman World." *Greece and Rome* 25: 1–15.

———. 2002. *The World of Odysseus.* Rev. ed. New York: New York Review Books.

———. 2008. "The Fifth-Century Athenian Empire: A Balance Sheet." Pages 14–37 in *The Athenian Empire.* Edited by Polly Low. Edinburgh Readings on the Ancient World. Edinburgh: Edinburgh University Press.

Fitzgerald, John T. 2010. "The Stoics and the Early Christians on the Treatment of Slaves." Pages 141–75 in *Stoicism in Early Christianity.* Edited by Tuomas Rasimus, Troels Engberg-Pedersen, and Ismo Dunderberg. Grand Rapids: Baker Academic.

Garfinkle, Steven. 2012. "Ur III Dynasty." Pages 6920–21 in *The Encyclopedia of Ancient History.* Edited by Roger S. Bagnall, Kai Brodersen, Craige B. Champion, Andrew Erskine, and Sabine R. Huebner. Malden, MA: Wiley-Blackwell.

Gómez-Lobo, Alfonso. 1989. "Colloquium 6: Philosophical Remarks on Thucydides' Melian Dialogue." *Proceedings of the Boston Area Colloquium in Ancient Philosophy* 5: 181–203.

Grene, David, trans. 1987. *Herodotus: The History.* Chicago: University of Chicago Press.

Gribble, David. 1997. "Rhetoric and History in [Andocides] 4, against Alcibiades." *Classical Quarterly* 47: 367–91.

Grinin, Leonid E. 2008. "Early State, Developed State, Mature State: The Statehood Evolutionary Sequence." *Social Evolution and History* 7: 67–81.

Gruen, Erich S. 1984. "The Roman Concept of Empire in the Age of Expansion." Pages 273–87 of vol. 1 of *The Hellenistic World and the Coming of Rome.* Berkeley: University of California Press.

Hallo, William W. 1960. "A Sumerian Amphictyony." *Journal of Cuneiform Studies* 14: 88–114.

Halstead, Paul. 2011. "Redistribution in Aegean Palatial Societies: Terminology, Scale, and Significance." *American Journal of Archaeology* 115: 229–35.

Hammond, N. G. L. 1967. "The Origins and Nature of the Athenian Alliance of 478/7 B.C." *Journal of Hellenic Studies* 87: 41–61.

Hanson, Victor Davis. 2008. "Introduction." Pages ix–xxiv in *The Landmark Thucydides: A Comprehensive Guide to the Peloponnesian War.* Edited by Robert B. Strassler. New York: Free Press.

Henderson, Jeffrey, trans. 2000. *Aristophanes: Birds, Lysistrata, Women at Thesmophoria.* Loeb Classical Library. Cambridge: Harvard University Press.

Hollander, David B. 2012. "Taxation, Roman." Pages 6551–3 in *The Encyclopedia of Ancient History*. Edited by Roger S. Bagnall, Kai Brodersen, Craige B. Champion, Andrew Erskine, and Sabine R. Huebner. Malden, MA: Wiley-Blackwell.

Hornblower, Simon. 2012. "Corinthian War." Page 386 in the *Oxford Classical Dictionary*. Edited by Simon Hornblower and Anthony Spawforth. 4th ed. Oxford: Oxford University Press.

Hudson, Michael. 2000. "Mesopotamia and Classical Antiquity." *American Journal of Economics and Sociology* 59, no. 5: 3–25.

Hudson-Williams, H. L. 1950. "Conventional Forms of Debate and the Melian Dialogue." *American Journal of Philology* 71: 156–69.

Jamzadeh, P. 1979. "The Apadana Stairway Reliefs and the Metaphor of Conquest." *Iranica Antiqua* 24: 125–47.

Jones, Horace L., trans. 1928. *Strabo: Geography: Books 10–12*. Loeb Classical Library. Cambridge: Harvard University Press.

Jowett, Benjamin, trans. 1881. *Thucydides*. 2 vols. Oxford: Clarendon.

Kelly, Thomas. 2003. "Persian Propaganda: A Neglected Factor in Xerxes' Invasion of Greece and Herodotus." *Iranica Antiqua* 38: 173–219.

Laks, André, and Glenn W. Most, ed. and trans. 2016. *Beginnings and Early Ionian Thinkers: Part 1*. Vol. 2 of *Early Greek Philosophers*. Loeb Classical Library. Cambridge: Harvard University Press.

Liebeschuetz, W. 1968. "The Structure and Function of the Melian Dialogue." *Journal of Hellenic Studies* 88: 73–7.

Liverani, Mario. 1992. *Topographical Analysis*. Vol. 2 of *Studies on the Annals of Ashurnasirpal II*. Quaderni di Geografica Storica 4. Rome: Università di Roma "La Sapienza."

Loomis, William T. 1992. *The Spartan War Fund: IG V 1, 1 and a New Fragment*. Historia 74. Stuttgart: Steiner.

Low, Polly, ed. 2008. *The Athenian Empire*. Edinburgh Readings on the Ancient World. Edinburgh: Edinburgh University Press.

Maeda, Tohru. 1994. "Bal-Ensi in the Drehem Texts." *Acta Sumerologica* 16: 115–64.

———. 1995. "Šà-bal-a in Umma Tablets: Bal-duty of the Ensí of Umma." *Acta Sumerologica* 17: 145–74.

Manning, Joseph G. 2018. *The Open Sea: The Economic Life of the Ancient Mediterranean World from the Iron Age to the Rise of Rome*. Princeton: Princeton University Press.

Matty, Nazek Khalid. 2016. *Sennacherib's Campaign against Judah and Jerusalem in 701 B.C.: A Historical Reconstruction*. Beihefte zur Zeitschrift für die alttestamentliche Wissenschaft 487. Berlin: De Gruyter.

Macleod, C. W. 1974. "Form and Meaning in the Melian Dialogue." *Historia* 23: 385–400.

Migeotte, Léopold. 1998. "Finances sacrées et finances publiques dans les cités grecques." Pages 181–5 in *Historia y arqueología*. Vol. 6 of *IX congreso español de estudios clásicos: Madrid, 27 al 30 de septiembre de 1995*. Edited by González Castro and José Francisco. Madrid: Ediciones Clásicas.

———. 2006. "La haute administration des finances publiques et sacrées dans les cités hellénistiques." *Chiron* 36: 379–94.

———. 2012. "Ateleia." Pages 895–6 in *The Encyclopedia of Ancient History*. Edited by Roger S. Bagnall, Kai Brodersen, Craige B. Champion, Andrew Erskine, and Sabine R. Huebner. Malden, MA: Wiley-Blackwell.

Miller, Walter, trans. 1913. *Cicero: On Duties*. Loeb Classical Library. Cambridge: Harvard University Press.

Moore, Clifford H., trans. 1931. *Tacitus: The Histories, Books IV–V*. Vol. 2 of *Tacitus*. Loeb Classical Library 249. Cambridge: Harvard University Press.

Norlin, George, trans. 1929. Vol. 3 of *Isocrates*. Loeb Classical Library. Cambridge: Harvard University Press.

Nylander, Carl. 1979. "Achaemenid Imperial Art." Pages 345–59 in *Power and Propaganda: A Symposium on Ancient Empires*. Edited by Mogens Trolle Larsen. Mesopotamia 7. Copenhagen: Akademisk Forlag.

Oppenheim, A. Leo. 1947. "A Fiscal Practice of the Ancient Near East." *Journal of Near Eastern Studies* 6: 116–20.

Orenstein, Henry. 1980. "Asymmetrical Reciprocity: A Contribution to the Theory of Political Legitimacy." *Current Anthropology* 21: 69–91.

Papazarkadas, Nikolaos. 2012a. "Delian League." Pages 1976–9 in *The Encyclopedia of Ancient History*. Edited by Roger S. Bagnall, Kai Brodersen, Craige B. Champion, Andrew Erskine, and Sabine R. Huebner. Malden: Wiley-Blackwell.

———. 2012b. "Tribute Lists, Athenian." Pages 6858–9 in *The Encyclopedia of Ancient History*. Edited by Roger S. Bagnall, Kai Brodersen, Craige B. Champion, Andrew Erskine, and Sabine R. Huebner. Malden: Wiley-Blackwell.

Pershits, Abraham J. 1979. "Tribute Relations." Pages 149–56 in *Political Anthropology: The State of the Art*. Edited by S. Lee Seaton and Henri J. M. Claessen. The Hague: Mouton.

Pritchard, David M. 2012. "Costing Festivals and War: Spending Priorities of the Athenian Democracy." *Historia* 61: 18–65.

Raaflaub, Kurt A. 2009. "Leaning from the Enemy: Athenian and Persian Instruments of Empire." Pages 89–124 in *Interpreting the Athenian Empire*. Edited by John Ma, Nikolaos Papazarkadas, and Robert Parker. London: Duckworth.

Rawson, Elizabeth. 1990. "The Antiquarian Tradition: Spoils and Representations of Foreign Armour." Pages 157–73 in *Staat und Staatlichkeit in der frühen römischen Republik*. Edited by Walter Eder. Stuttgart: Steiner.

Romer, F. E. 1994. "Atheism, Impiety and the *Limos Mēlios* in Aristophanes' *Birds*." *American Journal of Philology* 115: 351–65.

Root, Margaret Cool. 1979. *The King and Kingship in Achaemenid Art: Essays on the Creation of an Iconography of Empire*. Acta Iranica 19; Textes et Mémoires 9. Leiden: Brill.

———. 1985. "The Parthenon Frieze and the Apadana Reliefs at Persepolis: Reassessing a Programmatic Relationship." *American Journal of Archaeology* 89: 103–20.

Rose, Peter. 1995. "Cicero and the Rhetoric of Imperialism: Putting the Politics Back into Political Rhetoric." *Rhetorica* 13: 359–99.

Rutherford, Richard. 2010. "Voices of Resistance." Pages 312–30 in *Ancient Historiography and Its Contexts: Studies in Honour of A. J. Woodman*. Edited by Christina S. Kraus, John Marincola, and Christopher Pelling. Oxford: Oxford University Press.

Sallaberger, Walther. 1993. *Der kultischer Kalender der Ur III-Zeit*. 2 vols. Untersuchungen zur Assyriologie und vorderasiatischen Archäologie 7. Berlin: De Gruyter.

Schwartz, Daniel R. 2002. "Rome and the Jews: Josephus on 'Freedom' and 'Autonomy.'" Pages 65–81 in *Representations of Empire: Rome and the Mediterranean World*. Edited by Alan K. Bowman, et al. Oxford: Oxford University Press.

Scott, Lionel. 2005. *Historical Commentary on Herodotus, Book 6*. Leiden: Brill.

Seaman, Michael G. 1997. "The Athenian Expedition to Melos in 416 B.C." *Historia* 46: 385–418.

Shackleton-Bailey, D. R., ed. and trans. 2000. *Valerius Maximus: Memorable Doings and Sayings, Books I–V*. Loeb Classical Library. Cambridge: Harvard University Press.

Sharlach, Tonia M. 2004. *Provincial Taxation and the Ur III State*. Cuneiform Monographs 26. Leiden: Brill.

———. 2008. "'To Everything There Is a Season, Turn, Turn, Turn.'" Pages 79–98 in *The Growth of an Early State in Mesopotamia: Studies in Ur III Administration*. Edited by Steven J. Garfinkle and J. Cale Johnson. Biblioteca del Proximo Oriente Antiguo 5. Madrid: Consejo Superior de Investicaciones Científicas.

Smyth, Herbert W. 1956. *Greek Grammar*. Rev. Gordon M. Messing. Cambridge: Harvard University Press.

Städele, A. 1981. "Barbarenreden: Ein Beitrag zur Behandlung römischen Imperialismus im Lateinunterricht." *Anregung* 27: 248–58.

Steinkeller, Piotr. 1987. "The Administration and Economic Organization of the Ur III State: The Core and the Periphery." Pages 19–41 in *The Organization of Power: Aspects of Bureaucracy in the Ancient Near East*. Edited by McGuire Gibson and Robert D. Briggs. Studies in Ancient Oriental Civilizations 46. Chicago: Oriental Institute of the University of Chicago.

Stevens, Marty E. 2006. *Temple, Tithes, and Taxes: The Temple and the Economic Life of Ancient Israel*. Peabody, MA: Hendrickson.

Thapar, Romila. 1981. "The State as Empire." Pages 409–26 in the *Study of the State*. Edited by Henri J. M. Claessen and P. Skalník. New Babylon 35. The Hague: Mouton.

Trapp, Michael, ed. and trans. 2017. Vol. 1 of *Aelius Aristides: Orations*. Loeb Classical Library. Cambridge: Harvard University Press.

Usher, Stephen, ed. and trans. 1990. *Isocrates: Panegyricus and To Nicocles*. Greek Orators 3. Warminster: Aris & Phillips.

Van Hook, La Rue, trans. 1945. Vol. 3 of *Isocrates*. Loeb Classical Library. Cambridge: Harvard University Press.

Vickers, Michael. 1999. "Alcibiades and Melos: Thucydides 5.84–116." *Historia* 48: 265–81.

Vliet, Edward Ch. L. van der. 1990. "Early Rome and the Early State." Pages 233–57 in *Staat und Staatlichkeit in der frühen römischen Republik*. Edited by Walter Eder. Stuttgart: Steiner.

———. 2008. "The Early State, the Polis and State Formation in Early Greece." *Social Evolution and History* 7: 197–211.

Volk, Marie Therese. 1970. "The Melian Dialogue in Thucydides: A Structural Analysis." PhD diss., The Ohio State University.

Warner, Rex, trans. 1972. *Thucydides: History of the Peloponnesian War*. Rev. ed. Penguin Classics. Baltimore: Penguin.

Wassermann, Felix M. 1947. "The Melian Dialogue." *Transactions of the American Philological Association* 78: 18–36.

Yamada, Shigeo. 2000. *The Construction of the Assyrian Empire: A Historical Study of the Inscriptions of Shalmaneser III Relating to His Campaigns in the West*. Culture and History of the Ancient Near East 4. Boston: Brill.

2 The Check Is in the Mail

Assessing and Collecting Taxes in Ancient Egypt

Agnes Choi

Egypt has frequently been described as "the bread basket of the ancient world," for the crops raised in Egypt fed populations not only within, but also beyond, its borders. While earlier studies have considered the transport of foodstuffs from Egypt across the Mediterranean basin, less attention has been given to that which preceded the interregional journey at the intraregional level. While the adventures of sea travel certainly fire one's historical imagination, the more mundane activities of such individuals as the farmer and the tax collector illuminate our understanding of ancient society and the workings of its economy, for their work ensured nothing less than the food supply of the Greco-Roman world. Thus, this essay will consider the mechanics of assessing and collecting the taxes in kind in Ptolemaic and Roman Egypt that fueled her reputation as the ancient world's "bread basket." Special consideration will be given to the specific roles and responsibilities of the urban and rural figures involved, and it will be argued that urban-rural interaction was a common feature throughout the processes of tax assessment and tax collection. Before considering these two processes, it will be necessary to begin with a few words about the ancient system of tax farming.

Tax Farming in Antiquity

To the modern mind, it is perhaps surprising that taxes were not collected directly by civil servants.[1] Instead, the responsibility for tax collection was delegated through a system of tax farming that existed throughout the ancient world, including in Ptolemaic and Roman Egypt (Bingen, 2007: 160–63; Lewis, 1983: 161).[2] In this system, private individuals purchased at auction a lease to collect taxes and tolls. This tax farmer was responsible to the government for a particular tax or toll, essentially underwriting it: although he retained any surplus beyond the amount contracted, he was also responsible to pay any shortfall (Youtie, 1967: 7–8). Nevertheless, tax farming in Egypt differed from the better-known system in Rome in at

DOI: 10.4324/9781003041696-4

least one way: safeguards existed to protect the taxpayer (Youtie, 1967: 12). One safeguard related to the extent of the lease. While tax farmers submitted bids, the leases of the country were not sold to a single bidder. Instead, most leases were sold for the much smaller area of a single village. (On occasion, leases were sold for a nome or a meris.) Thus, it was quite likely that the tax farmer was resident in the district, if not the village itself, which had an important impact on tax collection. As Herbert Youtie states, "An absentee publicanus could face with equanimity the hatred of a far-off province, but any systematic attempt at extortion would make the Egyptian tax farmer a very unpopular and a very uncomfortable man" (Youtie, 1967: 13).

A second safeguard related to the compartmentalization and supervision involved in tax collection. Crown officials, who oversaw the auction of tax leases, were excluded from bidding at the annual auctions, serving as a partner in a tax-collection firm, or providing surety for a tax farmer (P.Rev. XV, 2–5; Youtie, 1967: 13; Harper, 1934b: 51–2). Further, the task of collecting taxes was not the tax farmer's responsibility. Instead, this task fell to tax collectors who were supervised by a tax farmer, but paid by the state (P.Rev. XII, 13). The individuals who worked as tax collectors were determined by government officials and tax farmers with the goal that "the staff should represent a stable element with no personal interest in the returns" (Youtie, 1967: 13–4; cf. Harper, 1934b: 52–5; Bingen, 2007: 166–9; Manning, 2010: 152–7).

Having in mind this brief overview of tax farming in Ptolemaic and Roman Egypt, we may now turn our attention to specific taxation-related tasks, their timing with respect to the agricultural calendar, and those responsible for carrying them out. Taxation-related tasks may be organized into two categories, namely tax assessment and tax collection, which will be considered in turn.

Tax Assessment in Egypt

Tax assessment was undertaken annually in Egypt in order to determine the tax and rental rates on agricultural produce. These varied from year to year, for the rates were determined on the basis of a number of variables, including: the category to which the land belonged; the physical condition of the land; the type of crop to be cultivated; and, most importantly, the extent of the flooding of the Nile in that year (Wallace, 1938: 6–7, 31; Johnson, 1959: 503).

Our understanding of the process and mechanics of tax assessment in Ptolemaic Egypt is illuminated by a careful reading of the so-called Menches archive. Between 120 and 110 BCE, Menches served as the village scribe (κωμογραμματεύς) of Kerkeosiris in the Polemon division of the

Arsinoite nome (in the southwest Fayum) (Verhoogt, 1998: 177). In this capacity, Menches's primary responsibility was the administration of the land of Kerkeosiris. This consisted of reporting on the land, land use, and agricultural produce of the village, as well as ensuring that the appropriate taxes and rents were paid (Harper, 1934a: 18; Verhoogt, 1998: 107–20).

In his study of Menches's documents, A. M. F. W. Verhoogt acknowledges the dangers of drawing conclusions about the work of village scribes on the basis of Menches's documents, not least because these documents do not actually constitute an archive. In fact, Menches's documents were first weeded by one of his successors, and the discarded documents were then reused by others who wrote their own private documents on the blank sides. Approximately twenty years later, these same pages were reused again, this time in the mummification of crocodiles that were buried southwest of Tebtynis (Verhoogt, 1998: 22–49). Verhoogt concedes, then, that "[t]he picture of the village scribe to be drawn from a collection of documents with these restrictions (regarding both nature and chronology), is likely to be restricted as well" (Verhoogt, 1998: 177). In the absence of comparative information, it is difficult to determine whether Menches was a typical village scribe. Nevertheless, Verhoogt correctly concludes that "[w]ith regard to the general framework of the land administration and its ultimate purpose (establishing the Crown revenues from the land), there will not have been much difference between Menches and other village scribes" (Verhoogt, 1998: 180). Thus, it is appropriate to use Menches's documents as evidence for the study of tax assessment in Ptolemaic Egypt.

The annual tax assessments took place in two stages, each involving a land survey, and the records arising from several of these land surveys have been preserved amongst Menches's papers.[3] The first survey was conducted in September at the beginning of Egypt's civil and agricultural year, and this survey involved a thorough inspection of the land associated with each village (Rathbone, Thompson, and Verhoogt, 2012: 244). This is indicated in the title of one cadastral survey: "Year 53, from Menches village scribe of Kerkeosiris, survey [*euthumetria*] by man (i.e., landholder) by basin [*perichoma*] *of the whole registered area around the village*" (P.Tebt. I 84a [September 118 BCE], emphasis added; Rathbone, Thompson, and Verhoogt, 2012: 244).

The details typically recorded in these cadastral surveys are amply illustrated in the survey conducted in September 119 BCE and published in P.Tebt. I 84b and IV 1117c (although these two texts were published separately, they, in fact, constitute a single text; Rathbone, Thompson, and Verhoogt, 2012: 243). The first column of this 260-line account reads as follows:[4]

βο(ρρᾶ) ἐχό(μεναι) ἐγβαί(νουσαι) ἀπη(λιώτου) παρὰ τὴν προγεγεω(μετρημένην) ἕως τοῦ
προγεγεω(μετρημένου) ἐξα(γωγοῦ)
ἐν τῶι καλουμένωι (τετάρτῳ) περιχώ(ματι) ἀρχό(μεναι) νό(του)
καὶ ἀπη(λιώτου) ὑπολό(γου) τοῦ ἕως τοῦ λθ (ἔτους) κατεξυ(σμένου) ⟦α ∠⟧ α ∠
⟦βο(ρρᾶ) ἐχό(μεναι) ἀρχό(μεναι) λι(βὸς) ὑπολό(γου) ἐμβρόχ(ου) τοῦ ἕως τοῦ λθ (ἔτους) ε δ⟧
⟦ἀπη(λιώτου) ἐχο(μένη) ἀρχο(μένη) νό(του) διῶρυξ β⟧
λι(βὸς) ἐχό(μενα) ⟦βο(ρρᾶ)⟧ ἀρ⟦ε⟧χό(μενα) ⸌νό(του)⸍ τὰ περὶ τὸν Ἰβιῶ(να) τῶν
(Εἰκοσιπενταρούρων) πε(δία)
/ βο(ρρᾶ) ἐχό(μεναι) Πετερμοῦθις Σιφμοῦτος γ ∠ ἀν(ὰ) δ ∠ γ´ ιˊβ´
βο(ρρᾶ) ἐχό(μεναι) ἀρχό(μεναι) ἀπη(λιώτου) ὑπολό(γου) ἁλμυ(ρίδος) τοῦ ἀπὸ τοῦ μ (ἔτους) β
/ λι(βὸς) ἐχό(μεναι) ἀρχό(μεναι) βο(ρρᾶ) ⸌Πετεσούχου θε(οῦ) κροκοδίλου διὰ⸍ Πετοσίρι<ο>ς
Ἀμεννέως ς ∠ ἀν(ὰ) δ ∠ γ´
/[νό(του)] ἐχό(μεναι) κ̣λ̣(ήρου) (ἑπτ[αρούρου)] Χ[ο(μήνιος)] Πασῶς μέ(γας) Φανήσιος ς ∠
[τοῦ] αὐ(τοῦ) βα(σιλικῆς) α ἀν(ὰ) ε
/ νό(του) ἐχό(μεναι) κλ(ήρου) [(ἑπταρούρου)] Χ̣[ο(μήνιος)] Ὀρσῆς Ἀ[ροννήσιος] ς̣ ∠
τοῦ α[ὐ(τοῦ) βα(σιλικῆς) α ἀν(ὰ) ε, (γίν.) ζ ∠]
/ νό(του) ἐχό(μεναι) κλ(ήρου) (τριακοντ[αρούρου) Χο(μήνιος) Ἁρυώτης Φαεῦτος ε]
⟦ . . . ⟧ τοῦ [αὐ(τοῦ) βα(σιλικῆς) β ἀν(ὰ) ε γ´, (γίν.) ζ]
/ νό(του) ἐχό(μεναι) κλ(ήρου) (ἑπταρούρου) [Χο(μήνιος) N.N. s. N.N.] ς ∠
/ νό(του) ἐχό(μεναι) ⸌ἀρχό(μεναι) [λι(βὸς)⸍] Κέ[ν]τι[ς Ὥ]ρ[ο]υ̣ β[α(σιλικῆς)] β
/ π[αρα(κείμενον) ἀπη(λιώτου)] ἐχό(μενον) κλ(ήρου) (ἑπταρούρου) Χο(μήνιος) Ἁρφαῆ[σις
Ὥρο]υ τὸ λο(ιπόν)
τοῦ αὐ(τοῦ) ⟨βα(σιλικῆς)⟩ β ἀν̣ὰ̣ [ε
ἀπη(λιώτου) ἐχό(μεναι) ἀρχό(μεναι) βο(ρρᾶ) [Ἁ]ρφαῆσις Πετοσίριος βα(σιλικῆς) α ∠ δ´
ἀν(ὰ) δ ∠ γ´ ιβ´
/ νό(του) ἐ[χ]ό(μεναι) [κλ(ήρου) (ἑπταρούρου) Χο(μήνιος) Πᾶσις μέ(γας) Κ]αλατύτιος ς ∠
[τοῦ αὐ(τοῦ) βα(σιλικῆς) β ἀν(ὰ)] ε̣, (γίν.) η ∠

Lying to the north, extending to the east, alongside the land already surveyed, as far as the
drainage channel already surveyed,
in the basin called Fourth, starting from the south
and east, eroded land out of account before year 39, [[1½]] 1½ (ar.).
[[Lying to the north, starting from the west, waterlogged land out of account before year
39, 5¼ (ar.).]]
[[Lying to the east, starting from the south, canal, 2 (ar.).]]
Lying to the west, starting from the south, the fields around Ibion Eikosipentarouron.
/ Lying to the north, Petermouthis son of Siphmous, 3½ (ar.) at 4½ + ⅓ + 1/12 (= 4 11/12 art.).
Lying to the north, starting from the east, salted land out of account since year 40, 2 (ar.).
/ Lying to the west, starting from the north, of Petesouchos, crocodile god, through Petosiris son
of Amenneus, 6½ (ar.) at 4½ + ⅓ (= 4 5/6 art.).
/ Lying [to the south] plot [of a 7-aroura man] of Chomenis, Pasos the elder son of
Phanesis, 6½ (ar.);
of the same man, royal land, 1 (ar.) at 5 (art.).
/ Lying to the south, plot [of a 7-aroura man] of Chomenis, Orses son of [Haronnesis], 6½ (ar.);
of the [same man, royal land, 1 (ar.) at 5 (art.), total 7½ (ar.)].
/ Lying to the south, plot of a 30-aroura man [of Chomenis, Haruotes son of Phaeus, 5 (ar.)];

of the [same man, royal land, 2 (ar.) at 5⅓ (art.), total 7 (ar.)].
/ Lying to the south, plot of a 7-aroura [man of Chomenis N.N. son of N.N.], 6½ (ar.).
/ Lying to the south, starting [from the west], Kentis son of Horos, royal land, 2 (ar.).
/ Adjoining, lying [to the east], plot of a 7-aroura man of Chomenis, Harphaesis son [of Horos], the remainder;
of the same man, royal land, 2 (ar.) at [5 (art.)].
Lying to the east, starting from the north, Harphaesis son of Petosiris, royal land, 1½ + ¼ (ar.) at 4½ + ⅓ + $^1/_{12}$ (art.).
/ Lying to the south, [plot of a 7-aroura man of Chomenis, Pasis the elder son] of Kalatutis, 6½ (ar.);
[of the same man, royal land, 2 (ar.) at] 5 (art.), total 8½ (ar.).

(Text and translation in Rathbone, Thompson, and Verhoogt, 2012: 246–7, 254)

Columns ii–xi continue in the same fashion: the basin being inspected is noted, followed by the recording of various details, including: the names of landholders; the dimensions and area of their land in arourae; details concerning the condition of the land (e.g., eroded, waterlogged, salted, unflooded), as well as any roads, dykes, canals, drains, or supply channels; the geographical relationship or orientation with respect to the previous plot of land; and the administrative category of each field, whether royal (βασιλική), sacred (ἱερά), or cleruchic (κληρουχική) (cf. Rostovtzeff, 1904: 201–3; Crawford, 1971: 10–14; Verhoogt, 1998: 142; Rathbone, Thompson, and Verhoogt, 2012: 244). It is evident, then, that the field-by-field survey (κατὰ περίχωμα) conducted each September was intended to be quite thorough.

The second stage of tax assessment took place in February prior to the harvest. An incomplete account of this type of survey is preserved in P.Tebt. IV 1122 (= P.Tebt. I 187 [late II BCE]), the first sixteen lines of which read as follows:

[ἀπη(λιώτου)] ẹχό(μεναι) ἐγβαί(νουσαι) ἀπη(λιώτου) παρὰ τὴν προγεγεω(μετρημένην) σχοι(νία)
β ∠ ις´
κλ(ήρου) (ἑπταρούρου) Χο(μήνιος) Ἀρυτῆς Ἀρυώτου ς ∠
ε ∠ δίς́ (∠ήίς́λ́β / ∠ίξ́λ́β) (πρὸς ἴσον), (γίνονται) γ∠δίς́λ́β́ (πυρῶι)
ἀπη(λιώτου) ἐχό(μεναι) ἀρχό(μεναι) νό(του) ηίς́ (πρὸς ἴσον), (γίνονται) ή
βο(ρρᾶ) ἐχό(μεναι) ἀρχό(μεναι) λι(βὸς) τοῦ αὐτοῦ
ίς́ ∠ (πρὸς ἴσον) ή, (γίνονται) λ́β́ξ́δ́
ἀπη(λιώτου) ἐχό(μεναι) ἐγβαί(νουσαι) βο(ρρᾶ) παρὰ τὰ περὶ τὸν Ἰβιῶ(να) τῶν
(εἰκοσιπεντ)[(αρούρων)]
πε(δία) σχοι(νίον) αή ⟦ἀρχό(μεναι) βο(ρρᾶ)⟧ α α∠ή (πρὸς ἴσον) . . . .
(γίνονται) αή
ἀπη(λιώτου) <ἐχό(μεναι)> εἰσ[βαί(νουσαι) . . ( )] παρὰ τὴν προγεγεω(μετρημένην) σ̣χοι(νίου) ∠ή
Ἀ̣ρ̣υ(ώτης) κ̣λ̣(ήρου) δίς́ α (πρὸς ἴσον) . . , (γίνονται) .ή̣ξ́δ̣́
(πυρῶι)
νό(του) ἐχό(μεναι) ἐγβαί(νουσαι) παρὰ τὴν προγεγεω(μετρημένην) σχοι(νίον) α
Ἀρυ(ώτης) κλ(ήρου) (ἑπταρούρου) Χο(μήνιος) τὸ λο(ιπὸν) τοῦ κλ(ήρου)
α̣∠δήίς́ (∠ήίς́χβ / ∠ίξ́χβ) αδίς́, (γίνονται) αήίς́
(γίνονται) τοῦ κλ(ήρου) ςδήίς́ (πυρῶι) γεω(ργὸς) [-ca.?-]

> Adjoining on the east, projecting $2\frac{9}{16}$ sconia east of the property previously surveyed, $6\frac{1}{2}$ arouras of an allotment for a 7-aroura cleruch of Chomenis, Haryotes son of Haryotes, measuring $5\frac{13}{16}$ X $5\frac{13}{16}$ X $\frac{23}{32}$ X $\frac{19}{32}$ scoinia, total $3\frac{27}{32}$ arouras, in wheat. Adjoining on the east, forming a southern boundary of the next lot, another bit of the allotment measuring $\frac{3}{16}$ X $\frac{3}{16}$ X $\frac{23}{32}$ X $\frac{23}{32}$, total $\frac{1}{8}$ aroura. Adjoining on the north, forming a western boundary of the next lot, belonging to the same man, another bit of the allotment measuring $\frac{1}{16}$ X $\frac{1}{8}$ X $\frac{1}{2}$ X $\frac{1}{2}$, total $\frac{3}{64}$. Adjoining on the east, projecting $1\frac{7}{8}$ schoinion north of the fields around Ibion Eikosipentarouron, another bit of the allotment measuring 1 X (?) X $1\frac{5}{8}$ X $1\frac{5}{8}$, total $1\frac{1}{8}$. Adjoining on the east, receding ... of the property previously surveyed for $\frac{5}{8}$ schoinion, another bit of Haryotes' allotment, measuring $\frac{5}{16}$ X (?) X 1 X 1, total $\frac{9}{64}$(?), in wheat. Adjoining on the south, projecting 1 schoinion beyond the property previously surveyed, the remainder of Haryotes' allotment as a 7-aroura cleruch of Chomenis, measuring $1\frac{15}{16}$ X $1\frac{15}{16}$ X $\frac{22}{32}$ X $\frac{19}{32}$, total $1\frac{3}{16}$. Total for the allotment, $6\frac{7}{16}$ arouras, in wheat, farmed by NN.
>
> (Text and translation in Keenan and Shelton, 1976: 177–80)

The survey conducted in February was not unlike that conducted in September in terms of the records kept about the landholders, the dimensions and area of their plots of land, and their orientation with respect to the previous plot of land. However, the survey conducted in February notes the crops, as well. In the survey quoted above, wheat was noted several times (ll. 3, 16); another survey noted lentils (P.Tebt. IV 1123 [late II BCE]). This second stage, then, consisted of a survey of agricultural produce (ἡ κατὰ φύλλον γεωμετρία) focused on cultivated land, detailing the crops grown in each field in order to determine the estimated yield and the anticipated revenue from each parcel of land (Rostovtzeff, 1904: 201–3; Harper, 1934a: 18; Crawford, 1971: 15–9; Verhoogt, 1998: 132, 143; Muhs, 2005: 18).

While the cadastral surveys reveal *how* tax assessment was conducted, accounts related to these surveys reveal *who* conducted them, and for this we are again indebted to Menches. In his accounts of the biannual surveys, he recorded the costs associated with conducting the cadastral surveys, including such necessary materials as papyrus and writing tablets, as well as other expenditures, such as a wide variety of foodstuffs, miscellaneous items (e.g., cooking pots, a mattress, wreaths), and various services (e.g., barber, bath manager, physician) (Verhoogt, 2005: 41–62). Because Menches's accounts also record to whom payments or reimbursements were made, we are able to identify the specific individuals who participated in conducting the cadastral surveys.

It quickly becomes clear that these surveys involved representatives from each of Egypt's three administrative levels. The nome level was represented by the nome's primary official, the βασιλικός γραμματεύς. That he was personally present is indicated by two mentions of the "reception of the *basilikos grammateus*" (P.Tebt. I 112, ll. 89, 131 [112 BCE]; cf. Verhoogt, 1998: 136; 2005: 29). On another occasion, Menches received from the βασιλικός γραμματεύς a notice to join him in order to survey the village (P.Tebt. I 12, ll. 6–7 [118 BCE]). Alternatively, the βασιλικός γραμματεύς might be represented by one of his officials. Several are mentioned in Menches's accounts as receiving payments, but it is his "usher" (εἰσαγγελεύς) who received the highest number of payments (Verhoogt, 1998: 136–7; 2005: 29). Verhoogt notes that three officials representing the βασιλικός γραμματεύς, namely, the "'chief-armed attendant', the 'recorder' and the 'letter-writer' were explicitly paid for the survey of agricultural produce, κατὰ φύλλον" (Verhoogt, 1998: 137).

The district level was represented by the τοπογραμματεύς (e.g., P.Tebt. I 149 [116–115 BCE]) or one of his representatives (e.g., P.Tebt. I 112, ll. 60–63, 81–83, 103 [112 BCE]; cf. Harper 1934a: 23; Verhoogt, 1998: 137; 2005: 30–31). Of his representatives, the scribe (γραμματεύς) of the τοπογραμματεύς received the highest number of payments (Verhoogt, 2005: 30).

The village level was represented by the village scribe, the κωμογραμματεύς (e.g., P.Tebt. I 12, ll. 7–8 [118 BCE], 72, ll. 189–190 [114–113 BCE]; Verhoogt, 1998: 137–9; Crawford, 1971: 29–30). This included not only the village scribe of the village being surveyed, but also those from other villages (Verhoogt, 1998: 137–8). In order to explain this curiosity, Verhoogt offers this suggestion: "Perhaps the presence of other village scribes should be ascribed to the general notion of the survey of agricultural produce as a nome activity, the shared responsibility of all officials who happened to be available" (Verhoogt, 1998: 139; cf. Verhoogt, 2005: 31–2).

That all three administrative levels participated in the cadastral surveys indicates that urban-rural interaction occurred during the biannual surveys as a result of urban-to-rural mobility. Moreover, this was not a passing interaction but involved at least several weeks in both September and February.

Urban-rural interaction also occurred as a result of rural-to-urban mobility. According to Menches's documents, following the survey of agricultural production, the village scribe composed several reports; and sometime during or around March, he traveled to Ptolemais Euergetis, the nome capital, in order to present to the βασιλικός γραμματεύς the information collected during the most recent survey (Harper, 1934a: 22–3; Crawford, 1971: 33; Verhoogt, 1998: 98–101, 143–4). There is also evidence that the village scribe took another journey in May or June, this time to Alexandria, in order to participate in an annual meeting with the διοικητής (e.g., P.Tebt. I 26 [113 BCE]; Crawford, 1971: 34–5; Verhoogt, 1998: 83–90). This meeting was referred to either as the "audit" (διάλογος) or the "public reading of the survey according to crops" (ἀνάγνωσις τῆς κατὰ φύλλον γεωμετρίας) (Verhoogt, 1998: 88). There were several reasons for this meeting: the outcome of the survey of agricultural produce was presented to the διοικητής and, if necessary, special cases were brought to his attention (προσαγγέλλω); the διοικητής read these reports (ἀνάγνωσις) and commented in the margins (παρεπιγράφω); and, following the meeting, administrative changes were incorporated into the appropriate documents (προσάγω) (Verhoogt, 1998: 88–9).

From this brief foray into Menches's papers, it seems clear that tax assessment involved urban-rural interaction at various times over the course of the year. Urban-to-rural mobility occurred as the βασιλικός γραμματεύς and τοπογραμματεύς (or their representatives) traveled to the villages for the biannual surveys. Rural-to-urban mobility occurred as the village scribes traveled to the nome capital and to Alexandria to present the findings of the survey of agricultural produce.[5] Urban-rural interaction was not confined to the activities of tax assessment, however, but also extended to the activities of tax collection, to which we now turn.

Tax Collection in Egypt

Taxes in kind were typically paid in wheat, though barley was occasionally substituted. In order to understand the process of tax collection and the opportunities for urban-rural interaction therein, it is necessary to begin with the various stages or steps involved in harvesting grain.

In Egypt, wheat was typically harvested in April (Packman, 1968: 59). The first step in this process was to reap the grain in the fields. Reapers used a sickle or a scythe to cut the stalks, and the cut stalks were subsequently bundled into sheaves and transported to the threshing floor (White, 1970: 182–3; Halstead and Jones, 1989: 43–4; Whittaker, 2000: 63).

The second step in this process was to thresh the grain at the threshing floor, which was typically "a roughly circular area with a smooth, compact surface" (White, 1970: 184). Crawford observes that at Kerkeosiris, "[c]lose by the village nucleus to the north-east was a further area of derelict land, of which 10 arouras formed the village threshing floor, ἅλων.... [T]his floor probably served the whole village" (Crawford, 1971: 47). The cereal was spread on the threshing floor and then trampled under the hooves of animals (oxen, cows, donkeys, or mules) in order to crush and break the stalks and to release the seed (White, 1970: 185–6; Halstead and Jones, 1989: 44). Alternatively, animals could draw a threshing sledge, that is, "a heavy wooden platform fitted on the underside with flint teeth" (White, 1970: 185). Both methods resulted in a mixture of grain, straw, chaff, and dirt (Schuman, 1961: 255; White, 1970: 186–7).

The third step consisted of winnowing in order to separate the grain from the straw and chaff, a task that required a breeze. A winnowing fork, a fork with a long handle and broad flat tines, was used to toss the threshed crop into the air. The grain and heavier chaff would fall back down to the threshing floor, while the straw and light chaff would be carried aside by the breeze (Schuman, 1961: 255; Halstead and Jones, 1989: 44).

The final step in this process was the sifting of the grain, which took place in two stages. A coarse or rough sifting was first completed using a sieve with a wider mesh (mesh size = approx. 6–10 mm). This was followed by a fine sifting with a fine sieve (mesh size = approx. 2.0–2.5 mm) (Schuman, 1961: 255–6; Halstead and Jones, 1989: 45–6). Fine sifting was not typically carried out at the threshing floor, but occurred throughout the year as part of the process of preparing food or the cleaning of seed corn (Halstead and Jones, 1989: 46).

The precise moment of tax collection is a matter of some debate. The cultivator bore the responsibility of transporting the sheaves from the field to the village threshing floor, and it has frequently been argued that taxes in kind were collected at the threshing floor throughout the Ptolemaic and Roman periods (e.g., Rostovtzeff, 1904: 204–5, 217; Wallace, 1938: 33–4; Crawford, 1971: 47). This position is supported by a series of four letters preserved in the papers of Menches concerning a certain Hermias, the overseer of the revenues (ἐπὶ τῶν προσόδων), and his failure to carry out his duties (P.Tebt. I 27 [113 BCE]). Despite several earlier warnings, Hermias had been negligent in his management of the crops and the appointment of subordinates. This final warning to Hermias included a list of specific tasks that he must carry out, including the following:

> πλὴ[ν] ἴσθι μὲν ἔγκλητος ὑπάρχων ἔτι δὲ καὶ νῦν διαλαβὼν μηδεμιᾶς τεύξεσθαι συνγνώμης ὀλιγωρηθέντος τινὸς ἵνα μὲν πρὸς ταῖς προειρημέναις χρείαις εὔθετοι κατασταθῶσιν προ̣. . λ̣ι̣ντη..ι[.]αι, ταξά[με]νος δὲ [τ]ὴν ἀδιαλίπτως προσφερομ[ένην σ]π̣[ο]υδὴν ἐν τοῖς ἀ̣[νήκουσιν εἰς] .τὴν τῆς φορολογίας ἐ̣π̣α[ύ]ξη̣σ̣ι̣ν καὶ παρὰ τῶ[ν κωμογραμ]ματέων ἐπιλαβὼν τὴν γραφὴν τῶν δυναμ[έ]νων ἐπι[σ]π[ασθ]ῆναι εἰς τὰς γενηματοφυλακίας ἀπό τε τ[ῶ]ν στρατευομένων καὶ τῶν ἄλλων τῶν τόπους κατ[ο]ικούντων καὶ ἐν περιστάσει κειμένων καὶ πίστει καὶ ἀσφαλ[ε]ίαι διαφερόντων καὶ τοὺς ἐπιτηδείους καταστήσας πρὸς ταῖς κατὰ κώμην καὶ παρὰ μὲν τούτων καὶ τῶν ἐν ἑκάστηι φυλ[α]κ̣ι[τῶν] λ̣α̣[β]ὼν χειρογραφίας ὅρκου βασιλικοῦ δισσὰς ἐπὶ τοῦ βελτίστου προσ̣τ̣ήσε̣σ̣[θαι τ]ῆς φυλ̣ακῆς καὶ μηθένα τῶν γεωργούντων τὴν βασιλικὴν καὶ τὴν ἐν ἀφέσει [γῆν] ἐφάψεσθαι τῶν χλωρῶν καὶ τῶν ἄλλων ἐπισπόρων πλὴν τῶν ε̣ἰ̣ς [τὰς] τροφὰς τῶν γεωργικῶν κτηνῶν ἃ καὶ με[τὰ] τῶν κωμογραμματέων π[ροσ]χορηγηθήσεται καὶ τῶν ἐγδιοικηθησομ[ένων] ὧν αἱ τειμαὶ καὶ το̣ύτων αἱ ἀσφάλ̣ε̣[ιαι δο]θεῖσαι κατατεθήσονται ἐπὶ [τ]ῶν τραπεζῶ[ν] πρὸς τὰ καθήκοντα εἰς τὸ β̣α̣[σιλικὸν] ἀκολούθως τοῖς προεγδεδομ[έ]νοις χρηματισ̣μ̣ο̣ῖ[ς] φροντίζειν ὅπως καὶ τἄ[λ]λα [γέν]ηται κατὰ θερείαν ἐξ ὑγιοῦς, παρακομ[ί]ζειν δὲ ἐπὶ τοὺς ἀποδεδειγμένους [τόπου]ς καὶ μηθὲν τούτων καταπ̣ρ̣ο̣ή̣σ̣ε[σθαι ἀλλὰ] ἐπὰν καὶ {περὶ} τὸ περὶ τῆς [ἀφέσε]ως πρόγραμμα ἐκτεθῆι ἐ̣ὰ̣ν μ̣ὴ̣ πάντ[ων] ὧν δέον ἐστὶ παραδοθέντω[ν καὶ] τῶν ἐφελκομένων πρὸς τοὺς ἔμ[π]ροσθεν χρόνους ἐκπληρωθέντων…

But be sure that you are liable to accusation; and, before it is too late, believing that you will receive no pardon for any neglect, see that suitable persons are appointed to the aforesaid offices, and display unremitting zeal in what tends to increase the revenue; and procure from the komogrammateis the list of those who can be made to undertake the custody of the produce from those in the army and the other inhabitants of the district who are living in the neighbourhood and are conspicuous for honesty and steadiness, and appoint those fit to the posts in the villages; take from them and the phylacitae in each village two declarations upon oath by the sovereigns that they will provide in the best possible manner for the guardianship; and will allow none of the cultivators of Crown land or land ἐν ἀφέσει to touch the green stuffs and the other second crops except those intended for the fodder of the animals used in agriculture, which shall be supplied with the approval of the komogrammateis, and except amounts to be collected for which the prices and securities shall be paid and deposited at the banks to meet the dues to the treasury in accordance with the regulations previously issued; and will take care that all else is rightly done in the summer, and will convey the produce to the appointed places, and let nothing go until the proclamation concerning the release of crops is published, and unless everything has been duly delivered and the demands for previous years paid up.

(Text and translation in Grenfell, Hunt, and Smyly, 1902: 107–12)

Of particular note is the task of appointing two men in each village "to undertake the custody of the produce … [who] will allow none of the cultivators of Crown land or land ἐν ἀφέσει to touch the green stuffs and the other second crops … and let nothing go until the proclamation concerning the release of crops is published" (ll. 53–64). The editors of this text state, "ἄφεσις in this connexion means the official release of the harvest *after* the claims of the government had been met" (emphasis added).

That taxes were collected at the threshing floor may also be indicated in a petition that Menches received from Horus the *kōmarch* and the elders of the farmers (πρεσβύτεροι τῶν γεωργῶν) of Kerkeosiris (P.Tebt. I 48 [ca. 113 BCE]):

κεχειρογραφηκότων ἡμῶν Πολέμωνι τῶι τοπάρχηι περὶ τοῦ παραδώσειν εἰς [τὸ] βασιλικὸν ἕως ι τοῦ Παχὼν πυροῦ (ἀρτάβας) Αφ περὶ ὧν καὶ προσεδρευόντων διά τε νυκτὸς καὶ ἡμέρας μέχρι τοῦ τὸ προκείμενον ἐκπληρῶσαι καὶ τὴν ἐπιγεγραμμένην πρὸς τὴν τοῦ βασιλέως παρουσίαν ἀγορὰν (πυροῦ) (ἀρταβῶν) π, τῆι δὲ γ τοῦ ὑποκειμένου μηνὸς ὄντων πρὸς τῆι παραδόσει τῶν ἐκφορίων καὶ τοῦ ἁλοητοῦ ἐπελθων ἐπὶ τὴν ἅλω Λύκος σὺν ἄλλοις ἐν ὅπλοις καὶ σπασαμένων τὰς μαχαίρας ἐπιλαβομένων τοῦ ἑ̣ν̣ὸ̣ς ἡμῶν Ὥρου κωμάρχου καὶ τούτου ἀγωγὴ̣ν μετὰ σκυλμοῦ ποιουμένων ῥίψαντα τὸ ἱμάτιον εἰς φυγὴν ὁρμῆσαι, καὶ ἡμᾶς τε σὺν τοῖς λοιποῖς γεωργοῖς ὑπόπτως σχόντας συνδεδραμηκέναι, διὰ δὲ ταύτην τὴν αἰτίαν ἐμποδισθῆναι ἐν τοῖς κατὰ τὴν παράδοσιν τῶν ἐκφορίων καὶ τῶν ἄλλων ἐπιγεγραμμένων.

> We signed an undertaking to Polemon the toparch that we would supply to the Treasury by the 10th of Pachon 1500 artabae of wheat, and we have been working night and day to make up the aforesaid amount and also the 80 artabae of wheat for the supplies imposed in connexion with the king's visit. On the 3rd of the month mentioned below while we were engaged in the receipt of the rents and the threshing expenses, Lycus proceeded to the threshing-floor with other persons armed, and drawing their swords they seized one of us, Horus the komarch, making a violent attempt to carry him off, so that he threw away his garment and took to flight, and we together with the rest of the cultivators having had our suspicions aroused ran off with him; for which reason we were hindered with regard to the receipt of the rents and other imposts.
>
> (Text and translation in Grenfell, Hunt, and Smyly, 1902: 155)

From this petition, we learn that a group of officials had been collecting wheat in preparation for the king's impending visit. Although this collection may not have been for the payment of annual taxes, it is important to note that the petitioners were assaulted by a group of people led by a certain Lycus as they collected wheat *at the threshing floor* (ἐπὶ τὴν ἅλω, l. 18).

The position that taxes continued to be collected at the threshing floor in Roman Egypt is supported by an oath taken by Aurelius Papontos, son of Theon, and Aurelius Horus, son of Archelaus, the *kōmarchs* of Ision Panga (P.Oxy. X 1255 [292 CE]). The body of the oath states:

> ἐπειθεμένου σου ἡμῖν
> ὥστε ἐν ἀσφαλεῖ ἔχειν τοὺς καρποὺς
> ἐν ταῖς ἁλωνίαις <ἐν> τοῖς ἡμετέροις παιδίοις
> ἄχρις ἂν πληρωθῶσι οἱ δεκάπρωτοι
> τῶν ἑκάστου δημοσίων τελεσμάτων
> ἐκ πλήρους, κατὰ τοῦτο ὁμολογουν ὀμνύν-
> τ̣ε̣ς τὴν τῶν κυρίων ἡμῶν Διοκλητιανοῦ
> καὶ Μαξιμιανοῦ Σεβαστῶν τύχην
> ἐπιτηρεῖν καὶ μηδενὶ ἐπιτρέψαι ἐφά-
> ψασθαι ἕως ἂν ἕκαστος τὸ ἐποφι-
> λόμενον μέτρον ἀποπληρώσῃ
> πρὸς τοὺς τῶν τόπων δεκαπρώ-
> τους, τῶν μετρημάτων γ̣[ι]ν̣ο̣μ̣ε̣ν̣ω̣[ν]
> εἰς τὸ μηδεμίαν μέμψιν ἐπα-
> κολουθῆσαι, ἢ ἔ̣ν̣οχ̣ο̣ι ε[ἴημ]ε̣ν
> τῷ ὅρκῳ.

> Having been enjoined by you to keep in safety the crops at the threshing-floors in our lands until the decaproti have received payment in full of the public taxes from each person, we accordingly agree, swearing by the fortune of our lords Diocletian and Maximian Augusti, to be on the watch and to permit no one to touch the produce until each person has paid to the local decaproti the amount due from him, the measurement being made so that no complaint may ensue; otherwise we may be liable to the penalties attaching to the oath.
>
> (Text and translation in Grenfell and Hunt, 1914: 173–4)

The oath of these *kōmarchs* specifies that crops were to remain at the threshing floors until the taxes due were paid. Only after payment for taxes had been received could the produce be removed from the threshing floor.

If taxes in kind were collected at the threshing floor, then urban-rural interaction would have taken place there between the urban officials supervising the process and the rural cultivators bringing in the harvest. There are at least three issues, however, complicating this proposal. First, if taxes in kind were collected at the threshing floor before the cultivator claimed his harvest, then it is difficult to explain the well-attested accumulation of arrears (e.g., *SB* I 5230 [10–11 CE]; cf. Wallace, 1938: 370, n. 22; Johnson, 1959: 490).

Second, the dates on the receipts issued for the payment of taxes and rents in kind do not usually coincide with the harvest season. In Zola Packman's *The Taxes in Grain in Ptolemaic Egypt*, we find a study of the receipts issued from the granary of Diospolis Magna from 164 to 88 BCE, including consideration of the date of tax payments. Although some receipts for payments in wheat for current taxes were dated to April, that is, during Egypt's wheat harvest, the vast majority of receipts for current wheat taxes were dated to the months of May through September, that is, weeks or months after the harvest (Packman, 1968: 59). According to Packman's analysis, the number of payments made each month were as follows: February = 1; March = 1; April = 10; May = 9; June = 27; July = 12; August = 16; September = 5 (Packman, 1968: Table 22). That payments were made even during July and August is evidence for the position that taxes were not collected at the threshing floor, for both fields and threshing floors were flooded by the Nile during these months. Thus, Packman concludes that taxes in kind were paid not at the threshing floor, but were paid in installments at the state granary weeks or even months after the harvest season (Packman, 1968: 63).

The third complication with the proposal of taxes being paid at the threshing floor pertains to the standard of quality that taxes in kind were required to meet. In Pharaonic and Ptolemaic Egypt, wheat and barley were cultivated as a maslin, that is, they were deliberately sown, reaped, and winnowed together as a single crop, thereby reducing the risk of crop failure (Mayerson, 2005: 51; cf. Halstead and Jones, 1995: 103–14; Mayerson, 2002: 210–13). Under the Romans, however, taxes paid in wheat were required to be pure or clean, rather than a mixture of wheat and barley (Mayerson, 2005: 51–4). This is illustrated, for example, in P.Oxy. IV 708 (188 CE), which consists of two letters from Antonius Aelianus to the strategus of the Diospolite nome in the Thebaid. The first of these letters reads as follows:

[Ἀντ]ώνιος Αἰλιανὸς στρα(τηγῷ) Διοπ(ολίτου) Θηβ(αίδος) χα(ίρειν).
[τοῦ] καταχθέντος γόμου ἐκ τοῦ ὑπὸ σοὶ νομοῦ
[διὰ .]αῦσιος Σιπῶτος καὶ τῶν σὺν αὐτῷ ἐν (πυροῦ) (ἀρτάβαις) Β
[ἐν τῇ] τ[ῶ]ν δειγμάτων ἄρσει οὐ καθαροῦ φανέντος
[ἐκ]έλευσα ἡμιαρτάβιον κριθολογηθῆναι
[καὶ] βωλολογηθῆναι, καὶ ἐξέβη ἔλασσον
[κρι]θῆς μὲν ⟦(ἀρτάβαι)⟧ ἑκατοσταὶ δύο βώλου δὲ ὁμοί-
[ως ἑ]κατοστῆς ἥμισυ. τοὺς [ο]ὖν τὸν πυρὸν [ἐ]μβα-
[λο]μένους σιτολόγους πρᾶξον τῷ σῷ κινδύνῳ
[τὰ]ς συναγο(μένας) σίτο(υ) διαφόρῳ (πυροῦ) (ἀρτάβας) ν (ἥμισυ) δ´ κα[ὶ] τὰ
[προ]σμ(ετρούμενα) καὶ τὰς ἄλλας δαπάνας, καὶ προσθέμε-
[νος] τῷ λόγῳ τοῦ χι(λιάρχου) δήλωσόν μοι.

Antonius Aelianus to the strategus of the Diospolite nome in the Thebaid, greeting. Since the cargo dispatched from the nome under you in charge of [.]ausis son of Sipos and his companions, amounting to 2000 artabae of wheat, appeared at the weighing of the samples to have been adulterated, I ordered that the amount of barley and earth in half an artaba of it should be ascertained, and it proved to be under measure

> by 2 per cent. of barley and likewise ½ per cent. of earth. Accordingly exact at your own risk from the sitologi who shipped the wheat the difference on the whole amount of the corn, 50¾ artabae of wheat, and the extra payments and other expenses, and when you have added this total to the account of the chiliarch let me know.
>
> (Text and translation in Grenfell and Hunt, 1904: 173)

The letter concerns a large shipment of wheat (2000 artabae) from which a half-artaba sample had been examined and found to contain 2 percent of barley and 0.5 percent of earth. Because this fell short of the expected standards, the strategus was instructed to exact 50¾ artabae of wheat from the sitologoi who had shipped this wheat in order to make up the difference (Mayerson, 2002: 112; 2005: 54).

That this shipment was deemed οὐ καθαροῦ (l. 5) raises the question of the standards for payments in wheat. The text of P.Oxy. XXXVIII 2874 (October 12, 108 CE) indicates that rent paid in grain "was commonly required to be clean, pure and winnowed before delivery" (Rowlandson, 1996: 225, n. 67). An extant lease of land is also helpful in this regard, for it stipulates that the lessor was to pay the annual rent in wheat that was νέος, καθαρός, ἄδολος, ἄκριθος, and κεκοσκινευμένος (P.Oxy. XVIII 2188 [107 CE], ll. 5–7). Verne B. Schuman (1961: 254, n. 2) defines these terms as follows:

> "New wheat" (νέος) must indicate grain from the harvest of the year for which the tax was paid; καθαρός, I believe, means that the individual grains of wheat must not be soiled in any way, e.g., by the animals used in the threshing process; ἄδολος indicates the absence of foreign matter of any kind; ἄκριθος, literally "without barley", [*sic*] can hardly mean that the wheat paid in taxes had to be entirely free of that grain, but that a very small proportion only was allowable; κεκοσκινευμένος, "sifted," i.e., processed in a sieve to remove any foreign matter not previously separated from the wheat.

Clearly, grain at the threshing floor would not meet this standard (Schuman, 1961: 255). While coarse sifting at the threshing floor removed some of the impurities from the grain, some would inevitably remain. Thus, a final cleaning of the grain would be necessary. Schuman's ultimate conclusion, with which Packman agreed, is that taxes in kind were not paid at the threshing floor, but weeks or months after the harvest. In this way, "ample time was thus given for bringing some substandard grain up to government specifications" (Schuman, 1961: 256).

In short, the moment that taxes in kind were collected, whether at the threshing floor or later at the granary, remains an open question. However, John C. Whittaker's ethnoarchaeological study of threshing in twentieth-century Cyprus may offer a solution: Whittaker observed that the threshed grain was measured and assessed for taxes at the threshing floor before it was taken home by the cultivator, apparently for cleaning (Whittaker, 2000: 64). Thus, it is conceivable that a similar procedure was followed in Ptolemaic and Roman Egypt, such that the amount of taxes to be paid was determined at the threshing floor, with payments being delivered to the granary after the grain was cleaned.

Regardless of whether taxes in kind were paid at the threshing floor or at the granary, urban-rural interaction occurred at the threshing floor. Moreover, the cultivator was responsible for transporting the grain to the granary; thus, urban-rural interaction also occurred at the granary between the rural farmers and the workers at the urban granary (Wallace, 1938: 34–5, 370, nn. 26 and 27).

Conclusion

The study of seemingly mundane areas of inquiry has revealed much about ancient society and its economy. The work of cultivating crops for the agricultural economy was clearly enormous. In addition to this, however, was the work by Crown officials, tax farmers, and tax collectors in assessing taxes, in order to determine how much of the harvest would enter the agricultural economy's supply chain, as well as in collecting those taxes, whether at the threshing floor or at the state granary. Long before grain could be loaded onto ships, this labor involved individuals of varying statuses, from both the urban and the rural populations, interacting extensively at regular and frequent intervals. Clearly, it was no mean feat, then, to serve as the ancient world's "bread basket," for it was, in fact, exceedingly laborious to put the check in the mail.

Notes

1. To be clear, "civil servants" in the ancient world were not precisely the same as the so-called "civil servants" in societies where bureaucracy was fully developed or well established.
2. While there were certainly differences between Ptolemaic and Roman Egypt's tax-farming systems, the mechanics of tax assessment and tax collection continued without significant changes. Livia Capponi has argued a similar point (2005: 123–56).
3. For tax assessment in the Thebaid in the same two-stage manner, see Vandorpe, 2000: 175, 186, and Christensen, Thompson, and Vandorpe, 2017: 9–12.
4. The notation \\/ indicates that what lies between them was inserted above the line.
5. These cadastral surveys continued in the Roman period without significant change (e.g., P.Berl.Leihg. 13). Cf. Rostovtzeff, 1904: 212–3, 217; Wallace, 1938: 7–8.

Bibliography

Bingen, Jean. 2007. *Hellenistic Egypt: Monarchy, Society, Economy, Culture.* Berkeley; Los Angeles: University of California Press.

Capponi, Livia. 2005. *Augustan Egypt: The Creation of a Roman Province*. Studies in Classics. London; New York: Routledge.

Christensen, Thorolf, Dorothy J. Thompson, and Katelijn Vandorpe. 2017. *Land and Taxes in Ptolemaic Egypt: An Edition, Translation and Commentary for the Edfu Land Survey (P.Haun. IV 70)*. Cambridge Classical Studies. Cambridge: Cambridge University Press.

Crawford, Dorothy. 1971. *Kerkeosiris: An Egyptian Village in the Ptolemaic Period*. Cambridge Classical Studies. Cambridge: Cambridge University Press.

Grenfell, Bernard P., Arthur S. Hunt, and J. Gilbart Smyly, eds. 1902. *The Tebtunis Papyri*. Vol. 1. London: Henry Frowde.

Grenfell, Bernard P., and Arthur S. Hunt, eds. 1904. *The Oxyrhynchus Papyri*. Vol. 4. London: Egypt Exploration Society.

———. 1914. *The Oxyrhynchus Papyri*. Vol. 10. London: Egypt Exploration Society.

Halstead, Paul, and Glynis Jones. 1989. "Agrarian Ecology in the Greek Islands: Time Stress, Scale and Risk." *Journal of Hellenic Studies* 109: 41–55.

———. 1995. "Maslins, Mixtures and Monocrops: On the Interpretation of Archaeobotanical Crop Samples of Heterogeneous Composition." *Journal of Archaeological Science* 22: 103–14.

Harper, G. M. 1934a. "Menches, *Komogrammateus* of Kerkeosiris." *Aegyptus* 14: 14–32.

———. 1934b. "Tax Contractors and Their Relation to Tax Collection in Ptolemaic Egypt." *Aegyptus* 14: 49–64.

Johnson, Allan Chester. 1959. *Roman Egypt to the Reign of Diocletian*. Vol. 2 of *An Economic Survey of Ancient Rome*. 6 vols. Edited by Tenney Frank. Paterson: Pageant Books.

Kalén, T. 1932. *Berliner Leihgabe griechischer Papyri*. Uppsala: Lundequist.

Keenan, J. G., and J. C. Shelton, eds. 1976. *The Tebtunis Papyri*. Vol. 4. London: Egypt Exploration Society.

Lewis, Naphtali. 1983. *Life in Egypt under Roman Rule*. Oxford: Clarendon Press.

Manning, J. G. 2010. *The Last Pharaohs: Egypt under the Ptolemies, 305–30 BC*. Princeton; Oxford: Princeton University Press.

Mayerson, Philip. 2002. "Three Pharaonic Crops in Ptolemaic Egypt: ῎ΟΛΥΡΑ (Emmer Wheat) and Maslins of ΚΡΙΘΟΠΥΡΟΝ and ᾿ΟΛΥΡΟΚΡΙΘΟΝ." *Zeitschrift für Papyrologie und Epigraphik* 141: 210–13.

———. 2005. "σῖτος/πυρός in Egypt as Deliberate Mixtures of Wheat with Barley." *Bulletin of the American Society of Papyrologists* 42: 51–62.

Muhs, Brian P. 2005. *Tax Receipts, Taxpayers, and Taxes in Early Ptolemaic Thebes*. Oriental Institute Publications 126. Chicago: University of Chicago.

Packman, Zola M. 1968. *The Taxes in Grain in Ptolemaic Egypt: Granary Receipts from Diospolis Magna, 164–88 B.C.* American Studies in Papyrology 4. New Haven: The American Society of Papyrologists.

Rathbone, Dominic W., Dorothy J. Thompson, and Arthur Verhoogt. 2012. "A Reconstructed Land Survey from Kerkeosiris." Pages 243–65 in *Papyrological Texts in Honor of Roger S. Bagnall*. Edited by Rodney Ast, Hélène Cuvigny, Todd M. Hicky, and Julia Lougovaya. Durham: The American Society of Papyrologists.

Rostovtzeff, Michael. 1904. "Kornerhebung und -transport im griechisch-römischen Ägypten." *Archiv für Papyrusforschung* 3: 201–24.

Rowlandson, Jane. 1996. *Landowners and Tenants in Roman Egypt: The Social Relations of Agriculture in the Oxyrhynchite Nome*. Oxford Classical Monographs. Oxford: Clarendon Press.

Schuman, Verne B. 1961. "Light on Taxes in Kind in Roman Egypt." Pages 254–6 in *Proceedings of the IX International Congress of Papyrology, Oslo, 19th–22nd August, 1958*. Edited by Leiv Amundsen and Vegard Skånland. Oslo: Norwegian Universities Press.

Vandorpe, Katelijn. 2000. "The Ptolemaic Epigraphe or Harvest Tax (*Shemu*)." *Archiv für Papyrusforschung* 46: 169–232.

Verhoogt, A. M. F. W. 1998. *Menches, Komogrammateus of Kerkeosiris: The Doings and Dealings of a Village Scribe in the Late Ptolemaic Period (120–110 B.C.)*. Papyrologica Lugduno-Batava 29. Leiden; New York; Köln: Brill.

———. 2005. *Regaling Officials in Ptolemaic Egypt: A Dramatic Reading of Official Accounts from the Menches Papers*. Papyrologica Lugduno-Batava 32. Leiden; Boston: Brill.

Wallace, Sherman LeRoy. 1938. *Taxation in Egypt from Augustus to Diocletian*. Princeton University Studies in Papyrology 2. Princeton: Princeton University Press.

White, K. D. 1970. *Roman Farming*. Ithaca: Cornell University Press.

Whittaker, John C. 2000. "*Alonia* and *Dhoukanes*: The Ethnoarchaeology of Threshing in Cyprus." *Near Eastern Archaeology* 63: 62–9.

Youtie, Herbert C. 1967. "Publicans and Sinners." *Zeitschrift für Papyrologie und Epigraphik* 1: 1–20.

3 Opaque, Inconsistent, and Unfair

Some Remarks on the Burden of Roman Taxation during the Principate

David B. Hollander

The undeniably poor reputation of Roman tax collectors might seem to suggest that Roman taxes were rather high, but recent history has shown that even relatively low taxes can generate considerable resistance and a substantial volume of complaints.[1] In fact, strong arguments have been marshaled in favor of the proposition that Roman taxes were fairly low at least in the Early Imperial period,[2] though, as with other critical questions concerning the ancient economy, the evidence is so poor and ambiguous as to support wildly divergent hypotheses. In what follows I will briefly review the case both for and against the proposition that Roman taxes were low, note what we can say with confidence about Roman taxation, and, finally, suggest how a different perspective can help us better assess the impact of taxation on Rome's subjects.

Probably the most well-known case for low Roman tax levels appeared as part of Keith Hopkins's highly influential 1980 article on "Taxes and Trade in the Roman Empire." His "proposition 7" was that Roman taxes were low. That is, "the effective tax rate was significantly less than 10 per cent of gross product" (Hopkins, 1980: 119–20). Hopkins arrived at this conclusion by working from estimates of Roman GDP and the imperial budget. Assuming that the largest single expense was the military—"the anchor of our calculations"—and that this expense could be estimated, he suggested a total annual budget "probably not much larger than 800 million HS in the early first century A.D." (Hopkins, 1980: 119). He came up with an estimate for GDP by combining population estimates with a guess about the extent to which production exceeded subsistence needs.[3] Hopkins did not claim that his numbers were highly accurate. Indeed, he called his conclusions "speculative and tentative" (1980: 119). He did, however, insist on their plausibility because "if either population or gross product had been much larger than these estimates, then effective tax-rates were unbelievably low compared with declared tax-rates" (Hopkins, 1980: 120). He further argued that the great wealth of provincial elites in the early empire constituted evidence for low Roman taxes (Hopkins, 1980: 122).

Most aspects of Hopkins's taxes-and-trade model have been the subject of lively debate in the intervening years, and Hopkins himself published several

DOI: 10.4324/9781003041696-5

follow-ups,[4] but here I will skip ahead to the much more recent arguments of Walter Scheidel (2015). Scheidel refined and expanded upon Hopkins's arguments about Roman taxation. He estimated annual Roman state expenses of around one billion sesterces and an imperial GDP of nearly 20 billion sesterces in the mid-second century CE.[5] If the Romans rarely had large surpluses, the annual budget would have to be close to annual tax revenue, suggesting net imperial tax revenue was 5 to 7 percent of Roman GDP.[6] At first sight, this is a remarkable claim, but there are several qualifications that have to be kept in mind. First, Scheidel was only talking about net revenue, the "income that was actually put at the disposal of the central authorities," not the nominal tax rates nor the gross revenue (2015: 230). Second, he was focused on the Early Imperial period in contrast to the civil wars of the late republic and the period of crisis that began in the late second century CE.[7] Third, and perhaps most importantly, Scheidel was concerned only with imperial tax revenue, not local or municipal taxation, which, along with rent-taking by agents, "would have raised the share of gross revenue extraction ... by a non-trivial margin" (2015: 244). So this is a narrower claim than it at first appears to be. Scheidel was looking at Roman taxation from the perspective of the imperial bureaucracy, not that of a provincial taxpayer.

Before I discuss the arguments for higher levels of Roman taxation, let me note three additional points Scheidel made in support of low taxes. First, there are signs that Augustus lowered some rates in Egypt after annexation.[8] Second, he argued that emperors "lacked a strong incentive to maximize (net) revenue" in the period from 30 BCE to 160 CE since there was an "absence of intense interstate competition" (Scheidel, 2015: 230). Third and finally, Scheidel echoed Hopkins in connecting "the conspicuous flourishing of cities ... to the successful retention of local surpluses" (2015: 251).

Though other scholars have made a case for oppressively high Roman taxation,[9] here I will review Alan Bowman's recent critique of Scheidel's arguments. Bowman argues for a "higher taxation model" (2018: 30), questioning the plausibility of an imperial budget under one billion sesterces, which he calls "unrealistically low" (Bowman, 2018: 30). For starters, he contends that the estimated cost of maintaining the Roman army does not fully account for the extent to which the army levied goods and services (Bowman, 2018: 37). He also argues that the "proponents of the 'low-tax economy'" have overlooked "several significant categories of revenue" (Bowman, 2018: 47): military requisitions/impositions and *munera*. Most importantly, however, Bowman points to the evidence from Egypt, which supports an "average per capita tax burden" of more than 20 percent (2018: 35).

The question of the typicality of Egypt as a Roman province—for which, of course, we have far more and better evidence than from anywhere else—is all too familiar to ancient historians.[10] Scheidel argued that Egypt was rather unusual, at least with respect to taxation. He suggested that its "deeply entrenched institutions of tracking and taxing an ecologically 'caged' population and its assets" made it a focus of Roman collection efforts (Scheidel, 2015: 248). Bowman, however, pointed to some statements in literary sources that seem to indicate that high rates were common throughout the empire. Most notably, Hyginus, probably writing in the second century CE and seemingly quite well informed, reports (*Const.* 205L) that in some provinces, the landowners pay one-fifth of their produce (20 percent); but in others, they pay one-seventh (about 14 percent). Ultimately, Bowman proposed that "the overall burden on the taxpayer in the High Empire was likely to average ±20 per cent and was very unlikely to be less than 15 per cent" (2018: 47). While there is a genuine disagreement here, it is worth noting that Bowman is more concerned with the perspective of the taxpayer, while Scheidel is focused on that of the imperial bureaucracy.

Absent the discovery of major new evidence, the debate over the level of Roman taxation may never be resolved to everyone's satisfaction. There are simply too many things we don't know.[11] These include:

- whether we know of all the taxes Rome imposed;[12]
- the rates of some known taxes;[13]
- when certain taxes were imposed;[14]
- when certain taxes were canceled;[15]
- when certain tax rates changed;[16]
- in what form certain taxes were collected (cash or in kind);[17]
- the extent to which it was possible for taxpayers to employ *adaeratio*;[18]
- the "success rate" of Roman tax collection efforts;[19]
- the revenue generated by particular taxes;[20] and
- the extent to which temples paid taxes.[21]

Aside from Egypt, most scholars would probably concede that our ignorance is vast and that this makes quantification extraordinarily difficult.[22] And, whether we want to understand the fiscal capabilities of the emperor or the burdens on the average subject, conventional taxation is only one part of the equation. The Roman state took in a wide variety of revenue. In addition to its various direct and indirect taxes,[23] Rome garnered revenue in some form from the following sources:

- Fines;[24]
- Fees;[25]
- Confiscated property;[26]
- Sales of imperial property;[27]
- Rents from imperial properties;[28]
- Rents on public land;[29]
- Moneylending;[30]
- Requisitions;[31]
- Liturgies, *munera,* and corvées;[32]
- State-owned mines and quarries;[33]

- *Aurum coronarium*;[34]
- Booty;[35] and
- Legacies.[36]

As with taxes, it is difficult to come up with estimates for these categories of revenue. Some of them must have been fairly regular, but others would have been quite inconsistent. It was obviously convenient to make the local elites perform important tasks like collecting imperial taxes on behalf of their communities, but how many *denarii* was that worth to the emperor? For the revenue generated by the emperor's *patrimonium*, however, there is hope for greater insight and perhaps even plausible estimates in the near future.[37] But there is more to economic history than quantification, and we actually have a (relatively) substantial amount of evidence for Roman taxation. References to tax collectors and discussions of taxation appear frequently in everything from Suetonius's biographies to the Synoptic Gospels. This evidence prompts me to suggest three nonquantitative propositions about Roman taxation.

Proposition 1: The Roman Tax System Was Routinely Opaque

Most Roman subjects probably shared our ignorance of the rates and regulations governing imperial taxation. Leaving aside the issue of literacy, sometimes the information was not made publicly available. Suetonius (*Cal.* 41) reports that Caligula once announced a variety of taxes but did not publish the details. When he finally did publish them, they were very hard to read, having been written in tiny letters and placed in a cramped location (*minutissimis litteris et angustissimo loco*). When Nero undertook tax reforms, one of his measures was simply to publish the customs regulations (*Ann.* 13.51). The *publicani* had apparently been making up additional charges.[38] Peter Brunt (1990: 358) noted a statement by the jurist Paul concerning the importance of custom "in nearly all taxes" (*Dig.* 39.4.4.2) and speculated that "it may well be that many rules were never defined in either laws or contracts." This, of course, would have provided tax collectors with many opportunities to take advantage of the ignorant.

Proposition 2: Roman Taxes Were Perversely Inconsistent

The evidence we possess is more than sufficient to demonstrate that variation was the norm.[39] Tax rates varied from province to province, and within provinces depending on a number of factors. In Pannonia, for example, Hyginus reports (*Const.* 205L), that the fertility of the land determined the tax rate. In Egypt, there were several different categories of land and a variety of attested rates (Wallace, 1938: 1–10). For Roman Palestine, Keddie (2019: 150) notes that an adult's "sum total of taxation" would vary depending on whether they were engaged in agriculture, how they were engaged in agriculture (i.e., as landowner or some type of tenant), the extent to which they engaged in commerce, their gender, and where they lived. Customs dues (*portoria*) also varied from place to place and depending on the nature of the goods. The *Monumentum Ephesenum* specifies a general 2.5 percent duty (11), but 5 percent for *murex* fish (20), and perhaps a flat fee for enslaved individuals (12). Some goods, however, were exempt, such as things being transported for religious purposes (58).[40] Most provinces seem to have shared Asia's 2.5 percent rate, but lower and higher rates are known, and there was a 25 percent duty on goods entering the empire in the east (De Romanis, 2020: 288–91). There were also municipal duties to worry about (France, 2017), not to mention the question of how goods were valued for tax purposes.

Proposition 3: Roman Taxes Were Flagrantly Unfair

A particularly important aspect of the variation in Roman taxes was the differential treatment of individuals and communities. Peoples and cities could be punished with additional taxes or receive preferential treatment. Dio Cassius (*Hist. rom.* 54.7.5) relates that in 20 BCE Augustus ordered some communities in Asia and Bithynia to pay more than their allotted tribute. The tax imposed on Jews after the First Revolt is perhaps the best-known instance of the Romans placing an additional tax burden on a particular group of subjects. By contrast, Volubilis received a ten-year exemption under Claudius.[41] Nero gave the people of Ilium immunity from taxation, apparently because of their legendary connection to Rome and the Julian family (*Ner.* 12.58). Citizenship also conferred tax privileges. In Egypt, for example, most adult males would pay *tributum capitis*, but not Roman citizens or the citizens of Alexandria and their slaves, as well as some Egyptian priests (Wallace, 1938: 116ff.; Capponi, 2005: 138). Tacitus (*Ann.* 13.51) says that soldiers were exempt from taxes except when they were transporting commercial goods. Roman citizens were exempt from some taxes, but liable for others that provincial noncitizens did not have to pay.[42]

Beyond the special privileges granted to certain groups of people and communities fortunate enough to win the favor of the emperor, it is likely that, since local elites did much of the tax collection on behalf of Rome, those without power or connections paid more than their fair share.[43] Scheidel is undoubtedly right to describe Roman taxation as "openly unfair" (2015: 253), but *flagrantly* unfair might be even better. The cruelty may have often been the point when the taxpayers were not Roman citizens.

The opaqueness of the regulations coupled with the inconsistent and unfair nature of the collection system suggest that a defining feature of Roman taxation from the perspective of the taxpayer was its unpredictability. Would the emperor raise, lower, or abolish particular taxes?[44] Would he demand *aurum coronarium* for some reason and, if so, how would one's community go about collecting it?[45] Would arrears be canceled or used to prosecute those who had fallen behind in their payments?[46] When would a census revise the tax rolls?[47] Would requests for relief be granted?[48] How would particular collectors go about the process of collection? How closely would the imperial bureaucracy supervise the collectors? Would the process itself change? Would Roman soldiers or magistrates pass through one's city or territory and, if they did, how would they behave? It would be hard, at least for nonelites, to be confident about any interaction with tax collectors, or to know in advance what they might be expected to pay in money, kind, or labor. This uncertainty would have generated considerable amounts of anxiety and resentment even *before* we factor in the resentment of those forced to pay taxes to their foreign overlords.

For some, the payment of taxes was a mark of servitude (Tertullian, *Apol.* 13.6) in addition to a financial burden; however, no one *liked* being taxed, not even Roman citizens in Italy, who enjoyed considerable privileges and were the clearest beneficiaries of empire. In 58 CE, in response to complaints about the *publicani*, Nero apparently put forward the idea of ending all indirect taxation, which he thought would constitute the most beautiful gift for mortals (*pulcherrimum donum generi mortalium*).[49] His advisors eventually talked him out of it, and he settled for a less radical set of reforms and reductions designed to limit the abuses of the tax collectors (*Ann.* 13.50–51). Nero and the Roman public shared the same low opinion of tax collectors that was apparently current in first-century CE Judea on the cusp of revolt. To judge by all the tax collectors associating with Jesus in the Synoptic Gospels, even some of *them* had misgivings about their profession.[50]

Conclusion

If we want to understand the role of taxation in the lives of Roman subjects, which is part of the mission of the Early Christianity and the Ancient Economy research project, the *experience* of taxpayers—something for which we have *abundant* evidence—is the most important question to investigate. We can consider some effects of the tax system without knowing precisely how much was paid. Behavioral Economics suggests that the *manner* in which taxes are extracted matters quite a bit.[51] The process, the conduct of the people implementing that process, the meanings attached to the act of payment, the looming consequences of a failure to comply, and the perceived "return" (in terms of government services) all contribute to the psychological impact of taxation.[52] The US system of payroll deductions coupled with refunds of excess payments after the filing of tax returns can transform an overpayment of taxes into an apparent bonus. The Roman system had no such feature.

Notes

1. See most of US history.

2. Hopkins (1980) is discussed below. Garnsey and Saller (1987: 103) qualify Hopkins's conclusion slightly, claiming that taxes were "relatively low, at least outside Egypt." Similarly, Rathbone and Temin (2008: 416) argue that the Romans had "a relatively low tax regime (especially for the wealthy)." Lo Cascio (2007: 622–5) argues that imperial tax revenue was well below 10 percent but cautioned against concluding that "the burden of taxation was light" because "the proportion of the imperial population as a whole which paid taxes was significantly lower than the gross total, and their tax burden must have been correspondingly heavier."
3. Hopkins (1980: 117–20) believed that "gross product averaged out at less than twice minimum subsistence" but refrained from offering a specific figure. His estimate for *minimum* gross product was HS 8,244 million. See Scheidel and Friesen (2009: 64–5) for an important critique of Hopkins's calculations.
4. For some discussions of the "taxes-and-trade" model see, e.g., Harris (1993: 14), Horden and Purcell (2000: 558), van Minnen (2000), Zelener (2000), and Silver (2008). Hopkins (1995/1996 and 2000: 253–4) revisit aspects of the model.
5. Scheidel, 2015: 243, citing Scheidel and Friesen, 2009: 73–4, for the GDP estimate.
6. Scheidel, 2015: 243–4. By way of contrast, Croatia had tax revenue of 46.1 percent of GDP in 2017.
7. Scheidel (2015: 230) argues that "the entire period from 30 BCE to 160 CE serves as an example of the phenomenon of relaxation of fiscal demands."
8. Scheidel, 2015: 233–4, citing Monson, 2015: 199–200.
9. See, e.g., MacMullen (1987) and Shaw (1988).
10. Discussed, e.g., in Brunt (1981: 162–3), Bowman and Rathbone (1992: 108), and Haug (2021: 518).
11. Duncan-Jones (1990: 187) noted that we have incomplete information about the details of "provincial taxation." Brunt (1990: 356) claims, "It is impossible to insist too strongly on the paucity of documentation for the imperial fiscal system."
12. Brunt (1990: 386–7) declares that "we cannot even draw up a complete list of all imperial taxes."
13. Suetonius (*Ner.* 10) says that Nero lowered some taxes, but doesn't tell us which ones.
14. It is not clear, for example, when exactly the *centesima rerum venalium* was instituted (Günther, 2016: 9). Rathbone (2010: 429) says Augustus extended the poll tax to all provinces, but Scheidel (2015: 237) is less confident. On the timing of censuses, see also Keddie (2019: 123, n. 35).
15. Suetonius (*Ner.* 10) says that Nero abolished some taxes. Which ones? Goodman (2004) suggests that Nerva may have canceled the Jewish tax only for Trajan to restore it.
16. We don't know in what year the sales tax on enslaved individuals was doubled to 4 percent (Günther, 2016: 10), nor when the eastern frontier customs duty was halved to 12.5 percent (De Romanis, 2020: 291).
17. Hopkins (2000: 255–6) claimed that at some point in the Principate "many provinces" went from in-kind payments of taxes to cash, but Hyginus (*Const.* 205L) says practices varied from province to province. Duncan-Jones (1990: 31) says it is "very uncertain" how much direct taxes were paid in money during the Principate. See also Rowlandson (2001: 147).
18. Rathbone (1997: 198).
19. Rathbone (2010: 431); see also Scheidel (2015: 248–9) on "limited compliance" and "concealment of taxable assets."

20. For example, Goldsmith (1987: 54) argues that the revenue from the tax on the sale of enslaved individuals was small, but Harris (1999: 75) suggests it was more substantial. McGinn (2011: 647) argues that the tax on prostitution instituted in 40 CE by Caligula, "generated enormous revenues."
21. See Dignas, 2005: 208.
22. Rathbone, 2010: 431. Bowman suggests that Egypt was the only province from which one could get "any clear ideas of tax revenues" (2018: 31), but Capponi has noted that aspects of even Egypt's tax system "remain obscure," especially in the early Roman period (2005: 123). Haug (2021) observes that while the Egyptian evidence is abundant, particular areas tend to dominate, and so we don't have a representative sample from the province.
23. Debate continues over how best to refer to certain Roman taxes. Should we classify *tributum* as a direct tax and *vectigal* as indirect? Because the Roman terminology doesn't align precisely with modern economic usage, Günther (2016: 2) argues that "a better translation nowadays would be 'so-called direct tax' for *tributum* and 'so-called indirect tax' for *vectigal*." See also Shaw (1988: 810), Rathbone (2008: 254), Dignas (2005: 216), and, on *portoria,* France (2017: 61–2).
24. Ulpian (*Dig.* 50.16.131) discusses fines.
25. For example, in Egypt, Wallace (1938: 279) notes the ἐπιστολικόν, a fee for sending "official documents to Alexandria." Tax collectors probably often charged "fees" simply to enhance their profits.
26. There is ample evidence for confiscation of elite property (e.g., Suetonius, *Tib.* 49, *Cal.* 41, and *Claud.* 25). Valuables were also confiscated from those condemned to death, and Ulpian says (*Dig.* 48.20.6) that governors often passed along such revenue to the imperial treasury, though they had considerable discretion with respect to its use.
27. Dio Cassius (*Hist. rom.* 72) reports that Marcus Aurelius sold πάντα τὸν βασιλικὸν κόσμον to finance a war. See García Morcillo (2008: 265) on auctions of imperial goods.
28. Through confiscation, conquest, and inheritance, Roman emperors came to hold tremendous amounts of land throughout the empire. Tacitus (*Ann.* 4.6.4) notes that early in the reign of Tiberius, the emperor did not possess much land in Italy and employed a limited household staff (*rari per Italiam Caesaris agri, modesta servitia, intra paucos libertos domus*). That would soon change dramatically (Drexhage et al., 2002: 45). On imperial estates in North Africa, see Kehoe (2021: 509ff.).
29. For *scripturae* (payments for the use of public pastures), see Rathbone (1996: 315).
30. The largest and clearest examples of imperial lending involve interest-free loans such as the hundred million *sesterces* distributed by Tiberius in 33 CE (Tacitus, *Ann.* 6.16–7; Suetonius, *Tib.* 48.2; and Dio Cassius, *Hist. rom.* 58.21.4–5). Still, loans through the emperor's agents were likely to have been common. Public funds might also be loaned out, as an exchange between Pliny the Younger and Trajan makes clear (*Ep.* 10.54–5). Since moneylending was common among the Roman elite, the confiscation of property would have regularly brought outstanding loans into the hands of the emperor. Dio Cassius (*Hist. rom.* 52.28.3–4) has Maecenas recommend to Augustus that he sell most of the land that the state had acquired and loan the proceeds at interest.
31. Requisitioned items might include horses, mules, and grain (*Dig.* 50.4.18). Billeting seems to have been a common requisition as well. The rules governing who was liable and who was exempt from what *munera* were complicated.

32. Tax collection itself, on behalf of the Roman state, was a liturgy that Rome increasingly imposed on its subjects in the early empire (van Nijf, 2008: 286; Shaw, 1988: 814). In Roman Egypt, there was a five-day corvée for dike maintenance, the πενθήμερος. See discussion in Capponi (2005: 75–6). Verboven and Laes (2017: 12) doubt *corvée* labor was "a central institution to the Roman economy," but note that "it was a common fiscal strategy" whose use probably extended beyond dykes to roads and other forms of infrastructure.
33. Mines would have been especially important. See discussion in, e.g., Shaw (1988: 815), Russell (2013), and Scheidel (2015: 245–6).
34. *Aurum coronarium* ("gifts" of gold for the emperor) was expected after an emperor's accession and on occasions such as triumphs. Wallace (1938: 282) notes that "late in the second half of the second century, the theory of the crown-tax was so far forgotten that the στεφανικόν became an annual exaction" in Egypt. See also Duncan-Jones (1980: 217).
35. Particularly, no doubt, in the form of the enslaved. Josephus (*B.J.* 7.132–52) indicates the variety of spoils from Jerusalem displayed in Vespasian's triumph.
36. For discussion, see Millar (1977: 153–5).
37. The PATRIMONIVM project (Geography and Economy of the Imperial Properties in the Roman World) is nearing completion. Their *Atlas patrimonii Caesaris* should prove particularly useful: https://patrimonium.huma-num.fr/atlas/. See also Maiuro (2012).
38. Nero's measures also gave priority to lawsuits against the *publicani.*
39. Shaw described Roman taxation as "a bewildering maze" (1988: 809), while Rathbone observed that there was "endless local variation" (2010: 429–30). Scheidel would presumably agree to some extent with this characterization since, as we have seen, he argues for the "disproportionate importance of revenue from key regions" (2015: 248). As has frequently been noted, one reason for the variation in taxation was the Roman tendency to adopt the collection practices in operation prior to conquest (Günther, 2016: 2), but there were certainly some adaptation and innovation as well.
40. For text, translation, and commentary: Cottier et al. (2008). See also Brunt (1990: 386–7) and Rathbone (1996: 314). Duncan-Jones (2006: 4) describes the structure of Roman customs rates as "very untidy."
41. *Inscriptions antiques du Maroc* 2.448 (Euzennat and Marion, 1982: no. 448).
42. Most famously, the inheritance tax. See de Blois (2014) for discussion of the *Constitutio Antoniniana.*
43. Shaw suggested that the "unprotected peasant proprietor" paid "closer to half than to a tenth of his total production" (1988: 824). Rathbone also believed that taxation "fell disproportionately on the poor" (2010: 431). See also Keddie (2019: 112).
44. While the details are often hazy, we frequently hear about the adjustments to taxation made by Roman emperors. Vespasian's unexpected accession brought a number of sudden changes. He restored the taxes canceled by Galba, instituted new taxes, and increased provincial tribute amounts (*Vesp.* 16). On a smaller scale, note that communities sometimes suspended customs and/or sales taxes during festivals (de Ligt, 1993: 229–34).
45. Pliny the Younger praised Trajan for declining *aurum coronarium* (*Pan.* 41.1).
46. Augustus burned old debts to the treasury (*Aug.* 32.2) as did Nero (*Ann.* 13.23). Claudius had created a senatorial commission to help collect arrears (Dio Cassius, *Hist. rom.* 60.10.4). Trajan (*Pan.* 40.2–5 and 55.5), Hadrian (*SHA Had.* 7.6; Dio Cassius, *Hist. rom.* 69.8, epit.), and Marcus Aurelius (Dio Cassius,

Hist. rom. 72.32.2) canceled some arrears. Cassius Dio says that Marcus Aurelius canceled forty-five years of arrears to both the emperor's treasury and the public treasury.

47. It is not clear that censuses were conducted on a regular basis (Shaw, 1988: 814).
48. Strabo (*Geogr.* 10.5.3) tells the story of a fisherman who was sent to Octavian to request a reduction of tribute. His village on the island of Gyaros in the Cyclades was having trouble paying the hundred and fifty drachmas demanded of them. In 17 CE, Syria and Judea requested that their taxes be reduced (Tacitus, *Ann.* 2.42).
49. Two emperors, Caligula and Galba, used coins to celebrate the abolition of a tax (Elkins, 2014).
50. The implication of Matt 9:10–12, Mark 2:15–17, and Luke 5:29–32 would seem to be that tax collectors sought out Jesus because of their sins. See also Matt 21:31–32 and, for the parable of the penitent tax collector, Luke 18:9–14. Tax collectors approached John the Baptist, too (Luke 3:12–13). However, some tax collectors were proud enough of their profession to have it recorded in inscriptions (van Nijf, 2008: 300).
51. See discussions of framing, loss aversion, and prospect theory in, e.g., Thaler (2015).
52. Happiness studies offers an exciting new perspective on the ancient economy by, among other things, taking a more holistic view of taxation. See, e.g., Vandorpe (2013) and Wyns (2018).

Bibliography

Blois, Lukas de. 2014. "The *Constitutio Antoniniana* (AD 212): Taxes or Religion?" *Mnemosyne* 67: 1014–21.

Bowman, Alan K. 2018. "The State and the Economy: Fiscality and Taxation." Pages 27–52 in *Trade, Commerce, and the State in the Roman World.* Edited by Andrew Wilson and Alan K. Bowman. Oxford: Oxford University Press.

Bowman, Alan K., and Dominic Rathbone. 1992. "Cities and Administration in Roman Egypt." *Journal of Roman Studies* 82: 107–27.

Brunt, Peter A. 1981. "The Revenues of Rome." *Journal of Roman Studies* 71: 161–72.

———. 1990. "Publicans in the Principate." Pages 354–432 in *Roman Imperial Themes.* Oxford: Clarendon.

Capponi, Livia. 2005. *Augustan Egypt: The Creation of a Roman Province.* New York: Routledge.

Cottier, M., Michael H. Crawford, C. V. Crowther, J.-L. Ferrary, Barbara Levick, O. Salomies, and M. Wörrle, eds. 2008. *The Customs Law of Asia.* Oxford: Oxford University Press.

De Romanis, Federico. 2020. *The Indo-Roman Pepper Trade and the Muziris Papyrus.* Oxford: Oxford University Press.

Dignas, Beate. 2005. "Sacred Revenues in Roman Hands: The Economic Dimension of Sanctuaries in Western Asia Minor." Pages 207–24 in *Patterns in the Economy of Roman Asia Minor.* Edited by Stephen Mitchell and Constantina Katsari. Swansea: The Classical Press of Wales.

Drexhage, Hans-Joachim, Heinrich Konen, and Kai Ruffing. 2002. *Die Wirtschaft des Römischen Reiches (1.–3. Jahrhundert).* Berlin: Akademie Verlag.

Duncan-Jones, Richard P. 1980. "The Wealth of Gaul." *Chiron* 11: 217–20.

———. 1990. *Structure and Scale in the Roman Economy*. Cambridge: Cambridge University Press.

———. 2006. "Roman Customs Dues: A Comparative View." *Latomus* 65: 3–16.

Elkins, Nathan T. 2014. "Taxes, Liberty, and the *Quadrantes* of Caligula." *Numismatic Chronicle* 174: 111–7.

Euzennat, Maurice, and Jean Marion, eds. 1982. *Inscriptions Latines*. Vol. 2 of *Inscriptions antiques du Maroc*. Paris: Centre National de la Recherche Scientifique.

France, Jérôme. 2017. *Finances Publiques, Intérêts Privés dans le Monde Romain*. Pessac: Ausonius Éditions.

García Morcillo, Marta. 2008. "Auctions, Bankers and Public Finances in the Roman World." Pages 256–75 in *Pistoi dia tèn technèn: Bankers, Loans and Archives in the Ancient World; Studies in Honour of Raymond Bogaert*. Edited by Koenraad Verboven, K. Vandorpe, and V. Chankowski. Leuven: Peeters.

Garnsey, Peter D. A., and Richard P. Saller. 1987. *The Roman Empire: Economy, Society and Culture*. Berkeley and Los Angeles: University of California Press.

Goldsmith, R. W. 1987. *Premodern Financial Systems: A Historical Comparative Study*. Cambridge: Cambridge University Press.

Goodman, Martin. 2004. "Trajan and the Origins of Roman Hostility to the Jews." *Past and Present* 182: 3–29.

Günther, Sven. 2016. "Taxation in the Greco-Roman World: The Roman Principate." in *Oxford Handbooks Online: Scholarly Research Reviews*. DOI: 10.1093/oxfordhb/9780199935390.013.38. Last accessed 2 August 2021.

Harris, William V. 1993. "Between Archaic and Modern: Problems in Roman Economic History." Pages 11–29 in *The Inscribed Economy: Production and Distribution in the Roman Empire in the Light of Instrumentum Domesticum*. Edited by William V. Harris. Ann Arbor: University of Michigan.

———. 1999. "Demography, Geography and the Sources of Roman Slaves." *Journal of Roman Studies* 89: 62–75.

Haug, Brendan. 2021. "Agriculture in Roman Egypt." Pages 517–38 in *A Companion to Ancient Agriculture*. Edited by David B. Hollander and Timothy Howe. Hoboken: Wiley Blackwell.

Hopkins, Keith. 1980. "Taxes and Trade in the Roman Empire (200 B.C.–A.D. 400)." *Journal of Roman Studies* 70: 101–25.

———. 1995/1996. "Rome, Taxes, Rents and Trade." *Kodai* 6/7: 41–75.

———. 2000. "Rents, Taxes, Trade and the City of Rome." Pages 253–67 in *Mercati permanenti e mercati periodici nel mondo Romano: Atti degli incontri Capresi di storia dell'economia antica (Capri 13–15 Ottobre 1997)*. Edited by Elio Lo Cascio. Bari: Edipuglia.

Horden, Peregrine, and Nicholas Purcell. 2000. *The Corrupting Sea: A Study of Mediterranean History*. Oxford: Blackwell.

Keddie, Anthony. 2019. *Class and Power in Roman Palestine: The Socioeconomic Setting of Judaism and Christian Origins*. Cambridge: Cambridge University Press.

Kehoe, Dennis P. 2021. "Agriculture in Roman North Africa." Pages 499–516 in *A Companion to Ancient Agriculture*. Edited by David B. Hollander and Timothy Howe. Hoboken: Wiley Blackwell.

Ligt, Luuk de. 1993. *Fairs and Markets in the Roman Empire: Economic and Social Aspects of Periodic Trade in a Pre-Industrial Society*. Amsterdam: Gieben.

Lo Cascio, Elio. 2007. "The Early Roman Empire: The State and the Economy." Pages 619–47 in *The Cambridge Economic History of the Greco-Roman World.* Edited by Walter Scheidel, Ian Morris, and Richard Saller. Cambridge: Cambridge University Press.

MacMullen, Ramsay. 1987. "Tax-Pressure in the Roman Empire." *Latomus* 46: 737–54.

Maiuro, Marco. 2012. *Res Caesaris: Ricerche sulla Proprietà Imperiale nel Principato.* Bari: Edipuglia.

McGinn, Thomas. 2011. "Roman Prostitutes and Marginalization." Pages 643–59 in *The Oxford Handbook of Social Relations in the Roman World.* Edited by Michael Peachin. Oxford: Oxford University Press.

Millar, Fergus. 1977. *The Emperor in the Roman World (31 BC–AD 337).* London: Duckworth.

Minnen, Peter van. 2000. "Agriculture and the 'Taxes-and-Trade' Model in Roman Egypt." *Zeitschrift für Papyrologie und Epigraphik* 133: 205–20.

Monson, Andrew. 2015. "Hellenistic Empires." Pages 169–207 in *Fiscal Regimes and the Political Economy of Premodern States.* Edited by Andrew Monson and Walter Scheidel. Cambridge: Cambridge University Press.

Nijf, Onno van. 2008. "The Social World of Tax Farmers and Their Personnel." Pages 279–311 in *The Customs Law of Asia.* Edited by M. Cottier, Michael H. Crawford, C. V. Crowther, J.-L. Ferrary, Barbara Levick, O. Salomies, and M. Wörrle. Oxford: Oxford University Press.

Rathbone, Dominic. 1996. "The Imperial Finances." Pages 309–23 in vol. 10 of *The Cambridge Ancient History.* Edited by A. Bowman, E. Champlin, and A. Lintott. Cambridge: Cambridge University Press.

———. 1997. "Prices and Price Formation in Roman Egypt." Pages 183–244 in *Économie Antique: Prix et formation des prix dans les économies antiques.* Edited by Jean Andreau, Pierre Briant, and Raymond Descat. Saint-Bertrand-de-Comminges: Musée Archéologique Départemental.

———. 2008. "Nero's Reforms of *Vectigalia* and the Inscription of the *Lex Portorii Asiae.*" Pages 251–78 in *The Customs Law of Asia.* Edited by M. Cottier, Michael H. Crawford, C. V. Crowther, J.-L. Ferrary, Barbara Levick, O. Salomies, and M. Wörrle. Oxford: Oxford University Press.

———. 2010. "Taxation, Roman." Pages 429–32 in vol. 6 of *The Oxford Encyclopedia of Ancient Greece and Rome.* 7 vols. Edited by M. Gargarin and E. Fantham. Oxford: Oxford University Press.

Rathbone, Dominic, and Peter Temin. 2008. "Financial Intermediation in First-Century AD Rome and Eighteenth-Century England." Pages 371–419 in *Pistoi dia tèn technèn: Bankers, Loans and Archives in the Ancient World; Studies in Honour of Raymond Bogaert.* Edited by Koenraad Verboven, K. Vandorpe, and V. Chankowski. Leuven: Peeters.

Rowlandson, Jane. 2001. "Money Use among the Peasantry of Ptolemaic and Roman Egypt." Pages 145–55 in *Money and Its Uses in the Ancient Greek World.* Edited by Andrew Meadows and Kirsty Shipton. Oxford: Oxford University Press.

Russell, Ben. 2013. *The Economics of the Roman Stone Trade.* Oxford: Oxford University Press.

Scheidel, Walter. 2015. "The Early Roman Monarchy." Pages 229–57 in *Fiscal Regimes and the Political Economy of Premodern States.* Edited by Andrew Monson and Walter Scheidel. Cambridge: Cambridge University Press.

Scheidel, Walter, and Steven J. Friesen. 2009. "The Size of the Economy and the Distribution of Income in the Roman Empire." *Journal of Roman Studies* 99: 61–91.

Shaw, Brent D. 1988. "Roman Taxation." Pages 809–27 in vol. 2 of *Civilization of the Ancient Mediterranean: Greece and Rome*. Edited by Michael Grant and Rachel Kitzinger. 2 vols. New York: Scribner's Sons.

Silver, Morris. 2008. "The Rise, Demise, and (Partial) Rehabilitation of the Peasant in Hopkins' Model of Roman Trade and Taxes." *Classics Ireland* 15: 1–33.

Thaler, Richard H. 2015. *Misbehaving: The Making of Behavioral Economics*. New York: Norton & Co.

Vandorpe, Katelijn. 2013. "A Happiness Index for Antiquity? Hellenistic Egypt as a Case-Study." Pages 91–103 in *Egitto: dai faraoni agli arabi. Atti del Convegno; Egitto: amministrazione, economia, società, cultura dai faraoni agli arabi / Égypte: administration, économie, société, culture des pharaons aux arabes; Milano, Università degli Studi, 7–9 gennaio 2013*. Edited by Silvia Bussi. Pisa: Fabrizio Serra Editore.

Verboven, Koenraad, and Christian Laes. 2017. "Work, Labour, Professions. What's in a Name?" Pages 1–19 in *Work, Labour, and Professions in the Roman World*. Edited by Koenraad Verboven and Christian Laes. Leiden: Brill.

Wallace, Sherman LeRoy. 1938. *Taxation in Egypt from Augustus to Diocletian*. Princeton: Princeton University Press.

Wyns, Valérie. 2018. "Happiness in the Kingdom of the Cleopatras: Examining Government Influence on Quality of Life in Hellenistic Egypt (332–30 BC)." *Historická Sociologie* 2: 9–26.

Zelener, Yan. 2000. "Market Dynamics in Roman North Africa." Pages 223–35 in *Mercati permanenti e mercati periodici nel mondo Romano: Atti degli incontri Capresi di storia dell'economia antica (Capri 13–15 Ottobre 1997)*. Edited by Elio Lo Cascio. Bari: Edipuglia.

4 Roman Provincial Censuses as Sociopolitical Regulation

Implications for Interpreting the Synoptic Gospels and Acts[1]

G. Anthony Keddie

In an impassioned editorial in *The Guardian*, the journalist and scholar Moustafa Bayoumi proclaimed, "I'm a brown Arab-American and the US census refuses to recognize me" (Bayoumi, 2019). The 2010 US census categories, which are being reused in the 2020 census despite considerable dissent, separate ethnicity and race and ask only about Hispanic, Latino, or Spanish ethnicity. The census questionnaire allows for four different races—White, Black or African American, American Indian or Alaskan Native, and "some other race." Records from the 2000 and 2010 censuses show that the "others" in this fourth category constitute the third largest racial demographic in the United States, and that those who selected this category were, in fact, 97 percent Hispanic, Latinx, or Spanish. Bayoumi noted that the race categories on the census not only force Latinxs into a category of "others," but they also misclassify other racial groups. In his words,

> According to the Office of Management and Budget's classifications, "white" refers to a person having origins in any of the original peoples of Europe, the Middle East, or North Africa. My origins are from Egypt. Every day, I live my life in America as a brown person. Defining me as white and likening me to a European, as the census does, is absurd.
>
> (Bayoumi, 2019)

In the months following the publication of Bayoumi's editorial, a federal judge prevented the Trump administration from adding a citizenship question to the 2020 census in what the leaked Hofeller files have exposed as a nefarious attempt to aid Republican redistricting efforts by scaring immigrants away from voting (Wines, 2019). As a result, it is clearer than ever that censuses are not an innocuous tool for collecting population statistics, for counting people.

Following recent debates about the US census while researching the economics of the Roman census has been unsettling, yet revealing. I now see that my positions of privilege as a white, male, US citizen have enabled me to overlook many of the ways that censuses institutionalize discriminatory discourses pertaining to gender, class, status, ethnicity, race, and citizenship. Censuses have been used in the United States to block people

DOI: 10.4324/9781003041696-6

of racially mixed ancestry from marrying whites (the so-called "one-drop rule"), to determine who counted as "Jewish" in Nazi Germany, to identify who counted as "Tutsi" during the genocide in Rwanda, and so on.[2]

Despite the widespread use of modern censuses to marginalize certain groups, scholars have scarcely explored this as a potential dimension of the Roman census. Mainstream New Testament scholarship has been too preoccupied with determining the authenticity of Luke's narrative about the Augustan census.[3] Beyond this search for authenticity, only two consequences of the census are usually taken into account: first, that Roman censuses were symptomatic of an increased tax burden under Roman rule; and second, that the Roman census symbolized the loss of national sovereignty through subjection to direct Roman rule (among others: Dunn, 2003: 310; Horsley, 2006). In this regard, many scholars have interpreted the impact of the census through the lens of Josephus's account of the Zealots emerging in response to the 6 CE census. If we only had Josephus, it would indeed appear that the census caused increased taxation and provoked widespread resentment toward Roman rule that culminated in the First Jewish Revolt.[4]

Fortunately, however, Egyptian and Arabian census documents can help us to fill out this picture. These are the main sources that I investigate in this paper. I begin by examining the economic implications of provincial censuses in the Roman East before turning to their sociopolitical effects. Inspired by Bayoumi's call to recognize how the US census regulates racial identities, I then proceed to identify ways in which the New Testament passages on the census may reflect this institution's marginalization of women, Jews, and other disadvantaged persons.

Economic Regulation

There are substantial gaps in our knowledge of Roman censuses, but one thing is very clear: census practices differed significantly from province to province and even from village to village. Luke's description of a universal Augustan census advances his own perception of how the census was organized. Documentary and inscriptional evidence shows, however, that censuses were administered differently by each province (Le Teuff, 2012: 299–344).[5] Augustus extended the census throughout the empire, but his provincial governors and their subordinates were responsible for conducting each province's census.

In the imperial era, the earliest known provincial census was taken in Gaul (and probably Spain) in 27 to 25 BCE (following a census of just Roman citizens in 28 BCE) (Le Teuff, 2012: 15–6). Some scholars have supposed that the Egyptian census, known as the "house-by house registration" (*kat' oikian apographē*), began around the same time, but 11/10 BCE is the earliest Egyptian census date known from the papyri. Securely dated documents indicate that the census was taken every seven years before a fourteen-year cycle began in 19/20 CE (Claytor and Bagnall, 2015). The eventual standardization of a fourteen-year cycle is an important clue that one of the main functions of the Egyptian census was to collect poll taxes: men were required to pay the poll tax from the age of 14, so the fourteen-year census ensured that all minors who would become eligible for the poll tax during the coming cycle would be counted.

Recent research by Andrew Monson (2012; 2014a; 2014b), among others, has problematized two traditional scholarly assumptions about the Egyptian census: first, that it was a Roman innovation; and second, that it was used as a tool of economic exploitation in the form of increasing the tax burden. In the first century BCE, Ptolemaic officials used censuses to collect a range of capitation taxes, such as the *syntaxis* and *epistatikon*. Much like under Augustus, Ptolemaic censuses and their related poll taxes were sometimes given the name *laographia*. A petition from an Egyptian priest to the prefect in 5/4 BCE assumes outright continuity between a type of *laographia* under Cleopatra and the one taken under Roman rule:

> To Gaius Turranius from Soterichos son of Nouchis, a priest chosen by his fellow priests Haryothes, Harsiesis, and Soterichos, priests of Isis, Sarapis, Harpsenesis, and Asklepios in Bousiris of the Herakleopolite nome beyond Memphis. Great governor, formerly even in the time of the queen [Cleopatra VII] until the 25th year of divine Caesar Augustus [6/5 BCE], we four priests out of the six who perform sacred services and carry out purifications and sacrifices two by two were undisturbed on account of the poll tax [*laographia*] but in the present 26th year of Caesar [5/4 BCE] because Epiodoros the royal scribe of the nome registered us for collection we were pressed into payment on account of the poll tax [*laographia*] for four years, each of us 64 silver drachmas [16 each], and on account of dike-taxes 108 silver drachmas. We therefore ask…
>
> (*BGU* IV 1198 [5/4 BCE, Herakleopolite nome];
> trans. Monson, 2014a: 150)

Acting as a representative for his fellow priests, Soterichos pursued the continuation of an exemption from the *laographia* for priests that was in place under Cleopatra VII, prior to Roman annexation. The request assumes that this exemption was maintained as part of the local census practice after annexation but was ignored for the first time in 5/4 BCE.

Literary and documentary sources show that the Ptolemaic censuses and concomitant capitation taxes had been highly irregular and were often abused by officials (Keddie, 2016: 204–6). Where sufficient data are available, it is now clear that the Augustan poll tax (most often 16 drachmas) represented either the same or a lesser burden than the Ptolemaic head taxes. In the Herakleopolite nome, for instance, it appears that the Roman government reduced the late Ptolemaic rate of 20 drachmas or higher per year to 16 drachmas (Monson, 2014a). These Egyptian data should make us cautious about assuming that any provincial censuses increased the local tax burden. Relative continuity was more likely the norm.

The declarations from the 127 CE census in Arabia suggest that the main purpose of censuses in *this* province was to collect land tributes, not poll taxes as in Egypt. The following declarations employ much of the same formulaic language, though gender may account for some key differences.[6]

> I, Sammouos son of Shim'on, of Maoza in the Zoarene district of the Petra administrative region, domiciled in my own private property [*oikōn* [*e*]*n idiois*] in the said Maoza, register myself [*apographomai emauton*], thirty years old, [as owner of a] half-share of a field…
>
> (P.Ḥev./Se. 62 [127 CE]; trans. Cotton, from Cotton and Yardeni, 1997, modified)

> I, Babatha daughter of Simon, of Maoza in the Zoarene district of the Petra administrative region, domiciled in my own private property [*oikousa en idiois*] in the said Maoza, register what I possess [*apographomai ha kektēmai*] (present with me as my guardian being Judanes son of Elazar, of the village of En-Gedi in the district of Jericho in Judea, domiciled in his own private property [*oikountos en idiois*] in the said Maoza).
>
> (P.Yad. 16 [127 CE]; trans. Lewis, 1989, modified)

On the basis of these two declarations, there is a debate about whether Babatha, and thus women in Arabia, were required to pay a poll tax. According to the third-century CE jurist Ulpian (*Dig.* 50.15.3), women paid poll taxes in Syria. This has led Udoh (2005: 218, 229), Cotton (2003), and others to conclude that they likely paid poll taxes in second-century CE Arabia (unlike in Egypt at the same time). The different language employed in the highly formulaic declarations of Babatha and Sammouos is striking, however. Whereas Sammouos's declaration says "I … register myself, thirty years old…," Babatha's says "I … register what I possess," names her legal guardian, and does not list her age. I am not convinced that we have enough information to say with any certainty whether women paid the poll tax in second-century CE Arabia, but the evidence that we do have suggests that they might not have done so (Lo Cascio, 1999: 201; cf. Lewis, 1988: 136; Cotton, 2003: 114–5; Udoh, 2005: 218; Le Teuff, 2012: 160–62).

Apart from the question of gender, the fact that these two declarants mentioned where they were domiciled and, at least in the case of men, their age, shows that the Arabian registrations involved more than just land tributes paid in kind. The demographic information these registrations collected would also have been used to continue the collection of certain Nabataean monetary taxes.[7] Unfortunately, based on the extant sources, we have no way of knowing how the rate of the land tribute in Arabia compared to its Nabataean antecedent.

The Syrian governor (technically, *legatus Augusti pro praetore*) Quirinius conducted the first Roman census of Judea in 6 CE. It involved the registration of property and thus served the purpose of collecting land tributes. Like its Arabian counterpart, this census collected information beyond what was necessary for land taxes. Note, for instance, that the epitaph of Quintus Aemilius Secundus recognizes an official's part in counting 117,000 people in Apamaea during Quirinius's census of Syria, presumably part of the same 6 CE census that impacted Judea: "On the orders of Quirinius, I was also the person who conducted the census of the city of Apamaea: 117 thousand citizens of both sexes" (*iussu Quirini censum egi Apamenae civitatis millium homin(um) civium CXVII*) (trans. Hall, 2004: 49, modified).[8] How would this population statistic have been known if the census were only for property registration? We cannot be certain that the Judean censuses were also used for capitation taxes, but I suspect that the information they collected was indeed used to resume the collection of Herodian capitation taxes; for example, the "house tax" remitted by Herod Agrippa I according to Josephus (*A.J.* 19.299).

What does this lacunose record of provincial censuses tell us about their functions and consequences? If we consider the Roman provincial census only as a mechanism for collecting taxes, we should conclude that it improved economic conditions in the provinces: it made tax collection more efficient, placed checks on administrative corruption, and standardized taxes at a rate equal or lower than that of previous regimes. In this sense, the provincial census was an institution whose function was economic regulation.

Scholarly theories of regulation are a nexus at which there is considerable convergence between New Institutional Economics and the Marxist *Régulation* School (Labrousse and Weisz, 2013). Both approaches are helpful for interpreting the institutional impact of the census. Proponents of the former identify the ways that institutions gradually reduce economic uncertainty in society by structuring human interaction. They argue that informal institutions such as cultural norms induce socioeconomic continuity and stability, even after political upheavals (among others: North, 1990). This New Institutional framework makes sense of the continuity between Ptolemaic and Roman census practices and the potentially positive effects of the introduction of regular census intervals and poll tax rates. Yet, the dialectical framework of Marxist *régulation* theory rightly reminds us that regulation is not always a blessing. As Roland Boer and Christina Petterson observe, "The solution is at one and the same time the cause of further problems" (2017: 46).

Sociopolitical Regulation

If the purpose of the census were only to collect head and land tributes, there would be no reason for census declarations to list people who were not liable to these taxes. In Egypt, only men between the ages of 14 and 62 had to pay the poll tax, yet census declarations also included women, minors, and elders. This is because the census was also a broad-ranging institution of population control, which generated and maintained norms. Building on

Foucault's (2007; 2008) interpretation of the census as a modality of biopower aimed at population control, some scholars of racial politics have described the US census as institutionalized discourse that prejudicially distributes privileges, regulates bodies, and shapes subjectivities (Nobles, 2000; Sandset, 2018). The census does not reflect reality; it constructs it. In different ways, this was also true of Roman provincial censuses.

The Egyptian census declarations list age, filiation, distinguishing physical marks such as scars and even moles, certain types of legal status, and in some cases professions (Capponi, 2005: 92). One of the most striking features of the census declarations is that they were often filed by the male head of the household (*pater familias*) on behalf of those in his home, his social subordinates. When there was no male head of the household, a female would register under the aegis of a legal guardian, as in the land registration of Babatha presented above and, for instance, in the census declaration of Tatubynchis of Philadelphia:

> To Eirenaios and Maron and Herakleides and Ammonios and Petesouchos, *laographoi*, and to Herakleides, village clerk of Philadelphia, from Tatybynchis, daughter of Mareis, of the same village, with my guardian, my relative Patouamtis, son of Ptollis. In the present twentieth year of Tiberius Caesar Augustus I register my son Panetbeueis, son of Kephalon, who lives in my own house; my above-mentioned son Panetbeueis, son of Kephalon, is 5 years old, and myself, Tatybynchis, daughter of Mareis, 35 years old, with a scar on my right thumb, together with my guardian, my relative Patouamtis, son of Ptollis, who is 36 years old and has a scar below his right brow.
>
> (*SB* I 5661 [34 CE, Philadelphia]; Huebner, 2019: 39)

After census declarations were received, tax officials glued them together into tax rolls called *tomoi* (Bagnall and Frier, 1994: 19–21, 28). This demographic information then served as a basis for generating lists of people liable to certain taxes or public liturgies and lists of those eligible for tax discounts. It also served as an official record for establishing inheritance rights.[9]

The only surviving document that might be related to the Judean census appears to be some sort of census-derived register. Discovered at Naḥal Ṣe'elim, this document was likely composed in Judea in the first half of the second century CE (though an Arabian origin is also possible). It lists at least 55 men along with their ages, all between the ages of 13 and 67 (see Table 4.1).

Hannah Cotton has demonstrated, through comparison with Egyptian tax registers, that the names are arranged by household (see Cotton's critical edition of the document in Charlesworth, 2000; cf. Cotton, 2003). The head of the household is listed first with a patronymic and is followed by the names of other male members of the household, which are indented by

Table 4.1 Excerpt of census list (P.Jud.Des.Misc. 4) from Judea or Arabia (Greek, first half of second cent. CE)[10]

Col. i	*Col. ii*	*Col. iii*
	[age] 25	
	[ag]e 13	[....]..[
	[ag]e 19	Yeshu'a, son of Levi
	[ag]e 41	[...]nor [son]
	[age]	Yosepos [another son]
	[age]	Yeshu'a, an[other son]
trace		Yosepos [another son]
son of [o]s	[age]	Aneinas [another son]
son of		Ellelos, an[other son]
[Shim']on (?)	age 61	Gaius, a[nother son]
		Se..os, son of Seima[
	age 67	A[
		K[
	[ ]	
	[ ]	
	[age] 22	
	[age] 36	
	[age] [?]2	

one centimeter.[11] Whether this very fragmentary document was indeed a tax register or served a different purpose (e.g., registration for public liturgies), the information on it was likely derived from census declarations.

In Egypt, *laographia* declarations appeared very similar to *epikrisis* declarations, and these terms were sometimes used interchangeably in official documents (Wallace, 1938: 109–12; Capponi, 2005: 92–5). Technically, an *epikrisis* was an examination of special statuses in order to determine tax discounts. Most of the same officials who oversaw the census were also involved in the *epikrisis*.

The *epikrisis* was an extension of the census that discriminated according to ethnicity. As Broux (2013; 2015) and others have argued, the Roman *epikrisis* practices gradually transformed the Ptolemaic head tax privileges for "settlers" (*katoikoi*) and those called "Greeks" (*hellēnes*), who may not have self-identified as Greek, into privileged rates for urban elites categorized as "metropolitans" or part of the gymnasial order.[12] Consider the following first-century CE record of an *epikrisis* of metropolitans and the gymnasial order in Hermopolis Magna, for example:

> To Antonius Ptolemaios, *strategos* of the Hermopolite nome. Those minors of the metropolis entering the age-group of fourteen years old in the *oktadrachmoi* [i.e., an order liable to pay only half of the poll tax rate—8 drachmas] and those of the order of the gymnasium, since they have to be scrutinized [i.e., *epikrisis*], if they preserve their metropolite

> descent from both parents, those from the gymnasium, if they are from that order itself. For the *epikrisis* of these (boys) it will be most necessary that it happens by worthy men of [70 (?)] years old.
>
> (*SB* V 8038 [first cent. CE, Hermopolis Magna]; trans. Broux, 2013: 147–8)

The institutional discourse advanced by provincial census and *epikrisis* practices thus construed Roman citizens and Alexandrian citizens, who were tax exempt, as superior to metropolitans and the gymnasial order in other Egyptian cities, who received tax discounts, and both of these brackets as superior to the majority of the population of Egypt (Broux, 2013).[13]

An *epikrisis* was not just a mechanism for examining privileged statuses, however. According to the lengthy Arsinoe papyrus of 73 CE, it was also used to collect the *Ioudaiōn telesma*, the tax exacted from *Ioudaioi* ("Judeans"/"Jews") throughout the empire following the First Revolt in Judea (Wallace 1938, 170–6; Heemstra, 2010; Keddie, 2018):

> The report of Herakleides, *amphodarchēs* of the quarter of "Apollonios Camp." The liability for the Jewish tax for the fifth year of the Emperor Caesar Vespasian Augustus being an abstract according to the statement of the fourth year. The number of Jews taken up by previous accounts are 5 adult males, 6 adult females, of whom one is over age and was adjudged as such, being 59 years of age in the fourth year, one minor, being four years of age in the fourth year, total of names 12. And those taken up through a transcript of the preceding *epikrisis* shown to be three years of age in the fourth year, being one year old in the second year. Males: Philiskos, son of Ptollas, grandson of Philiskos, mother Erotion. Females: Protous, daughter of Simon, son of Ptolemaios, mother Disarion, total 2, 14 in all, of these adult males 5, minor male 1, who in the fifth year was five years old, likewise 1 minor female four years old … total of names 14. In addition there is enrolled in the Jewish tax in the fifth year of Emperor Caesar Vespasian Augustus, of minors who in the third year were one year old and so in the fifth year three years old, of males taken up, Seuthes, son of Theodoros, grandson of Ptolemaios, mother Philous found to be two years old in the fourth year, in the *epikrisis* of the fourth year; total of names 15; of which adult males 5, 1 minor male who in the fifth year is five years old, adult females 6, 1 female minor who in the fifth year is five years old, adult females 6, 1 female minor who in the fifth year is five years old, likewise 1 four years old, total 15. Of these 5 adult males being of those in the list as liable to the maximum rate of the *laographia*, 5 names, and the remaining names 10….
>
> Together with the 5 names of those liable to the maximum rate of the *laographia*, total as above 15 names, at 8 drachmai and 2 oboloi each, 125 drachmai, for the *aparchai* 15 drachmai, total 140 drachmai. A similar copy has been deposited with the royal scribe through Amoutio … the scribe.
>
> (*CPJ* 2:421 [73 CE, Arsinoe]; trans. Tcherikover, 1957)

Whereas *Ioudaioi* were not required to list their ethnicity on census declarations, and they were issued special receipts for paying the Jewish tax, the Arsinoe papyrus shows that *laographia* and *epikrisis* data were used to exact this discriminatory tax. The *amphodarchēs* of Arsinoe who issued this report was responsible for creating lists of those eligible for all taxes, including the Jewish tax. Notably, this official indicates that he referred to "previous accounts" and "the preceding *epikrisis*" to determine the ages of those liable to a Jewish tax on top of the poll tax. Indeed, it appears from this document that local tax administrators closely examined information recorded on the *laographia* rolls to determine liability for the Jewish tax. This is noteworthy because the Jewish tax was collected from both men *and* women starting *at age 3*. Here, then, we can glimpse the dark side of regulation: by collecting census information that did not pertain to poll tax liability, the Roman administration was well equipped to exact a punitive tax on Jews, including women and minors. The imperial administration devised this tax to target *Ioudaioi* throughout the empire (regardless of whether they ever set foot in Judea) as culpable for the First Revolt. The tax not only cast all Jews as outsiders and potential rebels, but it also required them to show allegiance to the empire and its gods in the form of a tax to Jupiter Capitolinus, a god whom they rejected.[14]

Another corpus in which we can detect the repressive potential of the census institution is the Decian *libelli* of 250 CE. In response to Decius's edict that all citizens (except possibly Jews)[15] must offer a sacrifice, pour a libation, and partake of the offerings, the *pater familias* of a household wrote a petition to local officials to certify their declaration with a countersignature. The documents share much in common with the form of a census declaration, probably because they relied on the same bureaucratic apparatus maintained for the census: first, the *pater familias* issues the document on behalf of the entire household; second, the documents use stock phrases from the census declarations, such as "in accordance with what has been ordered" (and one of the documents is even labeled *apographē* on its verso);[16] third, the performance of allegiance to the emperor through sacrifice is an expansion—albeit a substantial one—of the oath sworn by the divine emperor in some of the census declarations (Rives, 1999: 148–50; Luijendijk, 2008: 167; Blumell and Wayment, 2015: 376). For example, an Egyptian census declaration from 12 CE records the following oath: "I, Harthotes, swear verily by Caesar Imperator Eleutherios, son of god, Zeus Augustus that I have submitted the previous declaration salutarily and truthfully, reserving nothing; if I have sworn truthfully may it be well with me, if falsely, the opposite" (P.Mil. I 3 + P.Col. inv. 8 [12 CE, Theadelphia]; trans. Bagnall, 1991). Notably, even the Jewish woman Babatha had to make such an oath "by the genius of the lord Caesar" when registering her land in Maoza. The surviving Greek translation of her Aramaic oath reads, "I, Babatha daughter of Simon, swear by the *genius* of our lord Caesar that I have in good faith [*omnymi tychēn kyriou Kaisaros kalēi pistei*] registered as has been written above..." (P.Yad. 16 [127 CE]; trans. Lewis, 1989). Taking such an oath, though formulaic, would have presented many Jews and Christians with a moral dilemma, as we know the later Decian *libelli* did for Christians.

Far beyond its regulation of earlier forms of registration and taxation, then, the provincial census was a powerful institution that relied on and reproduced a range of social distinctions, normalizing both privilege and marginalization.

Provincial Censuses in the Synoptic Gospels and Acts of the Apostles

Discussions of the handful of references to taxes and censuses in the New Testament tend to focus on critical issues pertaining to negotiations of imperial power and degrees of economic exploitation. In this section, I raise questions that begin to take account of the sociopolitical dimensions of censuses, complementing and moving beyond these issues. This preliminary survey focuses on passages in the Synoptic Gospels and the Acts of the Apostles that explicitly employ terminology invoking the census, but subsequent studies will be needed to expand this type of investigation with respect both to these passages and to other New Testament texts (e.g., Rom 13:6–7).

Jesus's teaching on taxes is a useful place to begin this investigation since it appears in each of the Synoptic Gospels. Because their subtle differences in language prove significant, Table 4.2 presents the full Greek text and English translation of each in parallel columns for comparison.[17]

Mark is our earliest witness to the Synoptic tradition of Jesus's famous "return to Caesar" teaching and the source of the other versions. In Mark's account, the Herodians and Pharisees acknowledge that Jesus does not regard people with partiality before asking him, "Is it lawful to give *kēnsos* to Caesar, or not?" The verb *exestin*, meaning "it is lawful," is often used to distinguish what is lawful for one person but not another, as in a letter in which Artemis of Karanis requests a legal representative "because it is not lawful [*ouk exesti*] for a woman to engage in a lawsuit without a legal representative" (P.Mich. VIII 507 [second/third cent. CE]; my trans.). As we have seen, women, minors, and certain high-status individuals were not legally required to pay poll taxes.

The Latin loanword *kēnsos* here must refer to taxes collected on the basis of census declarations, but specifically taxes collected in coin, since Jesus asks his interlocutors to bring him a denarius. As Zeichmann (2017b) has argued, in Mark's post-70 CE context, this could refer not only to a poll tax but also to the Jewish tax.[18] For the Markan author and earliest audiences, *kēnsos* may have encompassed the punitive tax levied on Jews. By validating the payment of census taxes, the Markan Jesus assented to an institution that normalized partiality. In this light, his clever response ("Return to Caesar the things that are Caesar's, and to God the things that are God's") is cast as

Table 4.2 Jesus's teaching on taxes in the Synoptic Gospels

Mark 12:13–17	*Matt 22:15–22*	*Luke 20:19–26*
13 Then they sent to him some Pharisees and some Herodians to trap him in what he said. 14 And they came and said to him, "Teacher, we know that you are sincere, and show deference to no one; for you do not regard people with partiality, but teach the way of God in accordance with truth. Is it lawful to give *kēnsos* to Caesar, or not? 15 Should we pay them, or should we not?" But knowing their hypocrisy, he said to them, "Why are you putting me to the test? Bring me a denarius and let me see it." 16 And they brought one. Then he said to them, "Whose head is this, and whose title?" They answered, "Caesar's." 17 Jesus said to them, "Return to Caesar the things that are Caesar's, and to God the things that are God's." And they were utterly amazed at him.	15 Then the Pharisees went and plotted to entrap him in what he said. 16 So they sent their disciples to him, along with the Herodians, saying, "Teacher, we know that you are sincere, and teach the way of God in accordance with truth, and show deference to no one; for you do not regard people with partiality. 17 Tell us, then, what you think. Is it lawful to give *kēnsos* to Caesar, or not?" 18 But Jesus, aware of their malice, said, "Why are you putting me to the test, you hypocrites? 19 Show me the coin of the *kēnsos*." And they brought him a denarius. 20 Then he said to them, "Whose head is this, and whose title?" 21 They answered, "Caesar's." Then he said to them, "Return therefore to Caesar the things that are Caesar's, and to God the things that are God's." 22 When they heard this, they were amazed; and they left him and went away.	19 When the scribes and chief priests realized that he had told this parable against them, they wanted to lay hands on him at that very hour, but they feared the people. 20 So they watched him and sent spies who pretended to be honest, in order to trap him by what he said, so as to hand him over to the jurisdiction and authority of the governor. 21 So they asked him, "Teacher, we know that you are right in what you say and teach, and you show deference to no one, but teach the way of God in accordance with truth. 22 Is it lawful for us to give *phoroi* to Caesar, or not?" 23 But he perceived their craftiness and said to them, 24 "Show me a denarius. Whose head and whose title does it bear?" They said, "Caesar's." 25 He said to them, "Then return to Caesar the things that are Caesar's, and to God the things that are God's." 26 And they were not able in the presence of the people to trap him by what he said; and being amazed by his answer, they became silent.

(Continued)

Table 4.2 Jesus's teaching on taxes in the Synoptic Gospels *(Continued)*

Mark 12:13–17	*Matt 22:15–22*	*Luke 20:19–26*
13 Καὶ ἀποστέλλουσιν πρός αὐτόν τινας τῶν Φαρισαίων καὶ τῶν Ἡρῳδιανῶν ἵνα αὐτὸν ἀγρεύσωσιν λόγῳ. 14 καὶ ἐλθόντες λέγουσιν αὐτῷ· διδάσκαλε, οἴδαμεν ὅτι ἀληθὴς εἶ καὶ οὐ μέλει σοι περὶ οὐδενός· οὐ γὰρ βλέπεις εἰς πρόσωπον ἀνθρώπων, ἀλλ' ἐπ' ἀληθείας τὴν ὁδὸν τοῦ θεοῦ διδάσκεις· ἔξεστιν δοῦναι κῆνσον Καίσαρι ἢ οὔ; δῶμεν ἢ μὴ δῶμεν; 15 Ὁ δὲ εἰδὼς αὐτῶν τὴν ὑπόκρισιν εἶπεν αὐτοῖς· τί με πειράζετε; φέρετέ μοι δηνάριον ἵνα ἴδω. 16 οἱ δὲ ἤνεγκαν. καὶ λέγει αὐτοῖς· τίνος ἡ εἰκὼν αὕτη καὶ ἡ ἐπιγραφή; οἱ δὲ εἶπαν αὐτῷ· Καίσαρος. 17 ὁ δὲ Ἰησοῦς εἶπεν αὐτοῖς· τὰ Καίσαρος ἀπόδοτε Καίσαρι καὶ τὰ τοῦ θεοῦ τῷ θεῷ. καὶ ἐξεθαύμαζον ἐπ' αὐτῷ.	15 Τότε πορευθέντες οἱ Φαρισαῖοι συμβούλιον ἔλαβον ὅπως αὐτὸν παγιδεύσωσιν ἐν λόγῳ. 16 καὶ ἀποστέλλουσιν αὐτῷ τοὺς μαθητὰς αὐτῶν μετὰ τῶν Ἡρῳδιανῶν λέγοντες· διδάσκαλε, οἴδαμεν ὅτι ἀληθὴς εἶ καὶ τὴν ὁδὸν τοῦ θεοῦ ἐν ἀληθείᾳ διδάσκεις καὶ οὐ μέλει σοι περὶ οὐδενός· οὐ γὰρ βλέπεις εἰς πρόσωπον ἀνθρώπων, 17 εἰπὲ οὖν ἡμῖν τί σοι δοκεῖ· ἔξεστιν δοῦναι κῆνσον Καίσαρι ἢ οὔ; 18 γνοὺς δὲ ὁ Ἰησοῦς τὴν πονηρίαν αὐτῶν εἶπεν· τί με πειράζετε, ὑποκριταί; 19 ἐπιδείξατέ μοι τὸ νόμισμα τοῦ κήνσου. οἱ δὲ προσήνεγκαν αὐτῷ δηνάριον. 20 καὶ λέγει αὐτοῖς· τίνος ἡ εἰκὼν αὕτη καὶ ἡ ἐπιγραφή; 21 λέγουσιν αὐτῷ· Καίσαρος. τότε λέγει αὐτοῖς· ἀπόδοτε οὖν τὰ Καίσαρος Καίσαρι καὶ τὰ τοῦ θεοῦ τῷ θεῷ. 22 καὶ ἀκούσαντες ἐθαύμασαν, καὶ ἀφέντες αὐτὸν ἀπῆλθαν.	19 Καὶ ἐζήτησαν οἱ γραμματεῖς καὶ οἱ ἀρχιερεῖς ἐπιβαλεῖν ἐπ' αὐτὸν τὰς χεῖρας ἐν αὐτῇ τῇ ὥρᾳ, καὶ ἐφοβήθησαν τὸν λαόν, ἔγνωσαν γὰρ ὅτι πρὸς αὐτοὺς εἶπεν τὴν παραβολὴν ταύτην. 20 Καὶ παρατηρήσαντες ἀπέστειλαν ἐγκαθέτους ὑποκρινομένους ἑαυτοὺς δικαίους εἶναι, ἵνα ἐπιλάβωνται αὐτοῦ λόγου, ὥστε παραδοῦναι αὐτὸν τῇ ἀρχῇ καὶ τῇ ἐξουσίᾳ τοῦ ἡγεμόνος. 21 καὶ ἐπηρώτησαν αὐτὸν λέγοντες· διδάσκαλε, οἴδαμεν ὅτι ὀρθῶς λέγεις καὶ διδάσκεις καὶ οὐ λαμβάνεις πρόσωπον, ἀλλ' ἐπ' ἀληθείας τὴν ὁδὸν τοῦ θεοῦ διδάσκεις· 22 ἔξεστιν ἡμᾶς Καίσαρι φόρον δοῦναι ἢ οὔ; 23 Κατανοήσας δὲ αὐτῶν τὴν πανουργίαν εἶπεν πρὸς αὐτούς· 24 δείξατέ μοι δηνάριον· τίνος ἔχει εἰκόνα καὶ ἐπιγραφήν; οἱ δὲ εἶπαν· Καίσαρος. 25 ὁ δὲ εἶπεν πρὸς αὐτούς· τοίνυν ἀπόδοτε τὰ Καίσαρος Καίσαρι καὶ τὰ τοῦ θεοῦ τῷ θεῷ. 26 καὶ οὐκ ἴσχυσαν ἐπιλαβέσθαι αὐτοῦ ῥήματος ἐναντίον τοῦ λαοῦ καὶ θαυμάσαντες ἐπὶ τῇ ἀποκρίσει αὐτοῦ ἐσίγησαν.

successful because Jesus does not show partiality that conflicted with census regulations. To those being taxed as *Ioudaioi* in Mark's audience, this might not have been satisfying. Perhaps, however, some would have taken solace in Jesus's implication that Caesar is not God, which undermines the oath taken in census declarations.[19]

Matthew's version of this teaching changes very little, though it is more explicit that the denarius is the "coin of the *kēnsos*." Earlier in his gospel, however, Matthean "special material" (i.e., material that only appears in the Gospel of Matthew among the gospels) primes readers to think of the *kēnsos* in terms of the Jewish tax (Matt 17:24–27):

> When they reached Capernaum, the collectors of the didrachma came to Peter and said, "Does your teacher not pay the didrachma?" [25] He said, "Yes, he does." And when he came home, Jesus spoke of it first, asking, "What do you think, Simon? From whom do kings of the earth take tolls or *kēnsos*? From their children or from others?" [26] When Peter said, "From others," Jesus said to him, "Then the children are free. [27] However, so that we do not give offense to them, go to the sea and cast a hook; take the first fish that comes up; and when you open its mouth, you will find a coin; take that and give it to them for you and me."
>
> Ἐλθόντων δὲ αὐτῶν εἰς Καφαρναοὺμ προσῆλθον οἱ τὰ δίδραχμα λαμβάνοντες τῷ Πέτρῳ καὶ εἶπαν· ὁ διδάσκαλος ὑμῶν οὐ τελεῖ [τὰ] δίδραχμα; [25] λέγει· ναί. καὶ ἐλθόντα εἰς τὴν οἰκίαν προέφθασεν αὐτὸν ὁ Ἰησοῦς λέγων· τί σοι δοκεῖ, Σίμων; οἱ βασιλεῖς τῆς γῆς ἀπὸ τίνων λαμβάνουσιν τέλη ἢ κῆνσον; ἀπὸ τῶν υἱῶν αὐτῶν ἢ ἀπὸ τῶν ἀλλοτρίων; [26] εἰπόντος δέ· ἀπὸ τῶν ἀλλοτρίων, ἔφη αὐτῷ ὁ Ἰησοῦς· ἄρα γε ἐλεύθεροί εἰσιν οἱ υἱοί. [27] ἵνα δὲ μὴ σκανδαλίσωμεν αὐτούς, πορευθεὶς εἰς θάλασσαν βάλε ἄγκιστρον καὶ τὸν ἀναβάντα πρῶτον ἰχθὺν ἆρον, καὶ ἀνοίξας τὸ στόμα αὐτοῦ εὑρήσεις στατῆρα· ἐκεῖνον λαβὼν δὸς αὐτοῖς ἀντὶ ἐμοῦ καὶ σοῦ.

English translations routinely obscure the specific monetary and institutional terms used here, rendering, for instance, "didrachma" as "temple tax" when the collector asks Jesus, "Does your teacher not pay the didrachma?" (Matt 17:24). Even if a lost earlier form of this story involved the annual didrachma (half-shekel) temple tax transmitted by Jews throughout the diaspora to the Jerusalem Temple, Matthew seems to have had the imperial Jewish tax in mind with his reference to the didrachma here. Jesus goes on to ask Simon, "From whom do the kings of the earth take tolls [*telē*] or *kēnsos*? From their children or from others?" Peter's response "From others" prompts Jesus to proclaim that the children are free.

Even though Jesus has Simon pay the tax for both of them with a *statēr* (two didrachmas) miraculously found in a fish's mouth (Matt 17:27), this teaching accuses the Roman kings of the earth of extracting taxes from various "others" instead of their children—that is, Roman citizens and other high-status individuals (Carter, 2000). Matthew then proceeds to rewrite Mark's pericope about greatness so as to emphasize that children are the greatest in the kingdom of heaven. After hearing the prohibitions on oaths in Matt 5:33–37 (another section of Matthean special material) and then this didrachma teaching, the subsequent "return to Caesar" teaching must have struck Matthew's earliest audiences as a rather critical appraisal of census practices, even if Jesus ultimately endorsed paying taxes.

In Luke-Acts, I detect little of the ambivalence toward the census found in Mark and especially Matthew. The Gospel of Luke ties the birth of Jesus to the registration itself, the *apographē*, in 2:1–5:

> In those days a decree went out from Caesar Augustus that all the world should be registered. [2] This was the first registration taken while Quirinius was ruling Syria. [3] All went to be registered, each to his own polis. [4] Joseph also went from the Galilee, from the polis of Nazareth, to Judea, to the polis of David called Bethlehem, because he was descended from the house and lineage of David. [5] He went to be registered with Mary, who was engaged to him and was pregnant.
>
> Ἐγένετο δὲ ἐν ταῖς ἡμέραις ἐκείναις ἐξῆλθεν δόγμα παρὰ Καίσαρος Αὐγούστου ἀπογράφεσθαι πᾶσαν τὴν οἰκουμένην. [2] αὕτη ἀπογραφὴ πρώτη ἐγένετο ἡγεμονεύοντος τῆς Συρίας Κυρηνίου. [3] καὶ ἐπορεύοντο πάντες ἀπογράφεσθαι, ἕκαστος εἰς τὴν ἑαυτοῦ πόλιν. [4] Ἀνέβη δὲ καὶ Ἰωσὴφ ἀπὸ τῆς Γαλιλαίας ἐκ πόλεως Ναζαρὲθ εἰς τὴν Ἰουδαίαν εἰς πόλιν Δαυὶδ ἥτις καλεῖται Βηθλέεμ, διὰ τὸ εἶναι αὐτὸν ἐξ οἴκου καὶ πατριᾶς Δαυίδ, [5] ἀπογράψασθαι σὺν Μαριὰμ τῇ ἐμνηστευμένῃ αὐτῷ, οὔσῃ ἐγκύῳ.

Birth and census dating issues aside, Huebner (2019: 41) is right that Luke and his audience must have viewed the census process described as *plausible*. Here, it is noteworthy that it is Joseph who needs to register and that he is described as being of the "house [*oikos*] and lineage [*patria*] of David," implying the patriarchal structure of registration by the *pater familias* on behalf of the household. As John Chrysostom later noted, Joseph would have needed to travel to register in Bethlehem because he was a citizen who owned property there (*Natal.* [PG 49, col. 351]; see Huebner, 2019: 42). Luke introduces Bethlehem as the polis of David, signifying that Joseph was a city-dwelling landowner, who may thus have been eligible for a tax discount.[20] This fits with Luke's project of elevating the socioeconomic status of Jesus and his family: in Luke, Jesus is the son of an urban landowner, not a village *tektōn* (i.e., a "carpenter" or "stone mason") (Keith, 2011: 71–123).[21]

Luke rewrote Mark's teaching about taxes accordingly. First, he replaced the term *kēnsos* with *phoros*, a word that could refer to the land or head tribute, but was more often used for the land tribute. Unlike Matthew, Luke does not connect the denarius directly to the tax, thereby allowing that *phoros* does refer to land tributes paid in kind. When Jesus is on trial, the chief priests and scribes falsely accuse him of "forbidding us to give tributes [*phoroi*] to Caesar" (*kōlyonta phorous Kaisari didonai*; Luke 23:2). Similarly, in Acts 5:37, Gamaliel's speech insinuates that Jesus's detractors thought of him as similar to Judas the Galilean, who "rose up in the days of the *apographē*."[22]

Luke-Acts insists that Jesus was not an opponent of the census and related tributes. There are no hints that this author or audience had to deal with the Jewish tax. And, instead of interrogating the partiality of census practices, Luke-Acts uses the census as a literary tool to raise the socioeconomic status of Jesus's family and to differentiate him from tax rebels and other low-status criminals (cf. Matthews, 2019).[23] Luke-Acts fully participates in the normalization of the discriminatory institutional discourse represented by the census.

Conclusion

I have argued in this essay that New Testament scholars, myself included, have been too quick to equate the census with increased taxation and the loss of national sovereignty. Documentary sources show that the Romans did not necessarily increase tax burdens in the provinces and tended to adapt local census and taxation practices rather than impose a fully new system.

The census was an institution that regulated economic practices such as taxation and transmissions of inheritance, but it also regulated social distinctions, institutionalizing patriarchal household structures, the division between city and country, citizenship privileges, and in one important instance, the ethnoreligious category *Ioudaios*. Much as the US census has forced people of color like Bayoumi to identify with racial categories that misrepresent their experiences, one has to wonder how much of a role Roman censuses played in reifying social identities that were in reality more fluid. Would Christians have gradually differentiated themselves from Jews if Roman census practices did not construct Jews as rebellious ethnic others in the aftermath of the First Revolt?[24] This is an impossible question to answer, of course, but I think it is a helpful reminder that censuses may play a much greater part in shaping social relations, subjectivities, and prejudices than we realize—both in the ancient world and today.

Notes

1. This paper is an extension and reframing of certain issues addressed in Keddie, 2019: 122–31. I am thankful to Lara-Sophie Boleslawsky for her superb research assistance. A version of this paper was presented in a session of the Early Christianity and the Ancient Economy unit at the Society of Biblical Literature Annual Meeting in San Diego on November 25, 2019. I am grateful to those present who offered feedback and suggestions.

2. For research on census data collection, especially in the United States, see Nobles, 2000; Rodríguez, 2000; Kertzer, 2002; Schor, 2017.
3. On authenticity (and its pursuit) as a racializing discourse in New Testament scholarship, see especially Kelley, 2002.
4. The main Josephan references are *B.J.* 2.117–118, 167; *A.J.* 17.354–18.10; 18.26–27.
5. Pearson (1999: 272–3) and Huebner (2019: 44, 48) have identified one example of the Roman administration imposing a census within a client-kingdom. According to Tacitus (*Ann.* 6.41), the Syrian governor Vitellius intervened in the client-kingdom of Cilicia Tracheia during the reign of Archelaus II in 36 CE, attacking a tribe because they refused to supply the king with property returns and taxes. This account does not constitute sufficient evidence to consider the Roman facilitation of censuses in client-kingdoms to have been the norm. Nonetheless, Roman client-kings (including the Herodian rulers) would have imposed their own census practices in their territories and would have called on the Roman military from time to time to help quell resistance (e.g., when the Syrian legate Varus intervened in Judea to quash a tax rebellion shortly after the death of King Herod; see Josephus, *A.J.* 17.205–320).
6. See also P.Ḥev./Se. 61, the fragmentary declaration of a "son of Levi," and P.Yad. 24, a deposition regarding property registered by this 127 CE census.
7. For instance, we know from the Arabian documents that the Roman administration continued the collection of the Nabatean *stephanikon*, a monetary tax. Though not a capitation tax proper, it demonstrates some continuity between Roman and Nabatean taxation in Arabia. For further discussion with references, see Keddie, 2019: 125–6.
8. Emphasizing the use of *homin(um)* in the inscription, Kennedy (2006) observes that this "high-count" must have included almost all free residents of the city and its *chōra* instead of just enfranchised citizens.
9. The records were kept in administrative archives in villages and/or cities (e.g., P.Yad. 16 notes that Babatha's declaration was held at the basilica in Rabbath-Moab). On the administration of the census in Egypt, see Wallace, 1938; Bagnall and Frier, 1994.
10. Trans. Cotton, from Charlesworth, 2000, modified.
11. Communications scholars have noted how modern census forms institutionalize social hierarchies through even the visual representation of data on census forms (see Balzhiser, Pimentel, and Scott, 2019). This does not apply in the same way for the ancient world, where low literacy rates required that scribes filled out forms for most declarants. Even still, it is worth noting that in both modern and ancient census documents (including tax registers), the form itself conveys considerable information about how social relations are understood.
12. For the Ptolemaic tax privileges, see Clarysse and Thompson, 2006: 123–205.
13. Note that in some regions, such as the Arsinoite nome, the use of *hellēnes* and *katoikoi* as tax discount categories continued into the early Roman period. In certain regions, moreover, names such as *oktadrachmoi* and *dōdekadrachmoi* were used instead of, or in tandem with, *mētropolitai* and *hoi apo gymnasiou* (e.g., Oxyrhynchus).
14. Dio Cassius, *Hist. rom.* 65.7.2; Martial, *Epig.* 7.55; 11.94; *Lib. spec.* 36. See Zeichmann, 2015.
15. The best evidence for the widely held scholarly assumption that Jews were exempt from these decrees is the lack of evidence. As Rives (1999: 138, n. 16) puts it, "This silence is so striking that we must assume an exemption." Usually, lack of evidence is not an effective argument. But, in this case, considering the prolific literary production of Jews and Christians (the latter often writing about Jews, polemically) in this period, it is remarkable that there are

no traces of evidence that Jews were forced to sacrifice. Yet, we could also say that it is striking that there is not much evidence for the exemption (except for one brief and late reference related to the Diocletianic persecution of Christians in y. Avod. Zar. 5.4, 44d). On the other hand, we have such a longstanding tradition of certain forms of toleration for Jews in the empire, dating back to Julius Caesar with few breaks along the way, that a case could be made that it would be strange if Jews were included.

16. P.Oxy. LVIII 3929, l. 22 (verso).
17. All New Testament translations in this paper are my own.
18. As suggested above, however, I am not as confident as Zeichmann (2017b) and Udoh (2005) that the poll tax or other capitation taxes were not collected in pre-70 CE Judea. On a post-70 CE provenance for Mark, see Kloppenborg, 2005; Zeichmann, 2017a.
19. Jesus's statement also implies that Jupiter, the technical recipient of the Jewish taxes, was not God. On the transmission of Jewish taxes to the temple of Jupiter Capitolinus, see Zeichmann, 2015.
20. Luke uses "polis" for places that were not proper cities by ancient or modern scholarly standards. He does distinguish, however, between a polis and a *kōmē* (a term he uses more than the other gospel authors: Luke 8:1; 9:52, 56; 10:38; 17:12; 19:30; 24:13; 24:28) or *agros* (Luke 8:34; 9:12). This suggests to me that his use of "polis" in a text for an audience that consisted of people who may never have been to Palestine may bear some significance in terms of social distinctions. Several scholars have argued that Luke wrote for an urban audience (e.g., Esler, 1989: 30). I suggest that this urban outlook likely also influenced how Luke described Joseph's registration.
21. Mark 6:3 describes Jesus as a *tektōn*, and Matt 13:55 describes him as the son of a *tektōn*, but Luke omitted this detail from his Markan source entirely. Luke's Gospel effectively raises the socioeconomic status of Jesus. As Matthews (2019) has shown, Luke also takes a "masterly point of view" in its depiction of Jesus's fellow victims of crucifixion as deserving of their low-status punishments. On *tektōn* as Jesus's profession, see further Fiensy, 2014: 5–55; Huebner, 2019: 65–86.
22. This is an important detail that Huebner (2019) overlooks in her argument that Luke 2:1–5 refers to the first of two censuses by Quirinius—a census she assigns to ca. 8 BCE. Huebner (2019: 46–8) also makes too much out of Luke's description of Quirinius as ἡγεμονεύοντος τῆς Συρίας (Luke 2:2). Luke's use of this quasi title, instead of *stratēgos*, is not such clear evidence that Luke refers to a time when Quirinius served as financial procurator under the Syrian governor Saturninus, ca. 9–6 BCE. Luke also refers, for instance, to Pilate with the same term: ἡγεμονεύοντος Ποντίου Πιλάτου τῆς Ἰουδαίας (Luke 3:1).
23. Luke rewrites Mark's language about not showing partiality (Mark 12:14: καὶ οὐ μέλει σοι περὶ οὐδενός· οὐ γὰρ βλέπεις εἰς πρόσωπον ἀνθρώπων) as καὶ οὐ λαμβάνεις πρόσωπον (Luke 20:21) in order to downplay Mark's connotation of partiality as something judged with respect to individuals or groups (viz. οὐδενός, ἀνθρώπων). Matthew, meanwhile, preserves Mark's language about partiality in full (Matt 22:16).
24. On this question, see the important contribution by Heemstra (2010).

Bibliography

Bagnall, Roger S. 1991 "The Beginnings of the Roman Census in Egypt." *Greek, Roman, and Byzantine Studies* 32: 255–65.

Bagnall, Roger S., and Bruce W. Frier. 1994. *The Demography of Roman Egypt*. Cambridge Studies in Population, Economy, and Society in Past Time 23. Cambridge: Cambridge University Press.

Balzhiser, Deborah, Charise Pimentel, and Amanda Scott. 2019. "Matters of Form: Questions of Race, Identity, Design, and the U.S. Census." *Technical Communication Quarterly* 28: 3–20.

Bayoumi, Moustafa. 2019. "I'm a Brown Arab-American and the US Census Refuses to Recognize Me." *The Guardian*, February 14, 2019. https://www.theguardian.com/commentisfree/2019/feb/14/arab-american-census-america-racism.

Blumell, Lincoln Harris, and Thomas A. Wayment. 2015. *Christian Oxyrhynchus: Texts, Documents, and Sources*. Waco: Baylor University Press.

Boer, Roland, and Christina Petterson. 2017. *Time of Troubles: A New Economic Framework for Early Christianity*. Minneapolis: Fortress.

Broux, Yanne. 2013. "Creating a New Local Elite: The Establishment of the Metropolitan Orders of Roman Egypt." *Archiv für Papyrusforschung* 59: 142–53.

———. 2015. *Double Names and Elite Strategy in Roman Egypt*. Studia Hellenistica 54. Leuven: Peeters.

Capponi, Livia. 2005. *Augustan Egypt: The Creation of a Roman Province*. London: Routledge.

Carter, Warren. 2000. "Paying the Tax to Rome as Subversive Praxis: Matthew 17.24–27." *Journal for the Study of the New Testament* 22: 3–31.

Charlesworth, James, ed. 2000. *Miscellaneous Texts from the Judaean Desert*. Discoveries in the Judaean Desert 38. Oxford: Clarendon Press.

Clarysse, Willy, and Dorothy J. Thompson. 2006. *Historical Studies*. Vol. 2 of *Counting the People in Hellenistic Egypt*. Cambridge: Cambridge University Press.

Claytor, W. Graham, and Roger S. Bagnall. 2015. "The Beginnings of the Roman Provincial Census: A New Declaration from 3 BCE." *Greek, Roman, and Byzantine Studies* 55: 637–53.

Cotton, Hannah M. 2003. "The Roman Census in the Papyri from the Judaean Desert and the Egyptian Κατ' Οἰκίαν Ἀπογραφή." Pages 105–22 in *Semitic Papyrology in Context*. Edited by Lawrence H. Schiffman. Culture and History of the Ancient Near East 14. Leiden: Brill.

Cotton, Hannah, and Ada Yardeni, eds. 1997. *Aramaic, Hebrew, and Greek Documentary Texts from Naḥal Ḥever and Other Sites: With an Appendix Containing Alleged Qumran Texts*. Discoveries in the Judaean Desert 27. Oxford: Clarendon.

Dunn, James D. G. 2003. *Jesus Remembered*. Vol. 1 of *Christianity in the Making*. Grand Rapids: Eerdmans.

Esler, Philip F. 1989. *Community and Gospel in Luke-Acts: The Social and Political Motivations of Lucan Theology*. Cambridge: Cambridge University Press.

Fiensy, David A. 2014. *Christian Origins and the Ancient Economy*. Eugene: Cascade.

Foucault, Michel. 2007. *Security, Territory, Population: Lectures at the Collège de France, 1977–78*. Dordrecht: Springer.

———. 2008. *The Birth of Biopolitics: Lectures at the Collège de France, 1978–1979*. New York: Springer.

Hall, Linda Jones. 2004. *Roman Berytus: Beirut in Late Antiquity*. London: Routledge.

Heemstra, Marius. 2010. *The Fiscus Judaicus and the Parting of the Ways*. Wissenschaftliche Untersuchungen zum Neuen Testament 277. Tübingen: Mohr Siebeck.

Horsley, Richard. 2006. *The Liberation of Christmas: The Infancy Narratives in Social Context*. Eugene, OR: Wipf & Stock.

Huebner, Sabine R. 2019. *Papyri and the Social World of the New Testament*. Cambridge: Cambridge University Press.

Keddie, Anthony. 2016. "Ptolemaic Sovereignty and the Political Unconscious of 3 Maccabees: Philopator's Decree (2:28–30) in Light of Late Ptolemaic *Asylia* Inscriptions." Pages 193–216 in *New Vistas on Early Judaism and Christianity: From Enoch to Montréal and Back*. Edited by Lorenzo DiTommaso and Gerbern Oegema. Jewish and Christian Texts in Context and Related Studies 22. London: T&T Clark.

———. 2018. "*Iudaea Capta* vs. Mother Zion: The Flavian Discourse on Judaeans and Its Delegitimation in 4 Ezra." *Journal for the Study of Judaism* 49: 498–550.

———. 2019. *Class and Power in Roman Palestine: The Socioeconomic Setting of Judaism and Christian Origins*. Cambridge: Cambridge University Press.

Keith, Chris. 2011. *Jesus' Literacy: Scribal Culture and the Teacher from Galilee*. London: Bloomsbury.

Kelley, Shawn. 2002. *Racializing Jesus: Race, Ideology, and the Formation of Modern Biblical Scholarship*. Biblical Limits. London: Routledge.

Kennedy, David. 2006. "Demography, the Population of Syria and the Census of Q. Aemilius Secundus." *Levant* 38: 109–24.

Kertzer, David, ed. 2002. *Census and Identity: The Politics of Race, Ethnicity, and Language in National Census*. Cambridge: Cambridge University Press.

Kloppenborg, John S. 2005. "*Evocatio Deorum* and the Date of Mark." *Journal of Biblical Literature* 124: 419–50.

Labrousse, Agnes, and Jean-Daniel Weisz. 2013. *Institutional Economics in France and Germany: German Ordoliberalism versus the French Regulation School*. Studies in Economic Ethics and Philosophy. Berlin: Springer.

Le Teuff, Béatrice. 2012. "Census: Les recensements dans les provinces de l'Empire Romain d'Auguste à Dioclétien." PhD diss., Bordeaux University.

Lewis, Naphtali. 1988. "A Jewish Landowner in the Province of Arabia." *Scripta Classica Israelica* 8–9: 132–7.

———, ed. 1989. *The Documents from the Bar Kokhba Period in the Cave of Letters*. Judean Desert Studies. Jerusalem: Israel Exploration Society.

Lo Cascio, Elio. 1999. "Census provinciale, imposizione fiscale e amministrazioni." Pages 197–212 in *Lokale Autonomie und römische Ordnungsmacht in den kaiserzeitlichen Provinzen vom 1. bis 3. Jahrhundert*. Edited by Werner Eck. Schriften des historischen Kollegs 42. Munich: Oldenbourg.

Luijendijk, AnneMarie. 2008. *Greetings in the Lord: Early Christians and the Oxyrhynchus Papyri*. Cambridge: Harvard University Press.

Matthews, Shelly. 2019. "The Lynching Tree and the Cross: James Cone, Historical Narrative, and the Ideology of Just Crucifixion (Luke 23:41)." Pages 147–70 in *The Narrative Self in Early Christianity: Essays in Honor of Judith Perkins*. Edited by Janet E. Spittler. Writings from the Greco-Roman World Supplements 15. Atlanta: SBL Press.

Monson, Andrew. 2012. *From the Ptolemies to the Romans: Political and Economic Change in Egypt*. Cambridge: Cambridge University Press.

———. 2014a. "Late Ptolemaic Capitation Taxes and the Poll Tax in Roman Egypt." *Bulletin of the American Society of Papyrologists* 51: 127–60.

———. 2014b. "Receipts for *Sitônion*, *Syntaxis*, and *Epistatikon* from Karanis." *Zeitschrift für Papyrologie und Epigraphik* 191: 207–30.

Nobles, Melissa. 2000. *Shades of Citizenship: Race and the Census in Modern Politics*. Stanford: Stanford University Press.

North, Douglass C. 1990. *Institutions, Institutional Change, and Economic Performance*. Political Economy of Institutions and Decisions. Cambridge: Cambridge University Press.

Pearson, Brook W. R. 1999. "The Lucan Censuses, Revisited." *Catholic Biblical Quarterly* 61: 262–82.

Rives, James B. 1999. "The Decree of Decius and the Religion of Empire." *Journal of Roman Studies* 89: 135–54.

Rodríguez, Clara E. 2000. *Changing Race: Latinos, the Census and the History of Ethnicity*. New York: NYU Press.

Sandset, Tony. 2018. *Color That Matters: A Comparative Approach to Mixed Race Identity and Nordic Exceptionalism*. London: Routledge.

Schor, Paul. 2017. *Counting Americans: How the US Census Classified the Nation*. New York: Oxford University Press.

Tcherikover, Victor A., ed. 1957–1964. *Corpus Papyrorum Judaicarum*. Cambridge: Harvard University Press.

Udoh, Fabian E. 2005. *To Caesar What Is Caesar's: Tribute, Taxes and Imperial Administration in Early Roman Palestine (63 B.C.E.–70 C.E.)*. Brown Judaic Studies 343. Providence: Brown Judaic Studies.

Wallace, Sherman LeRoy. 1938. *Taxation in Egypt from Augustus to Diocletian*. Princeton University Studies in Papyrology 2. Princeton: Princeton University Press.

Wines, Michael. 2019. "2020 Census Won't Have Citizenship Question as Trump Administration Drops Effort." *The New York Times*, July 2. https://www.nytimes.com/2019/07/02/us/trump-census-citizenship-question.html.

Zeichmann, Christopher B. 2015. "Martial and the *Fiscus Iudaicus* Once More." *Journal for the Study of the Pseudepigrapha* 25: 111–7.

———. 2017a. "Loanwords or Code-Switching? Latin Transliteration and the Setting of Mark's Composition." *Journal of the Jesus Movement in Its Jewish Setting* 4: 42–64.

———. 2017b. "The Date of Mark's Gospel Apart from the Temple and Rumors of War: The Taxation Episode (12:13–17) as Evidence." *Catholic Biblical Quarterly* 79: 422–37.

Part II

The Galilean Economy before and after the First Judean Revolt

5 The Economic Impact of the First Jewish Revolt on the Galilee

Mordechai Aviam

During the winter of 66 CE, Josephus Flavius, then Joseph, son of Mathaias, was sent to the Galilee as a governor by the Jerusalem revolt government. His mission, like all the other seven governors who were sent to their regions, was to take the reins of power from the Roman governing authorities. This included political leadership, sitting in judgment, collecting taxes, building a military power, and fortifying settlements.[1]

According to Josephus's account, in his days there were 204 cities, towns, and villages in the Galilee (and Golan, as part of his governing region). A study of this account succeeded in proving that the number is realistic (Ben David, 2011). This high number of settlements by itself is evidence of the strong economy of the Galilee during the 170 years since the annexation of the region to the Hasmonean kingdom (Aviam, 2004: 41–50; Leibner, 2009: 315–30).

To try and show the development and changes in economic terms of the Galilee before and after the war, I will use four excavated sites as test cases.

Archaeological Reflections on the Economic Situation of the Galilee before the War

Yodefat

The excavations of this site took place between 1992 and 1997 and were led by the author in the name of the Israel Antiquities Authority with the assistance of David Adan-Bayewitz from Bar Ilan University (for the first three seasons), Douglas R. Edwards from the University of Puget Sound (for the first season), J. Andrew Overman from the University of Rochester (for the first two seasons), and William Scott Green from the University of Rochester. Two short seasons continued during 2019 and 2020, led by the author in the name of Kinneret Institute for Galilean Archaeology, Kinneret College, in which the entire "fresco building" was uncovered. The results of the excavations at Yodefat showed that in the early first century BCE, the site captured the summit of the hill and was surrounded by a wall, probably as a Hasmonean stronghold.[2] During the second half of that century,

DOI: 10.4324/9781003041696-8

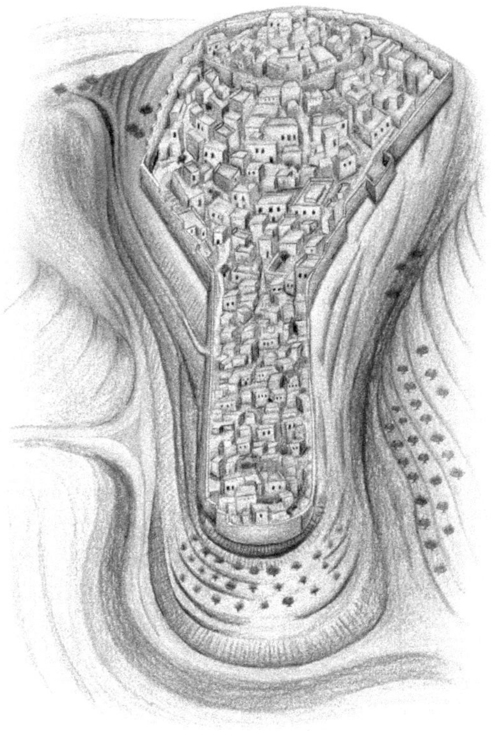

Figure 5.1 Yodefat, reconstruction: on the eve of the First Jewish Revolt.

Source: Drawing by T. Rom for the Yodefat project. Used by permission.

the town started to grow slowly to the eastern and southern slopes, and in the first half of the first century CE, it also included the southern range (Figure 5.1).

The most important evidence for the prosperity of the citizens of Yodefat in the early Roman period is the Fresco House, which was discovered on the northeastern slope. According to the foundations of the walls, this was a very large mansion, which had at least ten rooms in the lower floor and basements.

All four walls of one of the rooms were covered with frescos of the Second Pompeian Style, and surprisingly, its floor was frescoed as well (Figure 5.2). The frescos can date the establishment of this unit and the units around it, on the terrace, to the end of the first century BCE or the beginning of the following one. In summer 2019, we renewed the excavation of this house and found that the western wall was preserved to a height of more than 2 meters, and above the frescos, the upper part of the wall still carried stucco decoration. The adjacent room to the north is of an unusual size, approximately 5 by 10 meters, and its walls are covered with white plaster, designed as ashlars, in the Masonry Style.

Figure 5.2 Interior of Fresco House, with skeletal remains and Roman arrows.

Source: Photo by the author.

The houses along the eastern steep slope, such as the Fresco House, were based on large and massive terrace-walls, which supported the entire quarter. This could have been built only in an organized system with a serious investment of money. A few other luxury objects were found in other parts of the town: two iron door keys (thus, people had a reason to lock their doors); a pair of small (5 cm in diameter) bronze scales, which were probably used to weigh valuable objects or powder; a multinozzle gray "knife-pared" oil lamp imported from Jerusalem; two ritual baths (*miqvaot*) were found in one building (probably two apartments in one unit). Together with the Fresco House, this all points to the wealth in the town, beyond the simple housing system of walls covered with mud plaster, bitten earth, and smoothed rock floors.

Gamla

A very similar situation was discovered at Gamla. The synagogue at Gamla was established at the beginning of the first century CE. Compared with other excavated Second Temple synagogues, it is a large synagogue, an elaborate building with decorated stone architecture (Syon and Yavor, 2010). Such a building clearly reflects the financial power and ability of Gamla's population.

Figure 5.3 Gamla oil press.

Source: Photo by D. Syon. Used by permission.

In areas R and S, located on the western side of Gamla, many fragments of stucco and fresco were found, identifying the quarter as a rich commercial one, with elaborate rooms (Farhi, 2010). In this quarter, two workshops were discovered, a well-built oil press (Figure 5.3) and a flour mill operating at least two "Pompeian mills." Another decorated element found in this quarter is a lintel decorated with a rosette and a palm tree on each side of it. All reflect a life of prosperity (Syon and Yavor, 2010).

As at Yodefat, all areas that were excavated yielded a well-built and well-organized housing system.

Magdala

The third settlement from the first century BCE and first century CE that was largely excavated during the last decade is Magdala, on the shore of the Sea of Galilee.[3] Although Magdala was not a polis, it was larger and more organized than a Galilean town like Yodefat or Gamla. The city probably began as a late Hellenistic village of fishermen, and after the Hasmonean conquest it started to grow and developed as a regional capital as reflected by the first phase of the quay, which is dated to this period (Lena, 2018). A large domestic area was uncovered, and it clearly reflects two different social structures, similarly to Yodefat and Gamla (Zapata-Meza, 2018).

Area A yielded two large wealthy houses. Building E1 has a room (probably a *triclinium*) paved with a colored mosaic floor holding the design of a rosette surrounded by meanders. Two of its courtyards are paved with basal smoothed flagstones, and there are two *miqvaot* in this house. To the west, on the other side of the street is another house with paved courtyards and a *miqveh*. The fact that no earlier buildings were found beneath these houses proves that they were constructed at the end of the first century BCE or the beginning of the following one.

Areas B and C uncovered well-planned quarters with perpendicular streets on north-south and west-east orientations. In contrast with Area A, these are small, simple houses: small rooms, no mosaic floors, no paved courtyards, and no *miqvaot*.

An important place should be given to the synagogue. This is the northernmost building in the city. The excavators dated the building to the first decades of the first century CE, and reported that there is evidence for an earlier structure below it. It seems clear that the synagogue was established together with the neighborhood south of it, and developed through the first decades of the first century CE. Although it is not the largest synagogue from the Second Temple period, it is the most elaborate one. The walls are covered with frescos in the Second Pompeian Style, the columns are covered with both frescos and stucco, and a mosaic floor covers the footway between the upper and the lower benches. During salvage excavations at the end of 2021, a western neighborhood was uncovered, and as part of it, another synagogue was found, similar in size to the first one but not as elaborate (Winer, 2021).

Tel Rekhesh

The last example is the Jewish farmstead uncovered on the top of Tel Rekhesh in Lower Eastern Galilee (Aviam et al., 2019). On the summit of the biblical tell, there are the remains of a compound of walls and rooms on an area of approximately one acre. Excavations were conducted mainly in the northwestern corner, where few rooms were uncovered. In the debris of the second floor, many fragments of frescos as well as stucco were found, which point to an elaborate room on the second floor. We assume that this was the room of the owner of the farmstead, who was a wealthy man (Aviam et al., 2019).

According to the typical Galilean pottery, which includes storage jars, cooking pots and bowls, and oil lamps, the site was dated to the first and second centuries CE. This date is supported by the discovery of three coins from these centuries, the latest dating to 120 CE. The discovery of many chalk vessels shards supports the identification of the inhabitants as Jews. In the southwestern part of the site, an isolated room (9 by 9 m) was discovered, with benches of ashlar stones around the walls. Two stone bases probably supported a wooden/mud roof. We identified this room as a synagogue (Figure 5.4), and it is the only rural Galilean synagogue excavated to date (Aviam et al., 2019).

Figure 5.4 Aerial view of the synagogue at Tel Rekhesh.

Source: Photograph courtesy of the Tel Rekhesh Expedition. Used by permission.

The Preparations for the War

Josephus's description of the preparations for the war, by building a wall mainly around each settlement, was proven to be accurate in archaeological excavations and surveys (Aviam, 2008).

Yodefat

It was already noticed in earlier surveys that there is a wall around Yodefat, but it was only during our excavations (1992–1999) that we dated the wall and proved that this wall was built before and for the war (Aviam, 2015). The total length of the wall is more than 1 kilometer, and it is built with two techniques: in front of the accessible side in the north and in one part in the west, it is a casemate wall of about 4 meters wide; in other parts, it is a solid wall, 1.0–1.2 meters wide. It was built mainly along a topographical line in a pattern of "saw teeth" and a few towers. We found that the wall was built over some houses and dismantled a pottery kiln in the southeast. It also disconnected an oil press from the nearby house. The wall has very shallow foundations, and all together proved that it was built under pressure. We assume that more cisterns were cut, and we discovered one underground shelter, which was cut into the rock and contained a tunnel and caves in two layers.[4] It is very clear that such a building project requires many workers (including those with specialized skills), as well as a massive investment.

Gamla

The wall of Gamla was built only on the northeastern side, as all other sides were protected by nature with sheer cliffs and sharp slopes. The wall is about 200 meters in length. However, it is not a straight line, as it was created by blocking entrances between houses, filling up rooms, and building segments of wall. Like the wall built at Yodefat, this wall was built while cutting through existing rooms of houses (Syon and Yavor, 2010: 14–40).

Magdala

As Magdala is one of the settlements mentioned by Josephus as part of his fortifying project, the excavators suggest that the synagogue was purposely dismantled. It was taken apart because it was out of the line of the "emergency wall." Columns, covered with fresco and stucco similar to those fragments found in the synagogue, were found blocking the north-south street near the synagogue. The shops' entrances along the west-east street south of the synagogue were blocked. It seems possible that this evidence is connected to the fortifications of the city.[5]

In at least three or four sites identified as fortified by Josephus, evidence for fortifications were identified: Gischala, Beer Sheba of the Galilee, Mt. Nitai, and Mt. Tabor (Aviam, 2008: 39*–52*). Josephus mentioned that he "built a wall" on Mt. Tabor approximately 5 kilometers in length in forty days. The remains of a Hellenistic/Roman wall surrounding the top of the mountain was never properly excavated. It is less than 5 kilometers, but it is possible that Josephus reused a Hellenistic wall like he did at Yodefat and probably at Beer Sheba of the Galilee as well. In any case, reconstructing a long wall like this one requires a lot of manpower as well as financial resources.

As we can deduce from the archaeological evidence, it is clear that in the half year that Josephus spent in the Galilee from his arrival until the first battle at Yodefat, there was massive activity that required substantial financial resources. We can assume that this money came primarily from the taxes that Josephus collected (as reflected in *Vita* 63, 72). Instead of sending part of it to Jerusalem and part of it to the Roman authorities, it was now invested in building operations in the Galilee. It is also possible that each of the governors came to his region with money given to them from the "war government" in Jerusalem.

The Effects of the War

The war in the Galilee started in the summer of 67 CE, though there were a few clashes in Cestius Galus's attack in 66 CE, in which the village of Khabulon (Kabul) was destroyed (*B.J.* 2.503–505).

During the campaign of Vespasian and Titus, there were several battles: Yodefat, Yapha, Magdala (Tarichaea), Gamla, Mt. Tabor, and Gischala. Vespasian marched through the Galilee with an army of approximately 60,000 soldiers, and it is clear that this army caused a lot of damage and raided the villagers of the region. Josephus describes the beginning of the campaign as follows: "Both divisions made constant sallies and overran the surrounding country, causing trouble to Josephus and his men.... The Romans, enraged at his enterprise, never ceased, night and day, to devastate the plains and to pillage the property of the country-folk, invariably killing all capable of bearing arms and reducing the inefficient to servitude. Galilee from end to end became a scene of fire and blood" (*B.J.* 3.59–63).[6] On the way to the first battle at Yodefat, the Roman army attacked and destroyed the large village of Gabara; Vespasian also "burnt all villages and country towns in the neighborhood; some he found completely deserted, in the others he reduced the inhabitants to slavery" (*B.J.* 3.134). Although we do not have any archaeological evidence supporting these descriptions, they are probable given that the Roman military activity included the intimidation and terrorization of civilians in order to decrease their opponents' fighting ability before the Romans began their battles against the fortified towns and cities.

Yodefat

The first siege took place at Yodefat and, according to Josephus, who commanded the battle, it lasted forty-seven days. The topographical position of the town, its recently built walls, and the fighting spirit of the defenders were the reasons for the third-longest siege of the war, after Jerusalem and Masada. Josephus's narrative is dramatic, describing heavy bloodshed. At the end, after the Romans invaded the town, he described a heavy massacre (*B.J.* 3.336–339).

Over the years, many scholars have doubted Josephus's narrative of the war, but archaeological excavations point to the truth of Josephus's account. The town was found destroyed, with many fire marks; there are ballista stones all over the town; there are bow and catapult arrowheads everywhere. Surprisingly, we found human bones in every room we excavated and heaps of gathered bones in every cistern we checked (Aviam, 2002). Many of the bones carried violent marks, and all of these point to a heavy massacre of men, women, and children, as described by Josephus. Our estimation of the number of dead in the town is approximately 7,000 (it is clear that Josephus's number of 40,000 dead is purposely exaggerated) (Aviam, 2002). As the battle of Yodefat was the first one in the war, we think that the Jews did not want to surrender, and as the Roman army suffered a lot of casualties, the punishment was not only to slaughter many of the citizens, but also not to allow survivors to bury their dead: the bodies were left in the streets and houses to be a feast for the birds of the sky and the beasts.

The town was abandoned. Moreover, presumably as part of their punishment, Jews were not allowed to return and resettle in the town. According to Josephus's account, in addition to the 40,000 people killed, 1,200 were taken as prisoners of war (*B.J.* 3.337)

Yapha

During the siege of Yodefat, the Roman army launched a short attack on Yapha, a large village south of Yodefat and, in the end, the town was taken; and, according to Josephus, there were 15,000 dead and 1,130 prisoners (*B.J.* 3.289–306).

Gamla

After a siege lasting approximately three weeks, Gamla was conquered. According to Josephus's description, the Jews fled up the hill while the Roman soldiers were chasing them from the bottom. At the end, all of the survivors from the battle gathered on the rocky summit and threw themselves down the steep cliff. Josephus writes that there were 4,000 casualties in the battle, and that 5,000 took their own lives (*B.J.* 4.80). In contrast with Yodefat, the total number of casualties is not too exaggerated. If there was room for 3,000 people in the town during periods of peace, it is possible that there were 6,000 to 9,000 people in the town with the addition of refugees from the Jewish villages around the town.

The town was completely destroyed and has never been resettled. It is possible that, like Yodefat, the Roman authorities did not allow Jews to return, as a punishment. During the excavations, only one human jaw and a fragment of a skull were found (Syon, 2014: 17). It is possible that this lack of human bones in the town reflects Josephus's narrative of the end, where people were killed only on the summit. It is also important to know that, although two cisterns were discovered, neither was excavated, and we cannot tell if there were gathered bones there like at Yodefat.

Magdala

On its way towards Gamla, the Roman army surrounded Magdala. According to Josephus's story, there was an intense debate among the citizens of the town. The "foreigners" who had escaped to the town from Tiberias and other places supported participation in the war, while most of the original inhabitants were ready to give up. A short siege ended with a quick attack by the Roman cavalry, entering the town from the lakeside. The actual last battle took place on the water when the Zealots fled to the lake on boats, chased by Romans on boats and rafts. All of them were massacred: "One could see the whole lake red with blood and covered with corpses, for not a man escaped" (*B.J.* 3.529). According to Josephus, 6,700 people were killed in the first attack and on the water. Vespasian ordered the execution of 1,200 of the elderly and weak. Six thousand young men were sent to Rome, and 34,400 were sold to slavery, while others (no number) were sent to King Agrippa. All together, approximately 50,000 people were within the walls of the town, according to Josephus's account.

The archaeological discoveries did not identify any evidence of war in the town, but the boat excavated on the shore of Magdala was dated to the first century CE (Wachsmann, 1990). Arrowheads were found in this boat; thus, one might suggest a connection to the war on the lake (Syon, 1990).

The excavators suggest that the northern part of the town was an important commercial quarter with a market and shops, but it is clear that there was a rapid decline of this northern part of town in the late first century CE. This decline started with the abandonment of the synagogue, which was the northernmost building in the town, probably in the preparations for the war, and likely continued as a result of the battle. The rest of the town continued to exist (Zapata-Meza, 2018).

Conclusion

Since its creation as a Jewish region during the Hasmonean dynasty, the Galilee developed into a prosperous, highly populated area. The evolution of Sepphoris from a central town into a Roman-type polis and the establishment of a new Roman-style capital at Tiberias created a small region with two poleis surrounded by towns, villages, and a few farmsteads. The discoveries of richly decorated houses at Gamla and Yodefat, two field towns, emphasize the wealth that existed in many of the villages and undoubtedly extended into the cities. The two capitals had large public structures. A few of these are evident from archaeology, including theaters in Tiberias (Atrash, 2012) and Sepphoris,[7] and a stadium at Tiberias, as well as possible palatial structures in Tiberias (Jensen, 2006: 141–4) and Sepphoris (Weiss, 2015: 57).

Before the Roman invasion of the Galilee in 67 CE, as described clearly and in detail by Josephus Flavius, who, as a governor of the region, was an eyewitness, there was a large operation of fortifying cities, towns, and villages, as well as appropriate natural sites. A list of these sites appears in both *Life* and *Jewish War*, and was evident in archaeological surveys and excavations. These building projects, as well as the building of an army and other preparations for the war, required large sums of money, which probably came from local taxation.

A massive attack was launched on the Galilee for half a year. The two capitals surrendered to the Romans with no battle. There was siege war lasting forty-seven days at Yodefat, and at Gamla, there was an almost month-long siege. A few villages were burnt down (such as Gabara), while property, fields, and crops were plundered. If we calculate the total number of Galilean war casualties, according to Josephus, we shall come to a total of about 110,000 dead and sold into slavery. According to my analysis, the population of the Galilee and Golan before the war was approximately 184,000 (Aviam, 2005: 36). According to Uzi Leibner, the number of inhabitants in his survey area is between 9,000 (using the minimum estimation) and 35,500 (according to the maximum estimation), and the size of his surveyed area is approximately one-eighth of the size of Jewish Galilee and Golan (Leibner, 2009: 335). So, if we take the average number from Leibner and multiply it by eight, we will arrive at the number of 176,000 inhabitants.

It is therefore very clear that the numbers given by Josephus are highly exaggerated in order to emphasize the entire event of the war and its results. In fact, apart from Yodefat and Gamla (the two main battles of the Galilean campaign, which were destroyed and abandoned permanently) and the shrinking of Magdala, we have no other archaeological evidence for other catastrophes in the region. It is clear that many people were killed and many were sold into slavery; I estimated the number of humans lost at Yodefat to be 7,000 people. We can assume that a similar number was lost at Gamla, as well as at Magdala and Yapha.[8] According to my rough estimates, the victims of the war in the Galilee, including captives, numbered approximately 20,000 people. This amounts to approximately one-tenth of the population, which is a great loss. There was also a loss of property, but it seems as though the Galilee recovered very quickly from both losses.

The small farmstead of Tel Rekhesh is an example of continuity from the first to the second century CE, with no remains of destruction or abandonment in between. The walls that were built under Josephus, the governor of the Galilee, were partially demolished by the Romans as an act of victory (*B.J.* 4.117), and the rest of the walls were taken apart by the inhabitants themselves to be reused in new houses.[9] There was no more need for fortifications after the war.

We can also compare the results of the Galilean war with the results of the Judean campaign in the First Revolt and the results of the second. After the First Revolt, Jerusalem was completely destroyed by the Roman army and abandoned by its Jewish inhabitants. A Roman army camp was built inside, but the Judean villages recovered, like the Galilean. The results of the Second Revolt were different: all Judean villages were destroyed and abandoned.

Notes

1. For the division of the Jewish land into eight regions, the sending of governors, and Josephus's activity in the Galilee, see *B.J.* 2.562–584. For the understanding of the implementation of the fortification project as reflected from in all regions, see Aviam, 2008.
2. For a short summary of the excavation, see Aviam, 2015.
3. The best reference book is Bauckham, 2018.
4. For the preparations for the war, see Aviam, 2002.

5. This part of the excavation is not yet published, even in a preliminary report, but it is visible on site.
6. The translations of *Jewish War* are those of Henry St. John Thackeray (1927–1928).
7. The date of the theater in Sepphoris is still under debate. According to Weiss, it was built at the end of the first century CE. See Weiss, 2015.
8. Josephus also mentioned 6,000 dead at Gischala (*B.J.* 4.115), and "many" at Mt. Tabor (*B.J.* 4.54–61).
9. This is probably the reason why the remains of the walls were not discovered at Sepphoris, Tiberias, Gischala, and other sites, but clearly identified at Yodefat and Gamla, which were destroyed and abandoned.

Bibliography

Atrash, Walid. 2012. "The Roman Theater at Tiberias." *Qadmoniot* 144: 79–88.

Aviam, Mordechai. 2002. "Yodefat/Jotapata: The Archaeology of the First Battle." Pages 121–33 in *The First Jewish Revolt: Archaeology, History, and Ideology.* Edited by Andrea M. Berlin and J. Andrew Overman. London: Routledge.

———. 2004. *Jews, Pagans, and Christians in the Galilee: Twenty-Five Years of Archaeological Excavations and Surveys; Hellenistic to Byzantine Periods.* Rochester: University of Rochester Press.

———. 2005. "*Yodefat: A Case Study in the Development of Jewish Settlement in the Galilee during the Second Temple Period*" [Hebrew]. PhD diss., Bar Ilan University.

———. 2008. "The Fortified Settlements of Josephus Flavius and Their Significance against the Background of the Excavations of Yodefat and Gamla." Pages 39*–52* in *The Great Revolt in the Galilee.* Edited by Ofra Guri-Rimon. Haifa: Hecht Museum/University of Haifa.

———. 2015. "Yodefat-Jotapata: A Jewish Galilean Town at the End of the Second Temple Period; The Results of an Archaeological Project." Pages 109–26 in *The Archaeological Record from Cities, Towns, and Villages.* Vol. 2 of *Galilee in the Late Second Temple and Mishnaic Periods.* Edited by David A. Fiensy and James R. Strange. Minneapolis: Fortress.

Aviam, Mordechai, Hisao Kuwabara, Shuichi Hasegawa, and Yitzhak Paz. 2019. "A 1st–2nd Century CE Assembly Room (Synagogue?) in a Jewish Estate at Tel Rekhesh, Lower Galilee." *Tel Aviv* 46, no. 1: 128–42.

Bauckham, Richard, ed. 2018. *Magdala of Galilee: A Jewish City in the Hellenistic and Roman Period.* Waco: Baylor University Press.

Ben David, Chaim. 2011. "Were There 204 Settlements in Galilee at the Time of Josephus Flavius?" *Journal of Jewish Studies* 62: 21–36.

Farhi, Yoav. 2010. "Stucco Decorations from the Western Quarter." Pages 175–87 in *Gamla II: The Architecture; The Shmarya Gutmann Excavations 1978–1988.* Edited by Danny Syon and Zvi Yavor. Israel Antiquities Authority Reports 44. Jerusalem: Israel Antiquities Authority.

Jensen, Morten Hørning. 2006. *Herod Antipas in Galilee: The Literary and Archaeological Sources on the Reign of Herod Antipas and Its Socio-Economic Impact on Galilee.* Wissenschaftliche Untersuchungen zum Neuen Testament 2/215. Tübingen: Mohr Siebeck.

Leibner, Uzi. 2009. *Settlement and History in Hellenistic, Roman, and Byzantine Galilee: An Archaeological Survey of the Eastern Galilee.* Texts and Studies in Ancient Judaism. Tübingen: Mohr Siebeck.

Lena, Anna. 2018. "The Harbor." Pages 69–88 in *Magdala of Galilee: A Jewish City in the Hellenistic and Roman Period*. Edited by Richard Bauckham. Waco: Baylor University Press.

Syon, Danny. 1990. "The Arrowhead." Pages 99–100 in *The Excavations of an Ancient Boat in the Sea of Galilee (Lake Kinneret)*. Edited by Shelley Wachsmann. ʿAtiqot 19. Jerusalem: Israel Antiquities Authority.

———. 2014. *Gamla III: Finds and Studies IAA; The Shmarya Gutmann Excavations 1978–1988*. Israel Antiquities Authority Reports 56. Jerusalem: Israel Antiquities Authority.

Syon, Danny, and Zvi Yavor. 2010. *Gamla II: The Architecture; The Shmarya Gutmann Excavations 1978-1988*. Israel Antiquities Authority Reports 44. Jerusalem: Israel Antiquities Authority.

Thackeray, Henry St. John, ed. and trans. 1927–1928. *Josephus: The Jewish War*. Loeb Classical Library. Cambridge: Harvard University Press.

Wachsmann, Shelley, ed. 1990. *The Excavations of an Ancient Boat in the Sea of Galilee (Lake Kinneret)*. ʿAtiqot 19. Jerusalem: Israel Antiquities Authority.

Weiss, Zeev. 2015. "From Galilean Town to Roman City, 100 BCE–200 CE." Pages 53–75 in *The Archaeological Record from Cities, Towns, and Villages*. Vol. 2 of *Galilee in the Late Second Temple and Mishnaic Periods*. Edited by David A. Fiensy and James R. Strange. Minneapolis: Fortress.

Winer, Stuart. 2021. "Second Ancient Synagogue Found in Migdal Alters Ideas of Jewish Life 2,000 Years Ago." *The Times of Israel*. December 12. https://www.timesofisrael.com/second-ancient-synagogue-found-in-migdal-alters-ideas-of-jewish-life-2000-years-ago/.

Zapata-Meza, Marcela. 2018. "Domestic and Mercantile Areas." Pages 89–108 in *Magdala of Galilee: A Jewish City in the Hellenistic and Roman Period*. Edited by Richard Bauckham. Waco: Baylor University Press.

6 The Economic Transformation of an Early Roman Galilean Village

A Keynesian Approach

C. Thomas McCollough

This paper has as its primary goal the description and analysis of the changes in the economic posture of a small Jewish village in Lower Galilee over the period of the early first century CE to the end of that same century with a focus on the period after 70 CE. Given the dearth of written sources for doing such work, the material culture recovered in the excavations of Khirbet Qana between the years 1998 and 2008 will, naturally, be the primary source for describing the economic life of the village. The paper will argue that these data reveal a pattern of economic behavior that shows signs of significant change in the latter decades of the first century (ca. post-70 CE), and that the changes reflect a complex response to colonization that entails both accommodation and resistance.[1] The economic choices made in this period appear to defy the economic behavior model proposed in the classic work of Adam Smith and beg for the more dense model found in the work of John Maynard Keynes, and in particular the articulation of Keynes's work in the studies of Robert Shiller and George Akerlof. As will be shown, Keynes's inclusion of a notion of "animal spirits" provides insights into economic choices that seem to flout a rational negotiation of market forces, but rather reflect a more emotive or narrative-based approach to economic behavior.[2]

This study will also make the case for the importance of building an economic portrait of a region by beginning at the micro level and building out from that evidence to a more general theory of economic behavior. In the past, we have seen a persistent urban-centric bias in terms of the excavation of Roman and Byzantine sites in the Levant. Such concentration on urban remains excludes critical and inherently interesting information, and the sheer size and complexity of urban spaces inhibits a comprehensive understanding of the historical, social, and economic dynamics over time or in any given place. Evidence from village sites can contribute to a much more vivid picture of social forms of ranking, the nature and degree of integration into the larger political economy, and interconnections with commercial and cultural networks. Moreover, recent anthropological as well as historical studies of villages have argued against the long-held view that villages are essentially static entities, either in the sense of repositories of venerable

DOI: 10.4324/9781003041696-9

traditions (the so-called "little traditions") or in the sense of long-lived entities witnessing few changes in their material culture (Horden and Purcell, 2000). In the period that is relevant to this paper, for example, we find in the case of Upper Galilee in the transition from the Hellenistic to the Roman period, over a quarter of the villages ceased to exist, while other regions of the Galilee witnessed a spike in population and a correlate spike in the number of settlements and growth in preexisting settlement size (Frankel, Getzov, Aviam, and Degani, 2001; Edwards, 2007). Further, as the material remains from the villages have surfaced in greater quantity, narrow approaches to the economic landscape (e.g., the tendency to pigeonhole the economy of Roman Galilee as simply a political economy dominated by elites and imperial interests) have been challenged if not displaced by more complex and nuanced models. The data demand a model that can encompass evidence that shows signs of villages that "adapted and responded to their ecological circumstances influenced by their perception of the past, and their view of the future" (Edwards, 2009: 222). This can be manifest, for example, in indicators that villages were readily participating in patterns of trade and exchange in response to new infrastructure, greater monetization, and demographic shifts, while at the same time investing in structures and ways of life that ensure secure ties to a well-established if not ancient identity. The complexity of this economic landscape was succinctly captured in David Mattingly's observations about the Roman imperial economy:

> The pattern is one of a colorful mosaic of tied and free market activity.... We must conceptualize this in terms of a political economy that operated alongside a social economy that was in turn interleaved with a true market economy.
>
> (Mattingly, 2006: 295)

The Site of Khirbet Qana

Khirbet Qana ("the ruins of Cana") is located in the center of Lower Galilee, 7 kilometers north of the ancient city of Sepphoris and 15 kilometers west of Tiberias on the Sea of Galilee along a critical east-west corridor, the Beth Netofa Valley (see Figure 6.1). In terms of excavation history, no systematic survey or excavation of the site occurred until 1997, when Douglas R. Edwards initiated the University of Puget Sound excavations. That survey revealed plentiful evidence of human activity from the Neolithic through the Ottoman periods.

In terms of the identification of the site, there are grounds for associating this village with the New Testament Cana of Galilee (John 2:1–11), as well as Josephus's Cana (*Vita* 86).[3] Khirbet Qana's location on the edge of the Beth Netofa Valley just north of Nazareth and east of Sepphoris correlates well with the reference in Josephus.[4] The excavations have made evident that it was a substantial Jewish village in the first century CE, and there

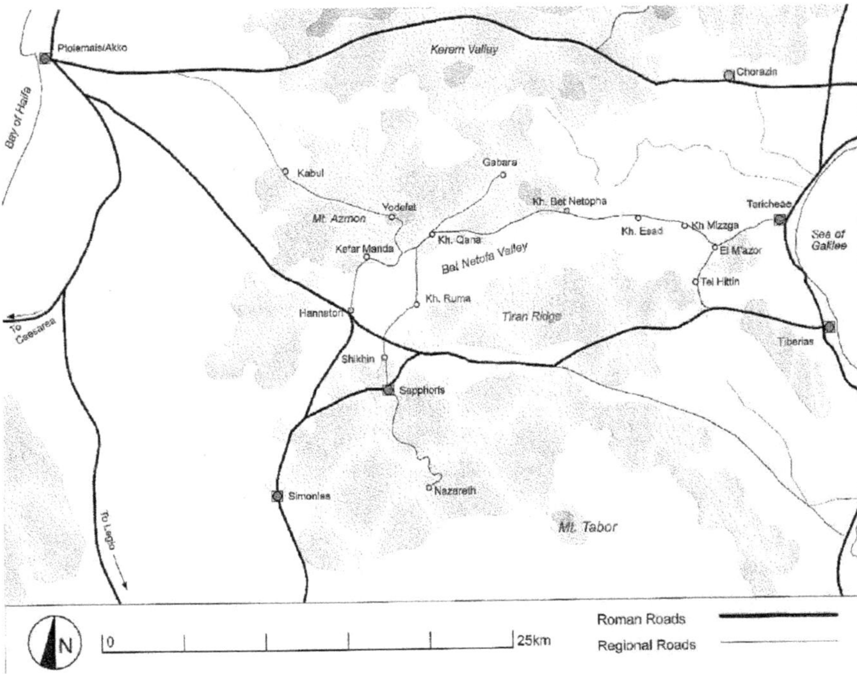

Figure 6.1 Map of Lower Galilee with Roman roads and paths.

Source: Drawing by James F. Strange. Used by permission.

is evidence of continuous Jewish presence until at least the sixth century CE (Edwards, 2002). Moreover, a thorough study of Christian pilgrims' references to visits to Cana of Galilee concluded that until the seventeenth century, there was only one Cana that the pilgrims visited, and that Cana correlates with the location of Khirbet Qana (Herrojo, 1999). The excavations of Khirbet Qana have further solidified the link between the Christian pilgrims' reports and this site by way of exposing an extensive veneration cave complex that included an altar-like structure with incised crosses, pilgrims' graffiti, and fragments of stone vessels dating from the sixth through the twelfth centuries.[5]

The excavations that began in 1999 have recovered no evidence of substantial remains from the Hellenistic period. There is significant numismatic material from the Hasmonean period, but there are no structures to connect this village with local representatives of Hasmonean power. The village begins to emerge architecturally in the Early Roman period (37 BCE–70 CE) and was concentrated on the acropolis and the north, east, and west slopes of the small hillock (see Figure 6.2). The steeper south slope (facing Sepphoris and the Beth Netofa Valley) has no buildings until one reaches a plateau halfway down, where a separate small village was built,

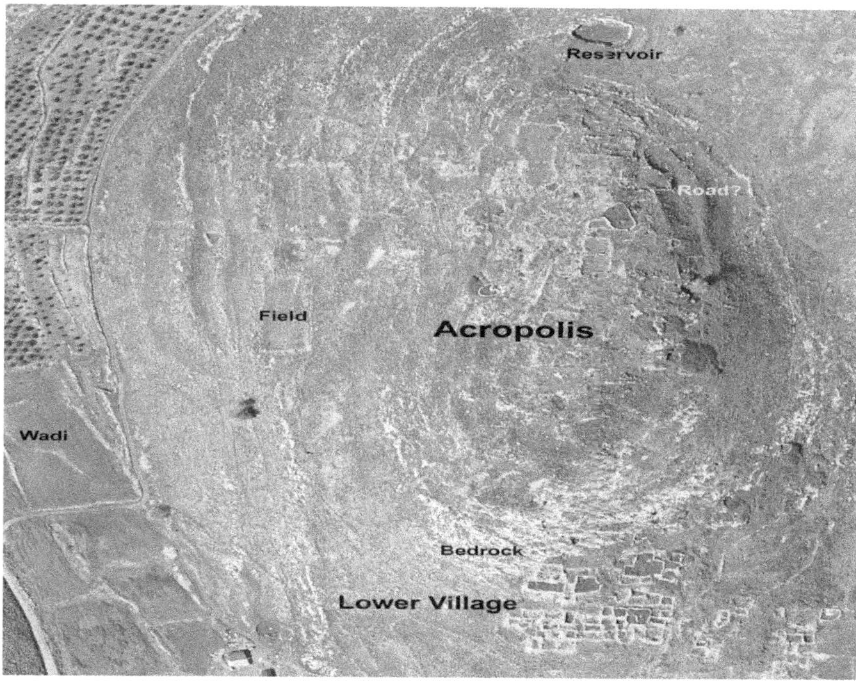

Figure 6.2 Aerial view of Khirbet Qana.

Source: Photo courtesy of University of Puget Sound Excavations. Used by permission.

perhaps as late as the early Ottoman period. The south slope was also the location of the multichambered veneration complex.

The village's location on the northern edge of the valley ensured access to one of the most fertile areas in the Galilee, second only to the Jezreel Valley (see Figure 6.3). Moreover, the valley served as the spatial framework within which the village operated and provided a natural approach to the Sea of Galilee and a visual connection to the urban center at Sepphoris.

Prior to the construction of a Roman road in the valley connecting Akko/Ptolemais with Tiberias (6 km south of Khirbet Qana) in the late first century CE, travel between Khirbet Qana and other places of significant human habitation seems to have been entirely dependent on footpaths. However, the construction of this road opened important new horizons for trade and other modes of interaction with other places and people outside the village proper. While sure evidence of the village being interwoven into the growing web of connections facilitated by the road have not been exposed, the map showing Khirbet Qana connected to a regional road network is feasible given the clues found in the *Tabula Imperii Romani: Iudaea, Palaestina* (Tsafrir, Di Segni, and Green, 1994) and the studies of Avi-Yonah on the Roman roads in the Galilee (Avi-Yonah, 1977).

Figure 6.3 Khirbet Qana and Beth Netofa Valley.

Source: Photo courtesy of University of Puget Sound Excavations. Used by permission.

The location of twelve tombs encircling the area of habitation has enabled an approximation of the size of the village. The Early Roman village covered approximately 5 hectares. By way of comparison, it was about the same size as the nearby village of Yodefat/Jotapata, a bit larger than Nazareth, and smaller than Capernaum, which measured about 17 hectares. It was significantly smaller than the urban center of Sepphoris, which measured about 60 hectares. Presuming a relatively dense population coefficiency (similar to that used by Spigel for Gamla), the population estimate by the end of the first century CE would be 1,200 (Spigel, 2012).

Khirbet Qana before 70 CE[6]

The artifacts and architecture recovered from the early decades of the first century CE exposed a modest village lacking any public structures and consisting of small, unexceptional domestic structures that are primarily if not exclusively built on slopes of the northeastern quadrant of the site (see Figure 6.4). These are houses without private courtyards, each of which uses the roof of the house below as its courtyard.

There is no architectural evidence for industry in this period. The village shows few signs of monetization. Interaction outside of subsistence agriculture appears to be largely limited to barter exchange within a network of Jewish villages, to include Kefar Hananya or perhaps, given the discovery of the pottery kilns at Yodefat, even more local. The coins that date

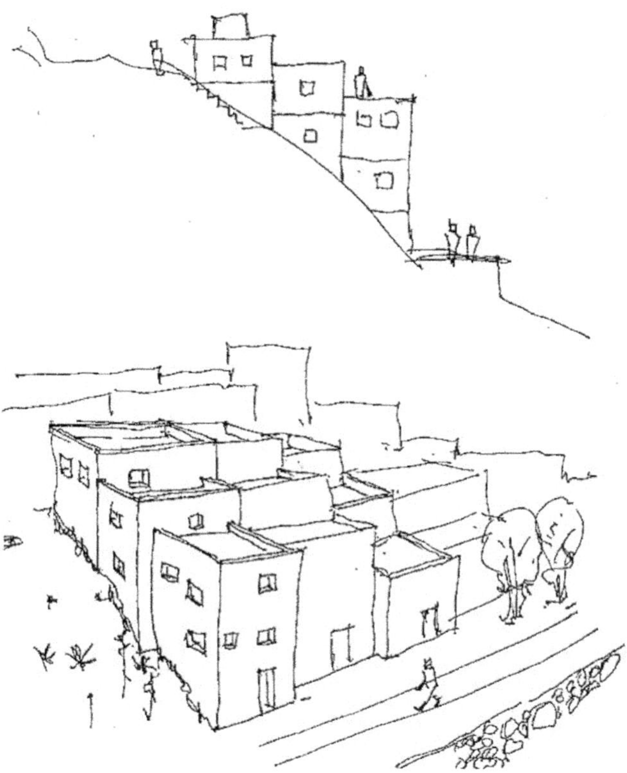

Figure 6.4 Drawing of houses without separate courtyards.

Source: Drawing by Peter Richardson for University of Puget Sound Excavations. Used by permission.

to this period are predominantly Seleucid (which Danny Syon describes as "found regularly in Galilee") and Jewish coins dating from 125 to 124 BCE (Syon, 2002). All indications are that the political economy manifest in the building of Sepphoris under Herod Antipas in the early decades of the first century CE had little impact on this village. In sum, the village appears to have been following a narrative that encouraged neither collaboration nor contestation, but a traditional, insular existence as the means for survival in an increasingly colonized landscape.

Khirbet Qana after 70 CE

The architecture and artifacts that emerge in the stratum that overlays this earliest phase of Roman period habitation show a striking shift in the enlargement of resources and expansion of trade relations, as well as deliberate efforts to retain a conservative/traditional Jewish identity. This is a layer that dates from roughly the mid-first century to the first two decades of the second century. In general, there are clear indications that the village was bolstered by human and material resources in the decades following the destruction of the temple in Jerusalem and the assault on and destruction of villages in the Galilee and Golan. The influx of assets may very well be related to the revolt and its aftermath (transfer of population and wealth from Judea and other villages), but in any case, these resources provided a basis for a transformation of the posture of the village from isolated to one of being connected and engaged in trade and industry. At the same time, as the village appeared to be tracking an economic course of action that was pragmatic and opportunistic, there also appeared to be countervailing dynamics that would ensure Jewish identity was preserved, especially at the intimate levels of foodways and sacred traditions. This type of hybridized posture of response to colonization reflected is not unique, as made evident by the work of Marianne Sawicki and, as noted previously, reflects economic behavior that incorporates a nonquantifiable "spirit" of resistance to the values and mores of the dominant power.

The first artifact that emerged which elucidates this complex dynamic are basalt grinders (both fragmentary and whole). In virtually every village that has been excavated in the Galilee, one will find grindstones and other implements (pounders, mills) made of basalt. When Jesus proclaimed that it is better that a millstone be placed around the neck of someone and be thrown into the deepest part of the sea rather than cause a child to sin (Mark 9:42), listeners would understand the sharp contrast of the heavy basalt millstone with leading a child astray. Despite the ubiquity of such stones and grinders, outcroppings of basalt in the Galilee are very rare; indeed only one clear example has been located, in eastern Galilee. Nearby, however, the Golan (ancient Gaulanitis) has a number of basalt outcroppings, making it the more likely point of origin for the basalt implements found in the Galilee. The raw basalt would need to be transported to workshops, and remnants of such workshops have been located around Capernaum (Xenophontos, Elliott, and Malpas, 1988). If the pattern of delivery from workshop to customer followed patterns revealed in texts recovered from Egypt as well as in the Mishnah, the artisan would take samples to villages and towns and then deliver the vessels by donkey train (Wolfe, 1952; Edwards, 2008). The basalt vessels found at Khirbet Qana have then arrived as the end point of an intricate arrangement of production and trade that shows no convincing evidence of being controlled by elites. As Edwards observed,

> The complexity of the economy within and between Galilean villages and cities has often been underestimated and inappropriately tagged with this loosely defined "political economy" label. In villages we find activities that indicate active engagement by villagers in the local and regional economy that belie direct involvement of local elites in the cities.
> (Edwards, 2007: 363)

The beginning point of Khirbet Qana's involvement in this thriving village economy is difficult to establish with certainty as the vessels were recovered in nonstratified contexts or in later use. One indicator that these vessels are part of the late first century CE context is to see their use in correlation with the transformation of water-holding cisterns to holding grain, which can be dated with some certainty to the late first century CE. While storing grain in large quantities may reflect a change in soil or environment, it is more likely evidence of a move from subsistence agriculture to market economy, which in turn demands the use of large vessels for grinding (Longstaff and Hussey, 1997; Schoenwetter and Geyer, 2000).

A second object of material culture that manifests the shift in economic posture is the large public building exposed on the southwest quadrant of the site's acropolis that has been identified as a synagogue (see Figure 6.5). The building was erected on a basilical plan. The large main hall (approx. 20 m by 15 m) is connected to a small room (approx. 3 m by 5 m) on the northeastern corner. The size of the main hall would have an estimated seating capacity of 225 to 250. The main hall is oriented north-south with an entry on the south wall. A Herodian-type bossed stone from the doorjamb was recovered on the floor of the main hall, suggesting a substantial and elaborate entryway. A sizeable fragment of a door lintel was also found. It is decorated with a rosette and garland. Several architectural elements (column base, flagstones) were found just outside the south entrance, suggesting a porch or courtyard on the south.

The outer walls of the putative synagogue are 1.5 meters wide and were plastered on both the exterior and interior. A hard-packed surface running along the outer western wall was exposed that sat directly upon quarried bedrock. It contained Early Roman period (37 BCE–70 CE) sherds. It appears to have served as a path or roadway. It is likely that the whole of the interior was painted, as fragments of the interior wall plaster were found decorated with red paint.

In the style consistent with other ancient synagogues, the interior of the building was divided into a central nave and two side aisles by way of eight interior columns. The foundation stones for the columns (footers) were recovered (5 m apart, north-south; and 2.5 m, east-west), as well as portions of column drums and stylobate fragments. A capital was uncovered that had been reused in the later transformation of the synagogue into domestic space. The capital's decorative elements place it in the Ionic order with recessed volutes. There are also carvings of fruit hanging from the volutes.

There was no sign of a mosaic having covered the floors of the earliest phase of the building, but the floors of the aisles were paved with plaster, while the floor of the nave was covered with flattened bedrock. In the northwest corner of the interior, a bench was constructed of small field stones, which were covered with plaster. In the northeast corner, bedrock was shaped into a bench and again was overlaid with plaster.

Figure 6.5 Aerial photo of possible synagogue.

Source: Photo by Skyview for University of Puget Sound Excavations. Used by permission.

As noted, a small room was connected to the exterior wall of the main hall at the northeast corner. Although the foundation of this room had been disturbed by Byzantine rebuilding, the excavations made clear that it was founded on quarried bedrock in the same manner as the large hall. In addition, the lowest level of debris within the room contained an overwhelming number of Late Hellenistic (152–37 BCE) and Early Roman sherds, suggesting that its original construction coincided with the building of the main hall. The room included a single low bench on three sides that was plastered. The plaster was subjected to radiocarbon (carbon-14) dating, and it yielded a date consistent with the floor of the main hall (100–300 CE). This, combined with the fact that the north wall of the room is not an extension of the north wall of the large building, suggests the room was added as part of the elaboration on the original building in the second century CE. The dating, size, position of the room in relation to the main building, and the inclusion of a bench aligns it with similar rooms uncovered in the course of the excavations of the Second Temple synagogues at Gamla (Syon and Yavor, 2010) and Wadi Hamam (Leibner, 2018). The Gamla room was identified as a "study room," and this room may also have functioned as a small *bet midrash* (Syon and Yavor, 2010: 55).

An additional architectural feature of importance is the *tegula*—ceramic roofing tiles. A portion of the tiles that were recovered in the earliest levels of debris was subjected to petrologic analysis to determine compositional characteristics and possible provenance. In terms of the latter, a significant percentage (55 percent) of the tiles proved to be imported, primarily from Cyprus. The utilization of imported tiles has several interesting possible implications to include locating the village in a much-expanded trade network, as well as pointing to enhanced economic resources and a decision to expend such resources on a public building that had high cultural/religious value.

In an effort to date the founding of the building, probes to foundation level were made. These probes revealed that the structure was built in an area that had previously served as a place for quarrying stone. The stones used at founding level had been mortared, and there was plaster adhering to the exterior and interior surfaces of this wall. The very few readable sherds recovered were from a bowl and a cooking pot that had a start date of the late first century BCE and an end date of the beginning of the second century CE. The excavation of the founding level also recovered a coin of Antiochus IV and a Hellenistic lamp fragment.

The mortar used in the construction of the foundation wall contained residue that was successfully subjected to radiocarbon (carbon-14) analysis. The analysis yielded a date of 4 to 235 CE (95 percent accuracy). Having exposed plaster on the interior floor of the building, it too was examined with radiocarbon analysis to assist in dating the structure. A sectioning of the floor exposed two layers, and the earliest layer was dated from 100 to 330 CE (95 percent accuracy). The soil beneath the lower floor contained a small number of datable forms that were similar to those found in conjunction with the foundation wall: spanning the late first century BCE to the second century CE.

This ensemble of evidence posed a founding date that spanned the spectrum from the early decades of the first century CE to the late first or early second century CE. The judgment was made that in sum, the evidence pointed to a founding in the late first to early second century CE, with full elaboration (i.e., plaster floors, columns, bench along walls, addition of a possible *bet midrash*) by the mid-second century CE. This dating would coincide with the dating of other architectural features and artifacts cited and discussed herein to include the basalt vessel, an industrial installation for processing wool, and the expansion of the domestic quarter.

The third material culture indicator of economic status and choice is in the realm of domestic structures. Peter Richardson's study of the domestic architecture of Khirbet Qana observed that by the end of the first century, the domestic area had expanded and, in addition to terrace housing without courtyards, included houses with side courtyards and at least one house with a central courtyard (Richardson, 2006). The houses that included courtyards located to the side of the main structure occupied the less steep northern slope. While these were simple houses with living space extending into the courtyard space, they were significantly larger than the terrace housing dated to the earlier decades of the first century CE. The courtyards included cisterns, and in one case, at least, we located a stepped pool that may have served as a *miqveh*.

The structure with the central courtyard was recovered on the northeast quadrant of the acropolis. Four large rubble core walls were uncovered that had been built to create a large room (12 m by 8 m). A pilaster built against the north wall appears to have been part of an arch supporting a second story. The pilaster is associated with a well-plastered floor still *in situ*. A small fragment of wall plaster with red paint along with pieces of marble were found in the fill nearby. The room was joined to a well-paved courtyard to the north and a small corridor to the west. A large, undecorated lintel was found resting on the courtyard pavers. Samples from the plaster floor that were subject to radiocarbon analysis dated them to the same period as the synagogue. While it is possible that this structure is a public building of some type, it appears more likely to be the remains of a large and somewhat opulent domestic structure similar to the elite house uncovered at Yodefat (Richardson, 2006).

The expansion and differentiation of domestic space provides further signs of a flourishing village, using its access to resources to enhance its living space, even at the cost of marking out social and economic differentiation. This is a pattern very similar to the one expounded by Sharon Lea Mattila in her studies of the domestic structures (and artifacts) uncovered in the Hellenistic- and Roman-period strata at Capernaum (Mattila, 2013). There is no indication of the owners/residents of this fine house, but it is worth noting that Cana is identified as one of the locations for the resettlement of the priestly course after the Great Revolt of 70 CE. Is it possible that this house, built in close proximity to the synagogue, is the home of the priestly family of Eliashib?[7]

The fourth and last of the economic indicators are the remnants of industrial activity. There are two such indicators, both located on the eastern slope. The first is a dovecote or columbarium. This is a bell-shaped dovecote that was hewn into the bedrock and plastered (see Figure 6.6). The form is typical of others found in Roman sites in Palestine and dated to the first centuries BCE/CE (Aviam, 2004).

The second industrial feature is a set of installations cut into the bedrock and built up with field stones that were then plastered (see Figure 6.7). These tub-like features are located near a large cistern. Two stepped structures that lead to underground chambers were built adjacent to these installations. One is just to the west and above the installations. It features five steps leading to a small (1 m by 1.7 m [east-west] by 2 m) underground plastered chamber. The second and larger stepped structure was uncovered 2.5 meters below and to the south of these installations. In this case, the five plastered steps lead to a circular underground chamber that measured 3 meters high

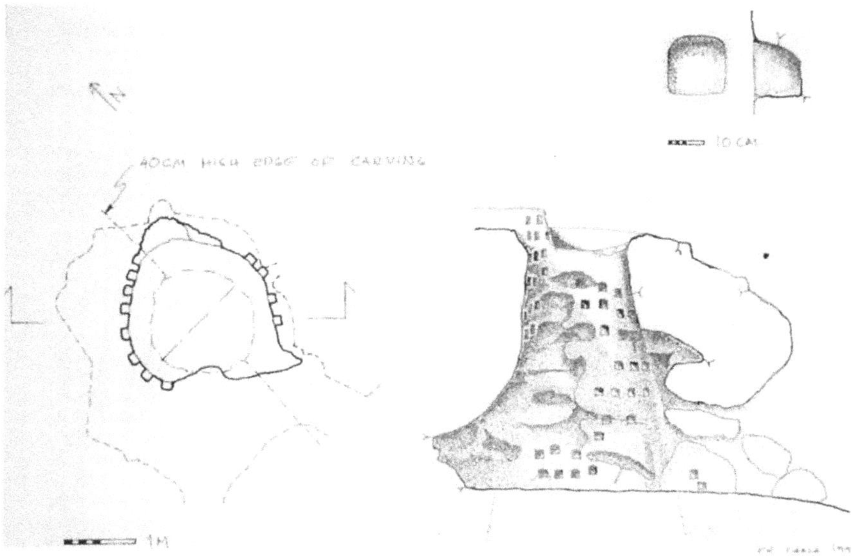

Figure 6.6 Drawing of a columbarium.

Source: Drawing by A. Sönderlund for University of Puget Sound Excavations. Used by permission.

and 4 meters in diameter. While the function of the installations is still not certain, recent research by Laura Mazow has pointed persuasively in the direction of use as fulleries (Mazow and Strathy, 2019). If this is the case, then the stepped structures may be *miqvaot* to serve purity demands for the workers, but it is more likely that they were used for storage and eventual distribution of the wool after processing. It is worth noting that among the artifacts reported to have been recovered at Khirbet Qana, there is a noticeable absence of indicators of spinning of wool (e.g., spindle whorls). On the other hand, at the nearby village of Yodefat/Jotapata, a number of items related to the spinning of wool were uncovered in the Early Roman layer of debris. Such finds fit with the growing body of evidence of craft and agricultural specialization as well as intentional complementarity among Galilean villages as they transitioned from subsistence and insularity to participating in trade and a market economy.[8]

These industrial features are, of course, important indicators of economic decision-making that manifest pivoting away from subsistence farming toward participation in trade and, on a limited scale, in the market economy. This pivot was certainly not unique to Khirbet Qana and in fact appears to have occurred earlier in other villages (Kefar Hananya, Capernaum) in response to the economic stimulation brought by the Hasmonean occupation of the Galilee and later Roman colonization. In the case of Khirbet

Figure 6.7 Photo of industrial area.

Source: Photo by Douglas R. Edwards for University of Puget Sound Excavations. Used by permission.

Qana, such developments appear to have awaited those that occurred in the post-revolt period to include the construction of roads and the shift of resources, human and otherwise, from south to north.

Conclusion: An Economy of Adaptation and "Animal Spirits"

In some ways, the pattern of transformation we have tracked at Khirbet Qana is predictable and not worthy of special note given the increase in infrastructure and monetary resources that flowed into the Galilee. What is remarkable is the evidence of what Mattila called an "introverted trade pattern," wherein the economic growth and dynamism is accompanied by what appears to be a deliberate pattern of inhibiting non-Jewish intrusion and by a determined effort of asserting the Jewish character of the village. We have noted the latter in architectural terms by way of the excavation of *miqvaot* and the synagogue. The latter can also be detected in the more intimate items of daily life such as ceramic forms, coins, and faunal data.

In terms of ceramic forms, through the middle of the second century CE, wares from the nearby Jewish villages of Kefar Hananya (and possibly if not probably Yodefat/Jotapata) and Shikhin make up the great majority of wares.[9] There is a noticeable absence of imported wares such as ETSA (Eastern Terra Sigillata A), as well as local wares produced in pagan contexts such as GCW (Galilean Coarse Ware). Aviam's summation of such a pattern of avoidance as a distinctive phenomenon of first-century CE Galilean Jewish villages, akin to avoidance of figurative art, seems apt for the results of the data from Khirbet Qana (Aviam, 2004). Given the evidence cited for economic growth and wealth, the absence of such wares does not appear to relate to cost, but rather points to a more deliberate decision. The issue of purity may factor into this choice, but I would agree with Andrea Berlin (2002, 2006) that nonpurity issues, including symbolic acts of resistance to Roman colonization, are at least as important, if not more so, in the choices made.[10]

The numismatic report simply reinforces the pattern detected above. As Danny Syon observed, the pattern at Khirbet Qana of Seleucid coins being gradually displaced by Hasmonean coins is consistent with other villages of the Galilee (Syon, 2002). What is noteworthy is the absence of a growth in Roman coins as the village moves into the early decades of Roman colonization. From the first three centuries of the Common Era, the excavations have recovered only one Herodian coin, four Early Roman coins, and, most conspicuously, no coins from neighboring Sepphoris. There was a significant number of Tyrian coins (and two from Akko/Ptolemais) that connotes active participation in trade, while at the same time spurning connections to Roman centers of economic activity.

And finally, the preliminary faunal report from the excavations revealed the absence of pig bones from the Early Roman assemblage. I take this to reinforce the arguments that while the village was taking advantage of opportunities to trade and to enhance the life of those living in the village, at the most intimate, immediate level of existence—coin exchange, pots and dishes for eating, cooking, storing—it was making deliberate choices to retain its cultural identity as a Jewish village.

The material culture uncovered in the excavation of this village perched on the edge of the Beth Netofa Valley in Lower Galilee discloses the dynamism and complexity of village life and, in particular, the economic and social dimensions of such in the Early Roman period. In the latter decades of the first century CE, this village pivoted from being a modest, insular entity to one crossing boundaries, taking advantage of new infrastructure, engaging in industrial endeavors, and reshaping itself architecturally. Indicators of social and economic differentiation also appear as a large public building in the heart of the village. Having survived virtually untouched by the upheavals of the mid-century, all the indicators point to a village that flourished by taking advantage of the opportunities that came its way. This is a set of choices that might easily be grasped in economic terms through the lens provided by Adam Smith's view of a market economy that presumes people rationally pursue their own interests. We have noted, however, that there is another facet to the pattern, and that is an investment in cultural and religious identity. These choices reflect on the one hand that aspect of economic decision-making that John Maynard Keynes called "animal spirits," a phrase based on the Latin *spiritus animalis*, meaning a basic mental energy or life force (Shiller, 2019: xvii). In terms of modern economic theory, the phrase has taken on the meaning of restless, inconsistent, ambiguous factors that at times trump rational selves in terms of economic choices. The purely rational self has to compete at times with the nonrational: the romantic, nostalgic, religious self. In the work of Shiller, he modifies the meaning a bit further to suggest that economic decisions are inextricably intertwined with the narratives that arise within a particular context and, when circulated orally or otherwise, give shape to economic decisions and changes:

> We need to incorporate the contagion of narratives into economic theory. Otherwise, we remain blind to a very real, very palpable, very important mechanism for economic change.... If we do not understand the spread of popular narratives, we do not fully understand changes in the economy and in economic behavior.
>
> (Shiller, 2019: xi)

While we do not have written narratives originating from this village as such, I believe we can detect the presence of "popular narratives" of resistance to identity dilution in the literature we do have from the latter decades of the first century CE and the decades immediately thereafter in the New Testament and Mishnah. For example, the New Testament's descriptions of Jesus's itinerant pathways show an avoidance of the new urban centers in Lower Galilee (Sepphoris and Tiberias), as well as the long-established urban areas of Tyre and Sidon. In the Mishnah, we witness a narrative that extends rabbinic influence "beyond purity and holy observances to such civil matters as marriages, the allotment of tithes and disputes over ownership and use of property" (Sawicki, 2000: 120). These narratives correlate with what we have revealed in the ruins of Khirbet Qana as the village constructed the architecture of resistance to a colonizing force that had pierced their land. The economic theories of Shiller (and Akerlof) thus provide an effective broadening to the analysis of economic decisions to capture the architectural and artifactual remains of this Jewish village in Lower Galilee as it found ways to live a life abundant and life of deep convictions while being swallowed up by a massive imperial enterprise.

Notes

1. Marianne Sawicki's (2000) analysis of the architecture of contact in her work *Crossing Galilee: The Architecture of Contact in the Occupied Land of Jesus* is especially insightful in mapping the strategies of response in Roman Galilee.
2. See the work of Akerlof and Shiller (2009) for their use of Keynes's notion of animal spirits in analyzing economic decisions.
3. There are four other sites that have over time been identified as Cana of Galilee. Three of the possible sites are, as expected, located in Lower Galilee, while one is found in what is today southern Lebanon. The location of this latter

contender is certainly odd, but its pedigree goes back to Eusebius of Caesarea's *Onomasticon*. Eusebius noted there were two Canas, one near Sidon ("Greater Cana") and another in the Galilee. Eusebius associates the water-to-wine miracle with Greater Cana, and this identification continues on in a few texts and maps into the medieval period. Given the biblical references (near Capernaum) as well as the references in Josephus (near Yodefat/Jotapata), Cana in Lebanon is no longer considered a viable candidate. The three sites in Galilee include Ain Qana, Kefar Kenna, and Karm er-Ras.

4. See Steve Mason's (2001) *Life of Josephus: Translation and Commentary*. Mason (2001: 69) remarks that Khirbet Qana has become the consensus location for Josephus's Cana and, given Khirbet Qana's "central location in Lower Galilee, with easy access routes, the nearby fortress [Iotapata/Yodefat], and a commanding view of both the main valley and the access to Iotapata, makes Cana an ideal location for Josephus." The claim that the identification of Khirbet Qana with Cana of Galilee is aligned with the consensus of scholarship is also cited in Strange, 1992; Mackowski, 1979; and Conway, 2006.
5. For a full description of the excavation of the cave complex and the correlation between the finds and the pilgrims' reports, see McCollough, 2015.
6. In terms of architectural remnants and artifacts, it is difficult to offer a definitive stratified portrait given the thin layer of soil that had accumulated over structures built into or on bedrock that consistently protrudes up toward the soil surface. Nonetheless, efforts were made to differentiate the strata relying on traditional ceramic and numismatic data combined with radiocarbon (carbon-14) results where possible.
7. The full list of the twenty-four priestly courses appears in piyyutim or liturgical poetry, and the one that locates the priestly family of Eliashib at Cana (קנה) is that composed by Eleasar Qalir in the ninth century. The credibility of the poet as accurately depicting earlier traditions has been given support by the discovery of a third-century mosaic at Caesarea that has a list indicating the location of the twenty-four priestly courses after 70 CE that coincides with Eleazar's lyrical poetry. For the ninth-century reference, see Klein, 1909; and for Caesarea, see Avi-Yonah, 1962.
8. Edwards (2007) gives a full exposition of the emergence of these patterns.
9. The discovery of pottery kilns at Yodefat/Jotapata producing forms similar to those produced at Kefar Hananya point to a broader level of village participation in the making and distributing of ceramics. See Aviam, 2014.
10. See both Berlin, 2002, and her update to this argument in Berlin, 2006.

Bibliography

Akerlof, George A., and Robert J. Shiller. 2009. *Animal Spirits: How Human Psychology Drives the Economy, and Why It Matters for Global Capitalism*. Princeton: Princeton University Press.

Aviam, Mordechai. 2004. "Columbaria in the Galilee." Pages 31–5 in *Jews, Pagans and Christians in the Galilee: 25 Years of Archaeological Excavations and Surveys; Hellenistic to Byzantine Periods*. Rochester: University of Rochester Press.

———. 2014. "Kefar Hananya Ware Made in Yodefat." Pages 139–46 in *Roman Pottery in the Near East: Local Production and Regional Trade; Proceedings of the Round Table Held in Berlin, 19–20 February 2010*. Edited by Bettina Fischer-Genz, Yvonne Gerber, and Hanna Hamel. Oxford: Archaeopress.

Avi-Yonah, Michael. 1962. "A List of Priestly Courses from Caesarea." *Israel Exploration Journal* 12: 137–9.

———. 1977. *The Holy Land, from the Persian to the Arab Conquest*. Rev. ed. Grand Rapids: Baker.

Berlin, Andrea. 2002. "Romanization and Anti-Romanization in Pre-Revolt Galilee." Pages 57–73 in *The First Jewish Revolt: Archaeology, History and Ideology*. Edited by Andrea Berlin and J. Andrew Overman. London: Routledge.

———. 2006. *Gamla I: The Pottery of the Second Temple Period*. Israel Antiquities Authority Report 29. Jerusalem: Israel Antiquities Authority.

Conway, Colleen. 2006. "Cana." Pages 531–2 in vol. 1 of *The New Interpreter's Dictionary of the Bible*. Edited by Katharine Doob Sakenfeld. Nashville: Abingdon.

Edwards, Douglas R. 2002. "Khirbet Qana: From Jewish Village to Christian Pilgrim Site." Pages 101–32 in vol. 3 of *The Roman and Byzantine Near East: Some Archaeological Research*. Edited by John Humphrey. Journal of Roman Archaeology Supplementary Series 49. Portsmouth, RI: Journal of Roman Archaeology.

———. 2007. "Identity and Social Location in Roman Galilean Villages." Pages 357–74 in *Religion, Ethnicity and Identity in Ancient Galilee*. Edited by Jürgen Zangenberg, Harold Attridge, and Dale Martin. Tübingen: Mohr Siebeck.

———. 2008. "Crossing Boundaries: Trade and Travel in Galilee and Its Environs." Haywood Lectures, April.

———. 2009. "Walking the Roman Landscape in Lower Galilee: Sepphoris, Jotapata, and Khirbet Qana." Pages 219–33 in *A Wandering Galilean: Essays in Honour of Seán Freyne*. Edited by Zuleika Rogers, Margaret Daly-Denton, and Anne Fitzpatrick McKinley. Journal for the Study of Judaism Supplement 132. Leiden: Brill.

Frankel, Raphael, Nimrod Getzov, Mordechai Aviam, and Avi Degani. 2001. *Settlement Dynamics and Regional Diversity in Ancient Upper Galilee*. Israel Antiquities Authority Reports 14. Jerusalem: Israel Antiquities Authority.

Herrojo, Julián. 1999. *Cana de Galilea y su localización: Un examen critico de las fuentes*. Paris: Gabalda.

Horden, Peregrine, and Nicolas Purcell. 2000. *The Corrupting Sea: A Study of Mediterranean History*. Malden, MA: Blackwell.

Klein, Samuel. 1909. *Beiträge zur Geographie und Geschichte*. Leipzig: Haupt.

Leibner, Uzi. 2018. *Khirbet Wadi Ḥamam: A Roman-Period Village and Synagogue in the Lower Galilee*. Jerusalem: Institute of Archaeology, the Hebrew University of Jerusalem/Israel Exploration Society.

Longstaff, Thomas, and Tristram Hussey. 1997. "Palynology and Cultural Process: An Exercise in the New Archaeology." Pages 151–62 in *Archaeology and the Galilee: Texts and Contexts in the Graeco-Roman and Byzantine Periods*. Edited by Douglas R. Edwards and C. Thomas McCollough. Atlanta: Scholars Press.

Mackowski, R. 1979. "'Scholars' Qanah': A Rexamination of the Evidence in Favor of Khirbet Qana." *Biblische Zeitschrift* 23: 278–84.

Mason, Steve. 2001. *Life of Josephus: Translation and Commentary*. Vol. 9 of *Flavius Josephus: Translation and Commentary*. Leiden: Brill.

Mattila, Sharon Lea. 2013. “Revisiting Jesus’ Capernaum: A Village of Only Subsistence-Level Fishers and Farmers?” Pages 75–138 in *The Galilean Economy in the Time of Jesus*. Edited by David A. Fiensy and Ralph K. Hawkins. Atlanta: Society of Biblical Literature.

Mattingly, David. 2006. “The Imperial Economy.” Pages 283–97 in *A Companion to the Roman Empire*. Edited by David Potter. Oxford: Blackwell.

Mazow, Laura B., and Diane Strathy. 2019. “Travelling on the Highway to the Fuller’s Field: Integrating Text and Archaeology to Reconstruct Wool Processing Technologies.” Paper presented at the American Schools of Oriental Research Southeastern Regional Meeting. Greenville, NC, March 9.

McCollough, C. Thomas. 2015. “Khirbet Qana.” Pages 127–45 in *The Archaeological Record from Cities, Towns, and Villages*. Vol. 2 of *Galilee in the Late Second Temple Period and Mishnaic Periods*. Edited by David A. Fiensy and James Riley Strange. Minneapolis: Fortress.

Richardson, Peter. 2006. “Khirbet Qana (and Other Villages) as a Context for Jesus.” Pages 120–44 in *Jesus and Archaeology*. Edited by James H. Charlesworth. Grand Rapids: Eerdmans.

Sawicki, Marianne. 2000. *Crossing Galilee: Architectures of Contact in the Occupied Land of Jesus*. Harrisburg, PA: Trinity Press International.

Schoenwetter, James, and Patrick Geyer. 2000. “Implications of Archaeological Palynology at Bethsaida, Israel.” *Journal of Field Archaeology* 27: 63–73.

Shiller, Robert J. 2019. *Narrative Economics: How Stories Go Viral and Drive Major Economic Events*. Princeton: Princeton University Press.

Spigel, Chad. 2012. *Ancient Synagogue Seating Capacities: Methodology, Analysis and Limits*. Tübingen: Mohr Siebeck.

Strange, James F. 1992. “Cana of Galilee.” Page 827 in vol. 1 of *The Anchor Bible Dictionary*. Edited by David Noel Freedman. New York: Doubleday.

Syon, Danny. “The Coins.” Appendix to “Khirbet Qana: From Jewish Village to Christian Pilgrim Site.” By Douglas Edwards. Pages 129–32 in vol. 3 of *The Roman and Byzantine Near East: Some Archaeological Research*. Edited by John Humphrey. Journal of Roman Archaeology Supplementary Series 49. Portsmouth, RI: Journal of Roman Archaeology.

Syon, Danny, and Zvi Yavor. 2010. *Gamla II: The Architecture*. Jerusalem: Israel Antiquities Society.

Tsafrir, Yoram, Leah Di Segni, and Judith Green. 1994. *Tabula Imperii Romani: Iudaea, Palaestina: Eretz Israel in the Hellenistic, Roman and Byzantine Periods; Maps and Gazetteer*. Jerusalem: Israel Academy of Sciences and Humanities.

Wolfe, Ethyl. 1952. “Transportation in Augustan Egypt.” *Transactions and Proceedings of the American Philological Association* 83: 80–99.

Xenophontos, Carolyn, Carolyn Elliott, and John Malpas. 1988. “Major and Trace-Element Geochemistry Used in Tracing the Provenance of Late Bronze Age and Roman Basalt Artefacts from Cyprus.” *Levant* 20: 169–83.

7 Bandits and the Galilean Economy

Was the Galilee Prosperous or Desperately Poor?

David A. Fiensy

There are two similar tales—perhaps legendary in nature—about bandits who lived five hundred years apart. In the first one, told by Augustine, Alexander the Great asks a pirate who has been captured what he meant by keeping hostile possession of the sea. The pirate answers that he means the same thing by his action that Alexander meant by his. "Because I do it with a petty ship, I am called a robber, while you who do it with a great fleet are styled emperor" (Augustine, *Civ.* 4.4; trans. Oates, 1948: 52).[1]

In the second story, the famous bandit chief, Bulla Felix (early third century CE)—whose very name, "Lucky Charm," seems something from a fairy tale—was captured and taken to a praetorian prefect. The prefect asked Bulla, "Why did you live the life of a bandit?" The classic answer: "Why are you a praetorian prefect?" (Dio Cassius, *Hist. rom.* 70.10).[2]

Interesting stories, but what do they mean? Some take them to mean that bandits were insisting on justice. They were, in this view, campaigners against the big guys of the earth. If Alexander and the Romans, represented by the praetorian prefect in the story, insist upon conquering people, these bandits, champions of the weak, will rise up to oppose them (Shaw, 1984: 52).[3]

But I see it differently. That interpretation is a superimposition of a certain cultural value on cross-cultural texts. To me, the answers are based on an ancient—and sometimes contemporary as well—value system. That value is: if one *can* gain power, one *should*. Why would you not? This is the value system of a warrior culture. Your mission in life is to conquer, to grasp for power. Thus, the praetorian prefect has risen in his world, in his system of power, just as Bulla Felix rose in his. The two are alike. Also, the pirate sought to rule the seas just as Alexander sought to rule the earth.[4] Each has sought power. What is the difference after all?

The stories illustrate one important feature. We can impose modern values and perspectives on ancient texts and persons. Such an imposition may be the model of social banditry invented by Eric Hobsbawm (1965; 2000) and advanced in New Testament studies by Richard Horsley (Horsley, 1979; 1981; 1987; 1988; and Horsley and Hanson, 1985) and others (Crossan, 1991; Hanson 2002). It is a model that has come under steady criticism—by social

DOI: 10.4324/9781003041696-10

scientists (Blok, 1972; Dodds, 2011; Leloup, Rousseaux, and Vrints, 2014), by classical historians (Shaw, 1984), and by both New Testament scholars and historians of Judaism (Donaldson, 1990; Freyne, 1988; Isaac, 1992; Kloppenberg, 2009; Rumple, 2005)—since it first appeared and that has been examined thoroughly in lengthy essays, in at least one master's thesis (Lincoln, 2005), and in at least one monograph (Grünewald, 1999).[5]

Horsley had started out, in his publications on social banditry, to counter the views of Hengel (1989 [orig. 1961]) and Rengstorf (1967 [orig. 1942]). They had maintained that in Josephus the bandits and the Zealots were one and the same. Horsley also took issue with the assertion that Josephus had used the term ληστής as a polemical term to discredit persons who were not, in actual fact, bandits. For Horsley, the bandits of Josephus were real bandits—and not freedom fighters or rebels—albeit a specific kind of bandit, the social bandit. Throughout his seminal essay of 1979, Horsley seems to assume that if he can credibly counter the first claim[6]—that the bandits were the same as the Zealots—he has also disproven the second—that many persons labeled bandits by Josephus were not actually bandits but were being tarred by the poisonous pen of the erstwhile Galilean general turned historian (Horsley, 1979). Since this article, Horsley has published numerous essays and monographs on the subject.

No one can discuss banditry in late Second Temple period Galilee and Judea without at least a respectable nod in Hobsbawm's and Horsley's direction. Both scholars are very creative and refreshing interpreters of history, and we, the scholarly world, owe them a large debt as we should owe anyone of equal creativity and innovation. However, one can both admire and critique.[7]

Did the economic situation in late Second Temple Galilee and Judea press young men (they were almost always men) into a life of banditry? Horsley argues that banditry arises in agrarian societies when peasants are exploited through economic crises (e.g., taxation, loss of land, famine, debt) and social disruption (e.g., war, foreign conquest, ineffective government).[8] He sees such exploitation in first-century CE Galilee and Judea: Many peasants fell into debt and had to forfeit their land. Vast numbers of peasants formed a proletariat and became day laborers. The Jewish ruling class and the Romans levied higher taxes (Horsley and Hanson maintain there was a 40 percent tax). And finally, there was a famine during part of this time period (Horsley and Hanson, 1985: 61).[9] Horsley and Hanson maintain that banditry arises directly from the peasants' inability to grow enough crops (Horsley and Hanson, 1985: 49–62). Thus, the peasants of Palestine faced a triple threat: alien rule, double taxation, and famine for at least part of this period. These conditions nourished a rise in epidemic banditry (Horsley, 1981: 412, 417–9; Horsley and Hanson, 1985: 49–50).

This description of conditions has sparked some pushback from other scholars who want to emphasize religious motivations in the first-century CE Jewish movements in Palestine (Isaac, 1992), who want to characterize the so-called bandit leaders in Palestine as rebels or political rivals (Grünewald, 1999), or who argue for a more nuanced assessment of the phenomenon of banditry in the ancient world (Shaw, 1984). These scholars observe that doubtless such conditions as economic stress increased the number of men seeking refuge in bandit gangs, but what about those men with families? The bandit route probably would not have been open to them. As historians have noted, many of the ancient persons came under economic stress, but a very small percentage of them turned to banditry (Grünewald, 1999: 17).[10] If we may accept Hobsbawm's figures, bandits in any society never exceed 1 percent of the total population and usually are half that or even less (Hobsbawm, 2000: 23–4).[11]

In this essay, I hope to answer one basic question about the phenomenon of ancient banditry in the Roman Empire, approximately contemporaneous with the events of first-century CE Palestine: Did a rise in banditry signify a concomitant governmental-economic collapse? In other words, can one reason backward: If there is a rise in banditry, then must there have been a preceding rise in the exploitation of the peasantry? To answer this question, I will offer four propositions:

1. Not everyone called a bandit really was one.
2. Bandits were everywhere in the Roman Empire; they did not just arise during economic stress.
3. Economic collapse was not necessarily the causal factor in becoming a bandit. There was a multitude of reasons for that life's choice.
4. A new economic theory may argue that it was/is not governmental-economic collapse that accounts for a rise in banditry, but rather a kind of "Goldilocks" societal situation that facilitates it.

Defining "Bandit"

First, not everyone called a bandit really was one. Let us begin by defining what a *latro*/ληστής was. Brent Shaw wrote that bandits were "men who threatened the social and moral order of the state by the use of *private violence* in the pursuit of their aims" (Shaw, 1984: 4; emphasis mine). The key words here are the ones highlighted: "private violence." The bandit engaged in armed robbery—often ending in murder—but represented no government. The bandit stood on a spectrum between one who committed ordinary "theft" (*furtum*) on the one end and being a legitimate "enemy" (*hostis*) on the other. The *latro*/ληστής committed serious armed robbery in a gang. He was usually upon capture executed by wild beast, burning, or crucifixion (Grünewald, 1999: 15; Shaw, 1984: 21–2; Hengel, 1989: 32; *pace* Hanson, 2002: 296).

"Every *latro* was a robber but not every robber was a *latro*," writes Thomas Grünewald (1999: 16). He offers a fourfold description of *latrones*/λησταί: (1) they used weapons; (2) they worked in gangs; (3) they aimed for plunder;

Table 7.1 Bandits in comparative overview

Hobsbawm (2000: 19–20, 23)	*Hanson* (2002: 293)[12]	*Grünewald* (1999: 3)[13]
Urban robbers		
Rural impoverished gentlemen		
Peasants		
Mere robbers	Thieves	Robbers ("real bandits")
	Haidukry	
Raiders	Raiders	
Social bandits	Social bandits	
Noble robbers		
Resistance fighters	Rebels	Rebels
Avengers		Avengers
	Revolutionaries	
		(Political) rivals

and (4) they showed "malice aforethought" (that is, they often murdered their victims; Grünewald, 1999: 16).

Before we ask why anyone would want to become a bandit—was it to correct injustice, to rob from the rich and give to the poor?—we might well delineate the types of persons labeled "bandit." Here we can profitably compare Hobsbawm's distinctions from his most recent and thorough critic, Grünewald. Table 7.1 (also including Hanson) quickly illustrates their similarities and differences.

As Table 7.1 demonstrates, both Hobsbawm and Grünewald assign a category to the pure bandit or criminal, as well as other categories in which the bandit is either "noble" or social (so Hobsbawm) or metaphorical (Grünewald); that is, the bandits are not really actual criminals, but rather political opponents and rebels according to Grünewald, or injustice rectifiers according to Hobsbawm.

If we are to credit the category of "social bandit" that Hobsbawm invented and that some New Testament scholars have accepted, then the origin of that group might be quite different from that of the real criminal. Horsley has argued, following Hobsbawm, that bandits appear in agrarian societies where peasants have been exploited, and their numbers increase in times of economic crisis and social disruption. In such conditions, social bandits arise to right the wrongs of society. These social bandits—like the legendary Robin Hood—defend the value of justice of the peasantry and punish the wealthy (Horsley, 1987: 39). Horsley holds up Eleazar ben Dinai, whose bandit group was active for around twenty years, as the Jewish Robin Hood (Horsley, 1981: 412–4).[14] During this period, "vast numbers" (so Horsley) of peasants were forced into a proletariat and became day laborers. It was a growing economic crisis (Horsley, 1981: 417).[15] Thus, Horsley would conclude, in answer to our question in the title of this essay, that the rising number of bandits in Palestine did indicate economic crisis.

Grünewald's position is that all of the persons labeled "bandit" in Josephus were actually rebels (i.e., political usurpers) or Josephus's own political rivals (Grünewald, 1999: 91–109).[16] To discuss a rise in banditry based on Josephus may be an exercise in futility since most were not actual bandits. It was common in the Roman Empire to label one's political rivals as *latrones*. Cicero, for example, observes Grünewald, called Catiline, his political enemy, a bandit. According to Grünewald, he referred to Mark Antony nearly forty times as a bandit (Grünewald 1999: 17, 161). It is common, even today, for nations to label troublesome rebels as "bandits" or "brigands."[17] Thus, we (and Josephus) use these terms metaphorically as a way of disparaging someone, argues Grünewald. So, when we ask who became a bandit, we need to be sure we are talking about real bandits.[18]

This practice—it seems to me—is something like our use of the term "thug." Many of the "bandits" in Josephus were bandits in the same way that calling a political rival a "thug" in American politics does not literally mean that the rival stands outside Walmart and physically assaults shoppers.

Banditry Was Widespread

Second, bandits were everywhere in the Roman Empire both before and after the first century CE. As Shaw observed: just as slavery affected the empire widely, so too banditry was integral to imperial society (Shaw, 1984: 8). Grünewald cites with disagreement the contention of the great historians Michael Rostovtzeff and Geza Alföldy that banditry broke out in the Roman Empire due to a crisis. Their mistake was to trust the flattering sycophants who claimed that Augustus had rid the world of bandits and pirates (Grünewald, 1999: 17).[19] He did not; they were always there.

The real bandits were very bad people who terrorized travelers[20]—both rich and poor—and preyed upon local farmers throughout the Roman Empire for centuries before and after the ministry of Jesus. So widespread was the phenomenon that Ulpian's *Digest* (13.6.5.4) lists as the common causes of death: old age, sickness, and bandits. It is even classed alongside natural causes of death such as storms, fire, and earthquakes (*Dig.* 13.6.18; Shaw, 1984: 9).

Both Paul (2 Cor 11:26) and Jesus (Luke 10:25–37) allude to the dangers of travel due to violent bandits. It was not uncommon for a person to set out on a journey and never be seen or heard from again. Pliny the Younger narrates the stories of two such individuals (*Ep.* 6.25).[21] It was so dangerous that poor persons would try to tag along behind wealthy ones because the latter traveled with armed guards,[22] or at least the poor attempted to travel together in an entourage (Epictetus, *Diatr.* 4.1.91–95). Some persons journeyed with a pack of dogs for protection. Still, that did not always help. Persons with guards—even military commanders with soldiers—could be intercepted by bandits, robbed, and killed (Grünewald, 1999: 20).

Death by bandits was one of the many dangers one faced in antiquity. One family, whose story is told in the Jewish tractate Semahot, suffered most of the horrors of the ancient world: the father was burned at the stake for heresy, the mother was killed by the sword, the daughter was given to prostitution, and the son was killed by bandits (Sem. 8.12; 12.13).

Sometimes entire families, including children, were simply wiped out by roving gangs of *latrones*. For example, an inscription states that a man, along with all seven of his children, was killed by bandits. Another inscription commemorates the death of a ten-year-old girl who was murdered by bandits just because she wore jewelry. In the fifth century CE, an entire monastery of Christian ascetics—"of the most perfect life and holiness"—living near the ancient village of Tekoa in Palestine, was slaughtered by Arab bandits (John Cassian, *Conf.* 6.1), causing the theologian to descend into troubled meditations. Even gladiators—trained in the art of fighting—would often be overcome by the gangs and killed by them. There are numerous tombstones from this period that attribute the death of the individual to bandits. Their tombstones read merely: *interfectus a latronibus*, "killed by bandits" (Shaw, 1984: 10).[23] Enough said; observers understood what the inscription meant.

So dangerous were the bandits that a whole class of skilled men arose: bandit hunters who tracked them down and brought them to justice. Alongside this class was the even more lethal "bandit killer," who skipped the bring-them-to-justice step and simply dispatched them immediately (Shaw, 1984: 14; MacMullen, 1966: 2–58).[24] It takes a brutal person to stop a brutal person was evidently the thinking. Often the Romans would station guards (called *stationarii*) at the worst spots for bandits. There are inscriptions celebrating certain of these guards for having killed many bandits (MacMullen, 1966: 259–60). The point is that banditry was ubiquitous in the Roman Empire, and "noble bandits" were rare, if indeed they even existed at all. These were bad people, feared, hated, and hunted (Shaw, 1984: 9–10; Grünewald, 1999: 24; MacMullen, 1966; Hengel, 1989: 35–8).

Both Shaw and Grünewald stress the ubiquity of banditry. There was no rise in banditry; it was always there. It had at least since the fifth century BCE in Greece been considered even an acceptable occupation. And in a warrior culture, raiding beyond one's borders was a given. Bandits did not arise suddenly because of social evils. They were already there, although their ranks might have swelled somewhat under certain social and political conditions (see below; Shaw, 1984: 25; Rengstorf, 1967: 257–8).[25]

Reasons for Banditry

Third, one did not necessarily become a bandit because of economic collapse. There were many reasons for choosing that lifestyle. We ask in this essay not who became a rebel or a political rival—who might be labeled a "bandit"—but who became a real bandit, a criminal who robbed with "malice aforethought," to use Grünewald's terminology. Grünewald eliminates from discussion at the outset many of the bandits described in Josephus. They were political rivals—so Grünewald—and not real criminals. As to why one rises up in rebellion or political rivalry, he leaves to us to opine (as I have done in the opening paragraphs of this essay). But his main interests are, first, describing real banditry and, second, showing the legendary character of the so-called noble bandit (or social bandit). The latter was a literary fiction, not a historical reality (Grünewald, 1999: 7–11, 161–2).[26]

So who became a criminal type bandit or "real bandit"? The following were the strongest candidates to join the ignominious group:

1. Fugitives from slavery
2. Army deserters and army veterans
3. Shepherds
4. Impoverished peasants (who could not find work in a farm)
5. Restless young men wanting freedom and adventure

Interestingly, these candidates are listed by both ancient historians and by Hobsbawm (Hobsbawm, 2000: 38–9; Grünewald, 1999: 57, 161; Hengel, 1989: 33). Enslaved individuals often fled to a life of banditry. The infamous Bulla Felix—referred to above—allegedly told a captured Roman centurion to go back and tell his enslavers to feed their enslaved people so that they would not become bandits (Dio Cassius, *Hist. rom.* 77.10.5). The implication is that harsh treatment of enslaved people often left them little choice but the dangerous route of banditry. When one escaped his enslaved life, where would he go? The options were limited if one wanted to avoid recapture.

Soldiers who found the rigors of army life unbearable and so deserted before their commitment was up naturally turned to a life of banditry. They probably calculated that either the harsh discipline or their chances of survival in battle did not warrant their continued loyalty to their military commitment. Further, many military veterans found that their retirement—in the form of land allotments—was not secured. The amount of land might not be enough or might even be denied at retirement. They needed to "supplement." They had military skills that were valuable to the bandit gangs and would have to endure much less discipline and perhaps endure less risk to their life than in the Roman army (Hobsbawm, 2000: 38; Shaw, 1984: 29).

Shepherds were tempted to engage in livestock rustling (cattle or sheep/goats) because of their proximity to other herds and the remoteness of their work in the mountains. Their nomadic life, moving along with the herds, afforded them less oversight. They then easily morphed from being a shepherd who occasionally rustled cattle to become a full-time bandit. This source of new bandits was perhaps the oldest one. Shepherds notoriously engaged in rustling since time immemorial (Lincoln, 2005: 53; Shaw, 1984: 31).

As the land increasingly was gobbled up both by large landowners and by the division of small farms among the heirs, there soon was not enough land to provide a living as a freeholder on one's own farm. Nor could one necessarily hire out as a day laborer. In some areas of the empire, there were not enough farming jobs to be had. What was a young man to do in that case? Among other options—which included fleeing to the city or selling himself into slavery—he could select a life of banditry.[27]

Finally, as Martin Hengel speculated, there were simply many young men who longed for more excitement and adventure in life than the yearly drudgery of farming. The critical age was between puberty and marriage, writes Hobsbawm (since most of the bandits were young and single). In those years—perhaps one could say from age thirteen to twenty—young men are most impressionable, most attracted to action (i.e., violence), and footloose (Hengel, 1989: 33; Hobsbawm, 2000: 36). But once he has a family, it is "harder for a man to revolt against the apparatus of power" (Hobsbawm, 1965: 18). Thus, many young men simply wanted adventure, and a period of time as a bandit seemed like a good idea.

These were desperate (or bored) persons who either needed to make a living and could find no other way to do so, who could no longer take the rigors of the military, who—as shepherds—were tempted into rustling livestock, or who found life on the farm in a backwater village too limiting and decided to see the world before they took upon themselves the "burden" of a wife and children. These were not noble bandits or social bandits. They took to a life of crime on this scale—a life of stealing that stood between petty thievery on the one hand and joining an enemy army on the other hand—for various reasons, none of which was to right the wrongs of society. Grünewald's argument is that brigandage (real banditry) was pervasive, and he doubts that it indicates very much about the effectiveness of the government or the efficiency of the economy of Palestine in the late Second Temple period.

But were there no Robin Hoods among them? Even Grünewald, Hobsbawm's most thorough critic, allows that there were avengers in their ranks. Usually, though, these were enslaved individuals getting revenge on their former, harsh enslavers. But it is doubtful, in his view, that there were social reformers—either in Palestine or elsewhere in the empire—like the social bandits envisioned by Hobsbawm (and Horsley and others). For one thing, all classes were attacked by bandits: enslaved persons, freedmen, household managers, entire families, soldiers, municipal officers, and so on (Shaw, 1984: 41; *pace* Horsley, 1979: 45). The bandits did not attack the rich to give to the poor (*pace* Horsley, 1979: 45). They attacked everyone to give to themselves.

The Goldilocks Criteria for the Presence of Brigandage

Fourth and finally, a new economic theory may have relevance to our discussion. Banditry had existed for centuries before the first century BCE in Palestine (Isaac, 1984; 1992). It did not suddenly arise to right the injustices of the world. Yet, it probably grew in numbers—although we should still think the numbers were very small—at certain points during that time period. If we accept Hobsbawm's own data (2000: 23–4),[28] that might mean that in the Galilee, for example, the total number of bandits grew from 175 (0.1 percent of the population) to 1400 (0.8 percent of the population) at the most, assuming a population of the Galilee during our period of 175,000 (Meyers, 1997: 59; Hoehner, 1972: 53).[29] Based on this type of banditry (i.e., real banditry), what did a rise in its numbers mean?

One gets the impression from Horsley and others that economic collapse brings on banditry, especially social banditry. But now there is a new economic theory that could have bearing on our understanding of banditry in first-century CE Palestine. This theory has been presented in a recent issue of the *Economist* magazine (anon., 2011). This article summarized a paper presented at Britain's Royal Economic Society (in 2011) by Olaf de Groot, Anja Shortland, and Matthew Rablen. They argued that even within a pirate-infested country like Somalia, most pirates come from the relatively stable part of the nation and not from the region characterized by anarchy. They argued that pirates (I presume the same for landlocked bandits) need a basic level of law and order in order to operate. There is a kind of "sweet spot" in the pirate-bandit career. Too much government effectiveness makes the outlaw life difficult, if not impossible. But too little government effectiveness can work the same way. These economists describe piracy as a "market-dependent" crime. One needs a fence or middleman, and one needs transport of stolen goods. These requirements depend on some basic rule of law. Paradoxically, you need some law in order to break the law with profit.

Thus, the economists prognosticate that for countries with very poor levels of governance (as measured by the World Bank Index), a bit of improvement in law enforcement, stability, and security will paradoxically lead to a rise in piracy: "Piracy can be endemic in weakly ruled states but rarely takes root in ones where the state has completely collapsed."[30] Thus, countries like Haiti, Liberia, and Sierra Leone will have few bandits since they are too dysfunctional. On the other hand, really well-governed countries produce few bandits. Thus, the presenters suggest, countries such as Cambodia and Cameroon will be overrun with bandits because they fit the "sweet spot" or Goldilocks criteria. One might diagram this theory as presented in Table 7.2.

If there is any merit to this theory, then a rise in banditry—per Josephus[31]—in Palestine in the first century CE was either due to a decrease in government efficiency (from strong Herodian rule to weaker Roman rule) or a slight

Table 7.2 Goldilocks criteria for the presence of brigandage

		Dysfunctional governments	*Weakly effective governments*	*Effective governments*
Level of brigandage	High		X	
	Low	X		X

increase in government effectiveness (from dysfunctional Herodian to weak Roman rule). Whatever the dynamic (I would think it was the former),[32] this theory argues not for a collapse in political-economic function—a period of "abnormal hardship" (Hobsbawm, 1965: 24)—but for a weak system, a system middling between effective government and dysfunctional government. The government and its presumed economically parallel result functioned fairly well—at least well enough. This "sweet spot" in government effectiveness allowed the banditry that was already present to grow in numbers somewhat. The other numerous references to bandits in Josephus were actually just name-calling of his rivals or an attempt to denigrate political rebels. They were not true bandits.

Conclusion

Thus, the assertion that Judea and/or the Galilee were in a state of near governmental anarchy and concomitant economic collapse or crisis ("abnormal hardship") seems exaggerated. The drastic polarities in my subtitle ("Prosperous or Desperately Poor?") are, as polarities usually are, hyperbolic. In truth, governmental effectiveness and economic efficiency were somewhere in the middle of those two opposites.

Conditions did change under the Romans, but probably not as much as we have heretofore believed due to the influence of Josephus. I think the strong rule of Herod the Great morphed into a somewhat weaker rule under the Romans, leading to a Goldilocks political-economic condition that nurtured a modest rise in banditry. Thus, the bandits you have always with you, but they do not always find the optimal conditions to pursue their career.

Notes

1. Edited for contemporary language.
2. My own translation. See Shaw (1984: 52) for these stories.
3. Shaw (1984: 51) writes: "The Bulla vignette is a variation on a common theme—that of popular insistence on a just order and a just rulership—that was picked up by the ruling classes for their own purposes."
4. This is the lesson Augustine draws from this story as well.
5. Grünewald's is the most comprehensive study of ancient banditry to date but can be profitably supplemented by Shaw, 1984; and MacMullen, 1966: 255–68.
6. For this effort, Horsley relies extensively on the conclusion of Morton Smith (1971) that the Zealots did not exist until just prior to the Jewish war.
7. Horsley has made a creative synthesis of broader historical events with Jewish history, offering plausible explanations based on a social-science model. Yet, his argument fails, in my opinion, with his endless speculations. See, e.g., Horsley and Hanson, 1985: "one likely effect" (57); "it is not difficult to imagine" (58); "would have been" (58); "probably" (63); "it is not difficult to deduce" (65); the bandits "must have" attacked the gentry and not the peasants (65); the rise in banditry was "almost certainly due to famine" (67).

8. Hobsbawm (1965: 24) affirmed that social banditry would most likely become a "major phenomenon" during periods of "abnormal hardship" such as famine and war.
9. They list two famines: one in 25–24 BCE and the other in the late 40s CE. Only the second would have had an effect on the Jewish society leading up to the war of 66–73 CE, if even that happened.
10. Grünewald (1999) considered the so-called *pax Augusta* to be only propaganda. The bandits and pirates were never under control.
11. Hobsbawm (2000: 23–4) says the rate of bandits for any society ranges from 0.1 percent to 0.8 percent.
12. Hanson's model is the most nuanced and complete (based on Hobsbawm).
13. Originally published in German under the title *Räuber, Rebellen, Rivalen, Rächer: Studien zu Latrones im Römischen Reich* (Grünewald, 1999).
14. For Eleazar ben Dinai, see Josephus, *A.J.* 20.118–136, 160–161 // *B.J.* 2.232–246, 253; m. Sotah 9:9 (he was a murderer); b. Ketub. 27a (he was a thief); Cant. Rab. 2.18 (he tried to liberate Israel). For a critique of this view of Eleazar, see Fiensy, 1991: 166–7. He was, according to Josephus, captured apparently shortly after Felix assumed his procuratorship and had engaged in his reign of terror for twenty years. The problem with dating is that we do not know exactly when Felix began his procuratorship (probably before 52 CE), but we do know when he ended it: 60 CE. See Braund, 1992: 783.
15. Elsewhere Horsley has maintained that banditry was both "endemic and epidemic" in Palestine (Horsley, 1988: 184). That is, that banditry was always there, but spiked due to economic crisis. The counsel of Morton Smith, uttered some twenty years ago, is worth repeating: "It would be foolish to suppose that only the poor used these opportunities [he means, as stated in *B.J.* 2.238]; in fact we soon hear of gangs organized by the rich, among them the high priests." See Smith, 1999: 516.
16. He maintains that all the bandits examined in Josephus had political ends. Josephus calls them bandits as "an expression of contempt" (Grünewald, 1999: 98). See also Shaw, 1993, and Rengstorf, 1967, who make much the same argument. Shaw's table (1993: 204) illustrates that Josephus used the term ληστής increasingly as he narrated the events of the Jewish war in *A.J.* 20. This was an attempt to discredit the Zealots and his own political rivals.
17. For a modern example of labeling rebels as bandits, see Russell, 2005. The Russians under Putin named the Chechen rebels "bandits." See also Cahen, 2002. One political party labeled a group of rebels "bandits" in Mozambique.
18. Several times Josephus refers to an infestation of bandits arising (e.g., in 62 CE when Albinus became procurator, *B.J.* 2.272; and in 64 CE just before Gessius Florus became procurator, *A.J.* 20.215). But one senses that this is simply Josephus's elitist dismissal of the rural population. The dirty rabble are all bandits, *pace* Horsley, 1979: 38.
19. He cites Seneca, Philo, Pliny the Elder, Epictetus, and Plutarch, among others who flattered Augustus (and the Julio-Claudians) in this way.
20. Juvenal, *Sat.* 10.19–22, writes that if a traveler carried even just a few plain silver items, he would shake with fear at the shadow of a wavering reed (thinking it might be a bandit). But a traveler with nothing in his hands would "whistle" at a robber (viz., be fearless).
21. One *eques* has disappeared, and Pliny speculates that the same fate has befallen him as another friend, one Metelius Crispus, who once set out with servants and was never heard from. Pliny does not know if he was killed "by his (enslaved people) or along with them." That is, did his enslaved people kill him and rob him or did bandits kill them all?

22. Seneca writes (*Ep.* 123.7) that no one travels without a Numidian escort in his day.
23. Shaw (1984: 12) counts twenty-four such inscriptions spread throughout the empire and comments that these are the mere "tip of the iceberg."
24. Fronto, *Anton. Pium* 8 and 18 (in inscriptions).
25. As Shaw points out, Aristotle listed banditry as one of the five traditional ways to make a living (along with pastoral nomadism, hunting, fishing, and farming). See Aristotle, *Pol.* 1256a–b; and Grünewald, 1999: 17–25. Also arguing for the ubiquity of banditry in the Roman Empire was MacMullen, 1966: 257–60.
26. The same point is made by Kloppenborg, 2009: 462.
27. See Isaac, 1992: 575–80, who observes that farmers in mountainous areas especially struggled to make a living, and bandits were more frequently recruited in those regions. Also see Hobsbawm, 2000: 35, on the shrinking job opportunities in rural regions as a major cause for banditry.
28. Hobsbawm says that the proportion of bandits to the total population of a society is from 0.1 percent to 0.8 percent.
29. Hoehner prefers the figure 200,000, and Meyers prefers 150,000 to 175,000.
30. The article measures government effectiveness according to "a commonly used World Bank index."
31. See *A.J.* 20.215 ("the land was filled with bandits" in ca. 64 CE); *B.J.* 2.272–273.
32. Because the Roman procurators seem to have misunderstood Jewish religious sensitivities and because many of the procurators were corrupt grifters. Shaw (1984: 33) maintains that the Roman civil war between Caesar and Pompey increased banditry. The government did not, of course, collapse, but there was a time of lessened effectiveness due to the inner conflicts of the republic.

Bibliography

Anonymous. 2011. "Brigands Seeking Harbours: Why Pirates Like a Little Law and Order." *The Economist*, April 20. http://www.economist.com/node/18586874.

Blok, Anton. 1972. "The Peasant and the Brigand: Social Banditry Reconsidered." *Comparative Studies in Society and History* 14, no. 4: 494–503.

Braund, David C. 1992. "Felix." Page 783 in vol. 2 of *The Anchor Bible Dictionary*. Edited by David Noel Freedman. New York: Doubleday.

Cahen, Michal. 2002. *Les Bandits: Un Historien au Mozambique, 1994*. Paris: Fundação Calouste Gulben Kian.

Crossan, John Dominic. 1991. *The Historical Jesus: The Life of a Mediterranean Jewish Peasant*. San Francisco: HarperSanFrancisco.

Dodds, Ben. 2011. "Jaime el Barbudo and Robin Hood: Bandit Narratives in Comparative Perspective." *Social History* 36, no. 4: 464–81.

Donaldson, T. L. 1990. "Rural Bandits, City Mobs and the Zealots." *Journal for the Study of Judaism* 21, no. 1: 19–40.

Fiensy, David A. 1991. *The Social History of Palestine in the Herodian Period: The Land Is Mine*. Lewiston, NY: Mellen.

Freyne, Seán. 1988. "Bandits in Galilee: A Contribution to the Study of Social Conditions in First-Century Palestine." Pages 50–68 in *The Social World of Formative Christianity and Judaism: Essays in Tribute to Howard Clark Kee*. Edited by Jacob Neusner and Peder Borgen. Philadelphia: Fortress.

Grünewald, Thomas. 1999. *Bandits in the Roman Empire: Myth and Reality*. London: Routledge. Trans. of *Räuber, Rebellen, Rivalen, Rächer: Studien zu Latrones im Römischen Reich*. Stuttgart: Steiner.

Hanson, K. C. 2002. "Jesus and the Social Bandits." Pages 283–300 in *The Social Setting of Jesus and the Gospels*. Edited by Wolfgang Stegemann, Bruce J. Malina, and Gerd Theissen. Minneapolis: Fortress.

Hengel, Martin. 1989 (1961). *The Zealots: Investigations into the Jewish Freedom Movement in the Period from Herod I Until 70 AD*. Edinburgh: T&T Clark.

Hobsbawm, Eric. 1965. *Primitive Rebels*. New York: Norton.

———. 2000. *Bandits*. New York: New Press.

Hoehner, Harold W. 1972. *Herod Antipas*. Cambridge: Cambridge University.

Horsley, Richard. 1979. "Josephus and the Bandits." *Journal for the Study of Judaism* 10, no. 1: 37–63.

———. 1981. "Ancient Jewish Banditry and the Revolt Against Rome, A.D. 66–70." *Catholic Biblical Quarterly* 43, no. 3: 409–32.

———. 1987. *Jesus and the Spiral of Violence: Popular Jewish Resistance in Roman Palestine*. Minneapolis: Fortress.

———. 1988. "Bandits, Messiahs, and Longshoremen: Popular Unrest in Galilee Around the Time of Jesus." *Society of Biblical Literature Seminar Papers* 27: 183–99.

Horsley, Richard, and John S. Hanson. 1985. *Bandits, Prophets, and Messiahs: Popular Movements at the Time of Jesus*. New York: Harper and Row.

Isaac, Benjamin. 1984. "Bandits in Judaea and Arabia." *Harvard Studies in Classical Philology* 88: 171–203.

———. 1992. "Banditry." Pages 575–80 in vol. 1 of *The Anchor Bible Dictionary*. Edited by David Noel Freedman. New York: Doubleday.

Kloppenborg, John S. 2009. "Unsocial Bandits." Pages 451–84 in *A Wandering Galilean: Essays in Honor of Seán Freyne*. Edited by Zuleika Rodgers, Margaret Daly-Denton, and Anne Fitzpatrick McKinley. Leiden: Brill.

Leloup, Pieter, Xavier Rousseaux, and Antoon Vrints. 2014. "Banditry in Occupied and Liberated Belgium, 1914–21: Social Practices and State Reactions." *Social History* 39, no. 1: 83–205.

Lincoln, Lawrence R. 2005. "Analysis of Jewish Banditry in First Century Palestine: 6 to 70 CE." MPhil thesis, University of Stellenbosch.

MacMullen, Ramsay. 1966. *Enemies of the Roman Order: Treason, Unrest, and Alienation in the Empire*. Cambridge: Harvard University Press.

Meyers, Eric M. 1997. "Jesus and His Galilean Context." Pages 57–66 in *Archaeology and the Galilee*. Edited by Douglas R. Edwards and C. Thomas McCollough. Atlanta: Scholars Press.

Oates, Whitney J., ed. 1948. *Basic Writings of Saint Augustine*. New York: Random House.

Rengstorf, Karl H. 1967 (1942). "λῃστής." Pages 257–62 in vol. 4 of *Theological Dictionary of the New Testament*. Edited by Gerhard Kittel and Geoffrey W. Bromiley. Grand Rapids: Eerdmans.

Rumple, John. 2005. "Galilee and Jewish Resistance Movements." *Stone-Campbell Journal* 8, no. 1: 55–72.

Russell, John. 2005. "Terrorists, Bandits, Spooks and Thieves: Russian Demonization of the Chechens Before and Since 9/11." *Third World Quarterly* 26, no. 1: 101–16.

Shaw, Brent. 1984. "Bandits in the Roman Empire." *Past and Present* 105: 3–52.

———. 1993. "Tyrants, Bandits, and Kings: Personal Power in Josephus." *Journal of Jewish Studies* 44, no. 2: 176–204.

Smith, Morton. 1971. "Zealots and Sicarii, Their Origins and Relation." *Harvard Theological Review* 64: 1–19.

———. 1999. "The Trouble Makers." Pages 501–68 in *The Early Roman Period*. Vol. 3 of *The Cambridge History of Judaism*. Edited by William Horbury, W. D. Davies, and John Sturdy. Cambridge: Cambridge University Press.

8 Refugees

The Missing Element in Discussions of the Galilean Economy in the Roman Period

James Riley Strange

Introduction

Refugee theory has developed within the social sciences for some decades, particularly in the fields of sociology and anthropology. More recently, geographers and archaeologists have joined the discussion, and the literature has grown and diversified. This increase may result in part from the many regions of the globe where political, social, and cultural issues of refugee migration have become acute, including countries in which these scholars live and in which they work. Archaeologists of the ancient Near East have also begun to deploy refugee theory to help them understand people movements caused by war, famine, natural disasters, and combinations of calamities as far back as the Bronze Age (Burke, 2011, 2018; Driessen, 2018). Refugee theory may therefore help archaeologists of later periods in this region as they refine their understandings of complex social systems, including economic exchange.

To that point, this paper is concerned with an archaeological problem: how to detect refugee movements in Palestine, out of Judea and into the Galilee, following the war with Rome near the end of the first century CE. Migrations of people within relatively short timespans create crises, and such crises happened frequently enough that they should be considered in discussions of the Galilean economy in the Hellenistic and Roman periods. For example, Hasmonean expansion northward near the turn of the first century BCE, the depopulating and repopulating of Sepphoris in 4 BCE, the building of Tiberias *de novo* in 18 CE, and the elevation and renaming of Bethsaida to the polis "Julias" (located in lower Gaulanitis, very close to the eastern border of the Galilee) circa 30 CE occurred before the two Judean wars with Rome, and archaeologists regularly interpret some material culture as evidence of population movements related to these events. Regarding migration generated by the trauma of war, there is good reason to anticipate finding evidence of refugees following 135 CE, when in response to the Bar Kokhba Revolt, Rome expelled Jews from Judea and forbade them from returning to Aelia, the former Jerusalem. Following 70 CE, however, the year in which the Romans destroyed Jerusalem and the Second Temple

DOI: 10.4324/9781003041696-11

but apparently did not expel people, it is less clear that refugees abandoned Judea; and if some did leave, detecting their arrival in the Galilee presents a challenge.

Our primary problem is that Judean refugees arriving in the Galilee during the late first and early second centuries CE ought to be virtually invisible to archaeologists, as we shall see. However, if we think it is plausible that some refugees moved into the region following 70 CE, then we ought to develop methods for detecting their arrival and the effects of their resettlement and integration, if that is indeed what they did, and if we can spot it. In this paper, I propose that an assemblage of finds from the site of Shikhin allows us to test a method for finding Judean refugees who arrived in the Galilee after the destruction of Jerusalem and the temple in 70 CE. That assemblage consists of a large number of fragments and complete specimens of a style of mold-made lamp (a "Darom," i.e., "Southern" lamp) (Sussman, 1982 [1972]), molds for forming these lamps carved into soft chalk, and a small kiln in which lamps of this type were fired (Strange and Aviam, 2017; Strange, n.d.).

Refugee Theory

The test begins by surveying some literature on refugee theory that frames the discussion of what to look for in the material record. We need an understanding of refugees and a model of population migration and resettlement that helps us generate hypotheses to explain how some Judeans could have integrated into the Galilean economy and to anticipate how that integration would have left a footprint in material culture.

Anthony Richmond's discussion is useful because, in contrast to some earlier studies, he avoids constructing an artificial dichotomy between refugees who choose to leave their homes and those who are forced to do so. He argues for "a continuum between the rational choice behaviour of *proactive* migrants seeking to maximize net advantage and the *reactive* behaviour of those whose degrees of freedom are severely constrained" (Richmond, 1993: 10; emphasis original). In the literature, we often see references to two separate categories: "economic" and "political" refugees. By contrast, Richmond explains, "Between these two extremes, many of the decisions made by both 'economic' and 'political' migrants are a response to diffuse anxiety generated by a failure of the social system to provide for the fundamental needs of the individual, biological, economic and social" (Richmond, 1988: 12).

Naturally, Richmond is drawing on data from modern refugee movements prior to 1993, and his model assumes migrations across modern nation-state borders. Nevertheless, the differences between modern economic, social, and political realities and those in Roman Palestine do not hinder an adaption of Richmond's model, which charts "the interaction between economic, political, social, environmental and bio-psychological determinants, on the one hand and, on the other, the importance of distinguishing predisposing factors, structural constraints, precipitating events, enabling circumstances and feedback effects of reactive migration" (Richmond, 1993: 12).

For our purposes, we can understand that the months-long siege of Jerusalem, the Zealots' destruction of the city's food stores, the 1.1 million people killed by famine and sword (Josephus, *B.J.* 6.420), the 97,000 enslaved (*B.J.* 6.420), the 11,000 captives who died while awaiting their fate during their incarceration in the temple's court of women (*B.J.* 6.419), the thorough destruction of the city, and Vespasian's confiscation and selling of land in Judea (*B.J.* 7.216–217) must have created a set of economic, political, social, environmental, and psychological circumstances that some chose to leave behind rather than to endure. This is the case even if we must greatly reduce the numbers that Josephus reports. It is plausible to anticipate that, if they were able to do so, those who experienced the aftermath of the war as a failure of the social system to provide for their fundamental biological, economic, and social needs would have left Judea to seek provision elsewhere.

According to Egon Kunz, once in a host society, "cultural compatibility" is the most influential factor leading to refugees' satisfactory resettlement:

> If … the refugees find a sufficient number of people in their new home who speak their language and share their values, traditions, lifestyle, religion, political views and food habits, and they are able to anticipate and evaluate their hosts' actions and responses, the integration will be accelerated.
>
> (Kunz, 1981: 47)

This cultural compatibility eases challenges for refugee integration while posing challenges for us, who look for evidence of new arrivals in material culture: both objects and ways of making objects that are new to the region. Richmond and Kunz tend to speak of decisions of individuals but let us think of decisions and movements made by households and extended families. Whereas we cannot account for the complex ways in which southerners and northerners felt about one another, or for the many different responses Galileans might have shown to an influx of Judeans (however many there were), or for how hosts and new arrivals negotiated power, we can use the archaeological record to look for Judean refugees in the Galilee after 70 CE.

Aaron Burke has proposed using Michael Cernea's Impoverishment Risks and Reconstruction (IRR) model (Cernea, 2000) to help detect evidence of refugees' flight from Israel and the city of Samaria, and their resettlement in and near Jerusalem following the eighth-century BCE Assyrian conquest. The IRR model is useful for this event because it identifies phenomena associated with refugees "that can be correlated with a line of archaeological evidence" (Burke, 2011: 44).

The eight phenomena of refugees are as follows.

1. *Landlessness* shows up in abandoned settlements and landscapes, especially if abandonment is matched by rapid expansion in other areas.
2. *Joblessness* in antiquity often becomes manifest in military conscription and projects that require large numbers of laborers. The rapid expansion of an industry might supply evidence of joblessness at Shikhin.
3. *Homelessness* is evident in attempts to mitigate it, usually through the expansion of settlements or rapid building of city neighborhoods, either within or outside the walls. At Shikhin, this might be seen in the construction of houses and the building or enlarging of an associated public building.
4. *Marginalization* presents a challenge for detection unless it results in concentrating, and hence isolating, the refugee population in certain neighborhoods.
5. *Food scarcity* may become manifest in effects that are difficult to detect, such as malnutrition or increased food production.
6. *Increased morbidity and mortality* can be inferred from additional burials or new cemeteries if they correspond with other phenomena.
7. *Access to common property assets* pertains to landscapes near villages and consists of land for pasture and crops, water supply, space to bury their dead, quarries, and similar resources. In the Galilee, an increase in cisterns, tombs, and quarried bedrock may indicate the arrival of refugees, but except for tombs, dating all of these features is notoriously difficult. At Shikhin specifically, we might include access to waste products from local industries as evidence of this phenomenon.
8. *Community or social disarticulation* refers to "a breakdown of kinship bonds" and "a loss of social capital," and the economic loss and social isolation that result (Burke, 2011: 45). As an isolated phenomenon, it will be hard to detect archaeologically.

Indeed, to be identified, either these phenomena must sufficiently alter settlements and landscapes of the host culture, or an expedition's methods must have what Burke calls "a high degree of resolution." As we shall see, in many cases, refugees moving north following the destruction of Jerusalem in 70 CE might have traveled in relatively small groups as extended families or individual households, and thus might not have left an obvious imprint.

The Challenges of Identifying Judean Refugees

At the outset, finding evidence of these phenomena in the material remains of the Galilee encounters several challenges. The initial challenge is that we are limited, first, to more or less permanent media—pottery, stone, metal, and bone; second, to those refugees who successfully integrated into the

Galilee; and third, to those who did so in sufficient numbers to make refugee migration a plausible explanation for what we find when we dig.

The second challenge is that refugees appear in literature only by innuendo. Josephus, our chief chronicler of the First Revolt, gives no details about migration northward. Rather, he mentions Sicarii who fled to Egypt and Cyrene following the sacking of Jerusalem (*B.J.* 7.10–11). Similarly, Vespasian's command to sell or lease "all Jewish territory" in Judea, which he now regarded as his private property, may have given some Judeans reason to leave (*B.J.* 7.216–217), but that is as confident as we can be. It also seems likely that the loss of Jerusalem and a large portion of its population would have created in Judea an economic hardship such that many would have abandoned it (*B.J.* 7.407–419, 437–442). Josephus neither confirms nor denies these suspicions.

For his part, Dio Cassius gives us much less information about the Bar Kokhba Revolt than we want, and none about refugees (*Hist. rom.* 69.12–14). It is the fourth-century CE historian Eusebius who tells us that Jews were banned from Aelia, the city that Hadrian built on the ruins of Jerusalem, but he says nothing about refugee flight and resettlement (*Hist. eccl.* 4.6). The Mishnah gives some evidence of sages who after 70 CE moved to Yavneh/Jamnia (see, for example, m. Sheqal. 1:4; m. Rosh Hash. 4:1; perhaps m. Yad. 3:5), which lies on the Belus River near the Mediterranean coast around 20 kilometers south of Yafo/Joppa (modern Jaffa; Figure 8.1). A Sanhedrin apparently reconstituted there, from which the Babylonian Talmud reports that it moved into the Galilee perhaps as early as a decade later: to Usha, back to Yavneh, back to Usha, thence to Shefar'am, Beth-She'arim, Ẓippori (Sepphoris), and Tiberias (b. Rosh Hash. 31a–b; Figure 8.2). The reference is late; the dates, educated conjecture. If the Sanhedrin moved from Yavneh to Usha between 80 and 140 CE, it may be evidence of ongoing migration northward and the need to establish a judicial body in the Galilee. The events of either 70 or 135 CE could have supplied the proximate cause.

From sixth-century liturgical poems (*piyyutim*, פיוטים), Samuel Klein reconstructed a list of Galilean towns in which priestly "courses" or divisions (*mishmarot*, משמרות) settled, and fragments of inscriptions found in Caesarea, Ashkelon, Kissufim, Tel Reḥov, and Yemen have supported his hypothesis (Klein, 1909: 66–7, 1923: 47; Avi-Yonah, 1962, 1964; Vardaman, 1964; Sukenik, 1926; Eshel, 1992; Dagen, 1973; Finegan, 1992; Miller, 2007: 375, n. 3). Listed in order, the towns are Meiron, Ẓippori (Sepphoris), Mafshitah, 'Iṭhalo(n), Bet Leḥem (Bethlehem), Yodefat, 'Eilabu(n), 'Uziyah, Arbel, Kabul, Qanah (Cana), Ẓfat (Zefat), Bet Ma'on, Shikhin, Yonit, Kefar Nimrah, Mamliaḥ, Naẓeret (Nazareth), 'Arav, Migdal Nunia (Magdala/Taricheae), Kefar Yoḥannah, Bet Ḥobaiah, Ẓalmin, and Ḥammat 'Ariaḥ (Avi-Yonah, 1962: 138, Figure 8.1). Some of these towns have been identified; Shikhin appears as the village in which the course of Jeshebeab (ישבאב) settled (Figure 8.2). There is some debate about whether the courses are

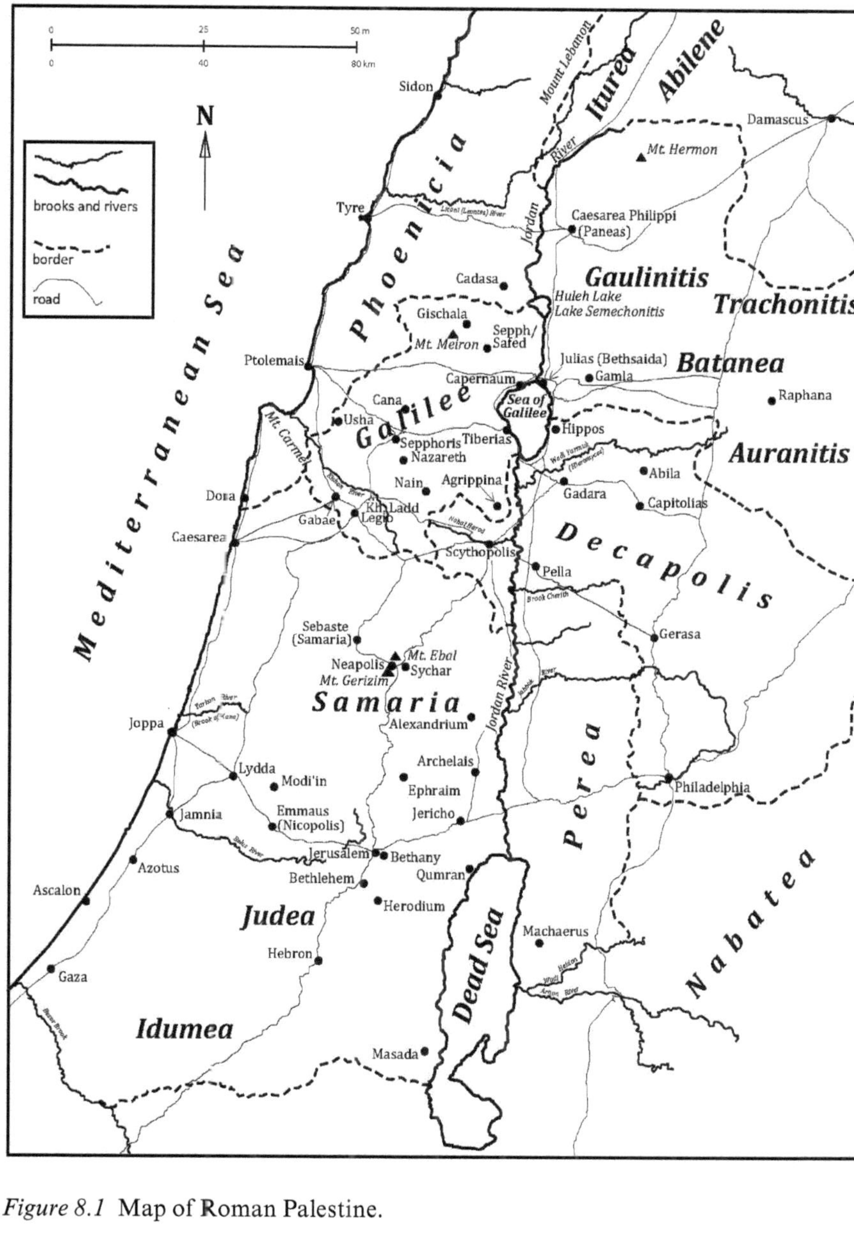

Figure 8.1 Map of Roman Palestine.

Source: Map by the author.

supposed to have settled following 70 or 135 CE. However, the presence on the list of Yodefat, which was destroyed in 68 CE and not resettled until people established a small village to the north of the ruined town in the late second or early third century CE, suggests that, if the roster is giving us

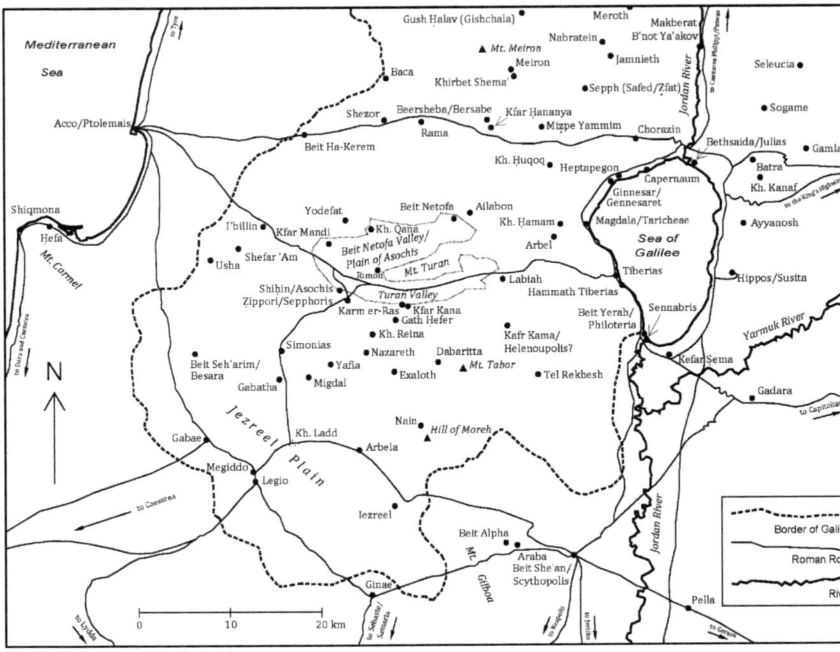

Figure 8.2 Map of the Galilee in the Roman Period.

Source: Map by the author.

good information, the migration may well have happened much earlier, in the Hasmonean period.[1]

Another inscription, this one in Greek and found on the lintel of an "elegantly styled" basalt mausoleum excavated near Tiberias in 1999, dates to the end of the second or beginning of the third century CE (Stepanski, 1999: 226). The façade of the mausoleum, which was the southernmost of a pair uncovered in a salvage excavation along Road 348, measured around 9 meters wide. The interior would have accommodated up to ten burial chambers (five, possibly six, were excavated). As with many other mausolea of the region and period, the door was carved to resemble a four-paneled wooden door with a keyhole. Nothing of the façade remained except the foundation and one nicely carved cornice stone, which indicates that the exterior was probably well decorated. The inscription may indicate the migration of a family of Judean refugees and their successful integration into the host society. If this is the case, we may speculate that cultural compatibility between Judeans and Galileans facilitated that integration. The inscription reads, 'Ιωσηπου 'Ελεα / ζαρου του Σειλου / 'Ωρησου ("[Tomb] of Joseph Eleazar / [son] of Silas / of Ḥoreshah") (Damati, 1999). Emmanuel Damati interprets Ḥoreshah as a town in Judea and speculates that Silas moved with his family from Ḥoreshah to Tiberias following the Bar Kokhba War.

He notes the significance that, if he is correct, by the third generation after their resettlement, the family's "economic achievements enabled it to establish a magnificent mausoleum" (Damati, 1999: 92*).

Inscriptional evidence brings archaeology into the discussion, and it raises the second challenge to detecting refugee movement from Judea into the Galilee. The refugees we seek have been least visible in the material culture. The first problem is that the archaeological evidence from Judea suggests that people returned to their villages rather than abandoning them (Zissu and Ganor, 2009; Magen, Tzionit, and Sirkis, 2004). Hence, we must confess that we do not expect to find in the Galilee evidence of large numbers of refugees following 70 CE.

The second problem is in knowing what to look for in the objects that survive and that we can recover. That is, the cultural compatibility that eases integration masks the arrival of the refugees we seek. Consider the shared material cultures of Judeans and Galileans in the first century BCE up until at least the late first century CE. Based on decades of surveys and digs, we now expect to find in both Judean and Galilean settlements of the period, and in southwestern Gaulanitis, a "household Judaism": a nearly identical assemblage of ceramic pots and lamps, chalk vessels, ritual baths, public buildings, and Hasmonean coins, and we expect them to be made in the same way (Berlin, 2005, 2014; see the recent challenge to this notion in Wassén, 2019). Without loupe or X-ray fluorescence gun in the field, or various forms of atomic spectroscopy in the lab, we cannot distinguish a storage jar found in Jerusalem from one found in Sepphoris. If Judean refugees took some of their things with them into the Galilee, many of the items vanished into their new environment. Expressions of regional distinctions in perishable media—clothing, hairstyles, makeup, and food preparation, for example—did not survive.

Consider the items left in the Cave of Letters during the Bar Kokhba War, particularly the wool and linen fabrics. All surely were in common use in both Judea and the Galilee (Yadin, 1963; see also Shivti'el, 2014, 2017; Shamir, 2018). The objects made from organic materials survived because of the arid climate near the Dead Sea. In the Galilee, these objects would not have lasted 1,900 years or so in the moist, alkaline soils. One thing that might survive and stand out is iron door keys, several of which were found in the Cave of Letters (Yadin, 1963: 94–9, figs. 33–7; Yadin published ten), and which are known from other hiding complexes (Tsafrir and Zissu, 2002). In the find spot of the cave, they indicate that people left their homes with hopes of returning. I am unaware of a cache of door keys found in towns or hiding complexes in the Galilee. One such key has been found at Yodefat (Aviam, 2015: 115–6, fig. G) and another at Shikhin. Without more information, however, one cannot say whether the key from Shikhin was brought from Judea, fit a door elsewhere, or belonged to a house at Shikhin.

Despite these distinctive challenges, it is useful to speculate about what we might find as evidence of Judean refugee migration into the Galilee. For example, we might find evidence of campsites beside known roadways where families and groups sheltered on their way north, particularly if such sites housed transients for decades (De León, 2013). It seems more likely, however, that we would find permanent evidence, such as signs of the phenomena associated with Cernea's Impoverishment Risks and Reconstruction model, or tomb inscriptions like the one in Tiberias that mention Judean towns as the family's place of origin. For an example of what inscriptions can indicate, consider the cache of bullae found near the City of David and bearing names of Israelite kings. That is, Judahites named their children for earlier Israelite kings: Pinchas, Menachem, and Ahiav (a variation of Ahab). The excavators interpret these names as evidence that Jerusalem accepted refugees from Israel following its eighth-century BCE destruction by Assyria (Mendel-Geberovich, Chalaf, and Uziel, 2020; Chalaf and Uziel, 2020). Along those lines, we might anticipate a proliferation of images of the menorah and other temple implements, as people expressed grief over their loss, hope that the temple would be rebuilt, cultural and religious identity, all of these attitudes, or others that underline the derelict temple's and ruined city's ongoing importance in Jewish life.

Can we say that images of temple implements proliferated after 70 CE? Based on objects found to date, we know that before 70, temple implements do appear in enduring media, but not commonly on lamps. A coin minted by Mattathias Antigonus (40–37 BCE) shows what are very probably the temple's seven-branched menorah on the reverse and the showbread table on the obverse. A famous fragment of a graffito etched in plaster found by Nahman Avigad in the Jewish Quarter of Jerusalem depicts a seven-branched menorah and what many interpret as the altar and the showbread table to the right of the menorah. A small, limestone sundial found in excavations near the Temple Mount bore an incised seven-branched menorah (for images, discussion, and bibliography, see Hachlili, 2001: 41–5). In addition to these, Ronny Reich and Eli Shukron found what looks like a five-branched menorah etched into a stone object in a drainage channel near the City of David (Reich, 2014). Sometime in the Second Temple or Bar Kokhba periods, a person etched a seven-branched menorah into the wall of a cistern at a site in the Judean Shephelah, near which someone else etched a cross, probably in the fourth century CE (Israel Antiquities Authority, [2017]). At Horvat Beth-Loya near Lachish, excavators found three seven-branched menorahs engraved into the doorjamb and lintel of the entrance to an underground olive press dating to the Early Roman period (Gutfeld, 2009). The seven-branched menorah on the limestone block found in the pre-70 CE synagogue at Magdala was an arresting discovery (Israel Antiquities Authority, [2009]). Rachel Hachlili notes that menorahs rarely appear on ossuaries, most of which date before 70 CE, and gives examples of three, one from before 68 CE and one dated by Rahmani between 70 and 135 CE (Hachlili, 2001: 45).

After 70 CE—perhaps within a decade—we do find images of temple implements and objects associated with pilgrim festivals on lamps of the new, so-called Darom ("Southern") type, the earliest examples of which are generally thought to have originated in the Daroma region of Judea, although very similar types are known to have been made in Scythopolis/Beth-She'an of the Decapolis and Shikhin of the Galilee (Strange, 2015; Strange and Aviam, 2017). Varda Sussman has published several examples of these lamps showing menorahs. Others depict ethrogs and lulavs invoking Sukkoth, baskets of fruits and the seven species invoking Shavuot, the matzah of Passover, altars, glass lamps, and one showing the ark of the law (Sussman, 1982; cf. Kaufman and Deutsch, 2012; Adler, 2004; Israel and Avida, 1988; Lapp, 2016). We must note that of the six lamps showing menorahs that Sussman published, only one depicts a lampstand with seven branches (admittedly, some of the pre-70 CE depictions of menorahs also do not show seven branches), and the altars we see might reflect Greco-Roman motifs rather than the Jerusalem Temple's altar. One lamp depicts door keys, which may indicate a hope of return to Jerusalem or a lingering connection to the city, with or without such hope (Sussman, 1982: 70, no. 92).

Darom-style ("Northern Darom") lamps also appear in the Galilee at around the same time, but I am unaware of published examples that depict door keys. At Shikhin, we have found a single example of a lamp fragment with an image of a seven-branched menorah flanked by palm fronds, and others showing what are probably ethrogs (Figure 8.3; see the discussion of this fragment in Sussman, 2017b: 410–13; fig. 22). Based on the projected diameters of the lamps, the flatness of the shoulders in relation to the fill holes, the fabric, and the location and profile of the missing handle on the ethrog fragment, both appear to be from Darom lamps. A complete Darom lamp depicts myrtle leaves and berries, which may indicate an association with the festival of Sukkoth (Figure 8.4). A complete mold for making

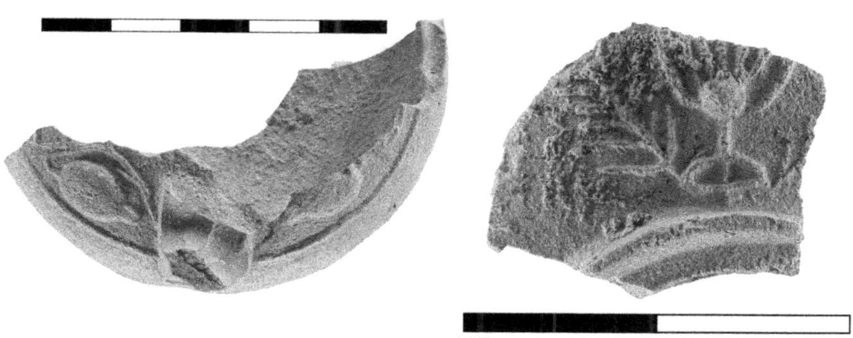

Figure 8.3 Right: a lamp fragment from Shikhin showing a seven-branched menorah flanked by palm branches. Left: a lamp fragment from Shikhin depicting ethrogs.

Source: Photos by Gabi Laron. Used with permission.

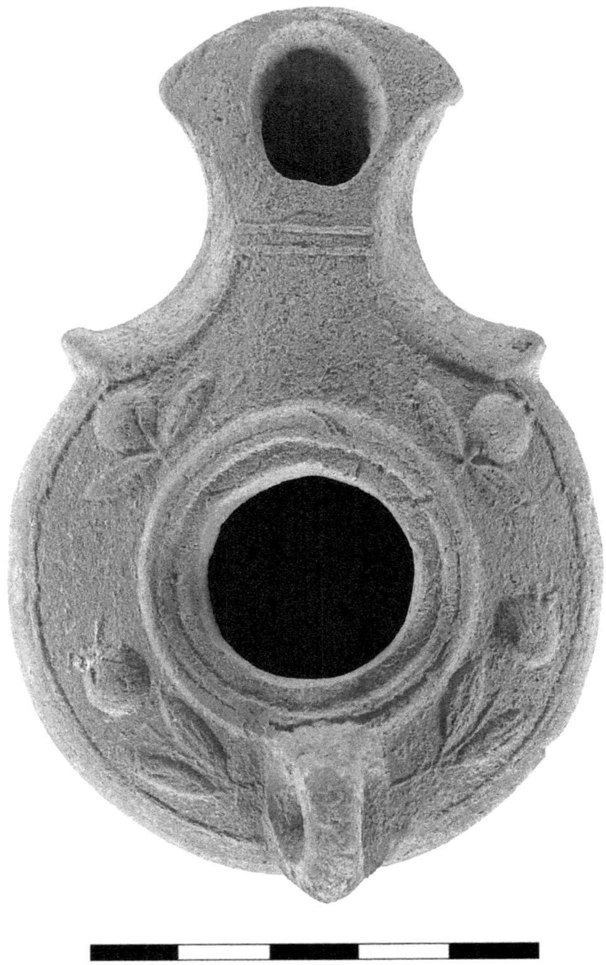

Figure 8.4 Northern Darom lamp from Shikhin depicting myrtle leaves and berries.

Source: Photo by Gabi Laron. Used with permission.

the top part of a Northern Darom lamp (Figure 8.5) has also been found at Shikhin. The decoration (carved intaglio into the mold, resulting in images in relief in the finished lamp) depicted tendrils with grape leaves and grape clusters with an amphora below the nozzle. The leaves and amphora on the mold resemble the decorations struck into the obverse and reverse of prutahs of year two of the Great Revolt, whereas the ethrogs on the lamp fragment resemble the design on the reverse of some prutahs of year four.[2] These decorations continue to be found in Jewish art of the region for some centuries.

Figure 8.5 Mold from Shikhin for making the top part of a Northern Darom lamp; the decoration shows tendrils, grape leaves and clusters, and an amphora or vase below the space for the fill hole.

Source: Photo by Yeshu Dray. Used with permission.

But what can isolated objects tell us about the Galilean economy and the effect on it that Judean refugees might have had? After all, depictions of the menorah continue to appear on lamps of many different types for centuries (Kaufman and Deutsch, 2012; Sussman, 2017a; Lapp, 2016) and in many other media.

Proposal

The remainder of this paper presents material remains from the site of Shikhin that suggest that after 70 CE, some Judean refugees settled in the village and found ways to integrate into Lower Galilee's economic system. If they achieved economic integration, they probably succeeded in other ways as well.

The 1988 and 2011 surveys of Shikhin and its environs produced a similar preliminary profile of settlement (J. F. Strange, Groh, and Longstaff, 1994 and 1995; Strange, 2012): human activity dates as early as the Iron II period (probably Iron IIC, 700–586 BCE) with indications of continued, sparse occupation in the Persian (586–333 BCE) and Early Hellenistic (333 to mid-second century BCE) periods. The number of Late Hellenistic sherds increases by about 38 percent, which suggests an increase in population sometime between the mid-second and mid-first centuries BCE. The number of Early Roman (mid-first century BCE to late first century CE) pottery forms increases by almost 60 percent, whereas the numbers of sherds dating to the Middle Roman (late first to mid-third centuries CE) and Late Roman (mid-third to mid-fourth centuries CE) periods steadily decline (about 20 percent in the Middle Roman period and about 16 percent in the Late Roman period). There were 40 percent fewer sherds dating to the Early Byzantine period (mid-fourth to mid-fifth centuries CE). In simpler terms, the survey teams found one sherd of the Late Byzantine period (mid-fifth to mid-seventh centuries) and none of the Early Islamic period (mid-seventh to mid-tenth centuries) (Strange, 2012). Field readings of pottery from excavations beginning in 2012 have largely borne out this initial picture with some refinements.[3]

The first hypothesis to explain the dramatic surge in the number of Early Roman sherds proposed two primary causes: a population increase coinciding with the resettlement of nearby Sepphoris when Herod Antipas rebuilt it in 4 BCE and the beginning of pottery production for regional distribution at around the same time. In Field I of the Shikhin Excavation Project, pottery manufacturing waste used to fill up a house's basement preserved some important data that require the reconsideration of that hypothesis.

In the surveys and first two seasons of excavation, as a point of reference to test in the field, the directors adopted the archaeological periods derived from the findings of the Meiron Excavation Project and adapted by the University of South Florida Excavations at Sepphoris: the working hypothesis was that the Early Roman period lasted from circa 37 BCE to circa 70 CE, or from the beginning of Herod's reign as a Roman client king to the Roman destruction of Jerusalem and the temple. For example, according to field readings, the lowest thirty buckets of pottery from the excavation of the fill in a house's basement contained sherds dating from the Late Hellenistic to the Early Roman period, with not a single sherd read in the field as later. This pottery included hundreds of wasters from pottery production. With no coins from the context to help refine the dating, the initial assessment assigned the production of this waste to sometime in the decades between 37 BCE and 70 CE. However, these thirty buckets of pottery waste also contained fragments of Herodian/knife-pared lamps and of Northern Darom lamps. Based on evidence first gathered in Judea, Varda Sussman, Eric Lapp, and other lychnologists (specialists in ancient lamps and lighting techniques) have been dating the production of Darom lamps between 70 and 135 CE, the ends of the two local wars with Rome, with some speculation that Darom lamp manufacture continued after 135 CE (Sussman, 1982:

16; Lapp, 2016: 5, Table 1). Accordingly, the evidence recovered from the pottery dump at Shikhin required either dating the beginning of Northern Darom lamp manufacturing earlier, before 70 CE, or extending the Early Roman period beyond 70 CE (Strange and Aviam, 2017).

Some clues suggest the latter solution. The most important is that many of the Northern Darom nozzles recovered from these buckets show no signs of use, as is the case with a very large, black fragment of a Herodian lamp from the same dump (Figure 8.6) (Strange and Aviam, 2017; Strange, n.d.). The lack of burning on so many lamp nozzles suggests that the lamp fragments are also from production waste. That conclusion is strengthened by the discovery of molds for making Northern Darom lamps at Shikhin and wasters of Northern Darom lamps. If Sussman and others are right that Northern Darom lamp manufacture in the Galilee followed the origin of the style in Judea, then Shikhin provides evidence that its potters continued to produce Early Roman period common pottery forms beyond 70 CE, perhaps because of Shikhin's close association with Sepphoris, which made peace with the Romans as war was breaking out in the Galilee (Meyers, 1999; Rapuano, 2013). Coins would help tremendously in shoring up this hypothesis; regrettably, none was found in that archaeological context.

The manufacture of Northern Darom lamps at Shikhin also suggests that Judeans migrated into the Galilee in the decades following the year 70 CE, and that some became involved in local industries. That involvement undoubtedly would have been complex, as Galilean social systems accommodated, as they were able, the arrival of new peoples. For example, there is some evidence that Shikhin's kilns manufactured and distributed lamps before 70 CE, in which case Judeans would have joined and expanded an existing industry.

As they developed their Northern Darom lamp production, Shikhin's artisans began producing another type of mold-made lamp, Sussman's "Northern undecorated" type (Sussman, 2012). The lamp resembles a knife-pared Herodian lamp that was formed in a mold rather than on a wheel (Figure 8.7). Even though the body and nozzle were formed as a unit in the mold, makers of Northern undecorated lamps also pared the nozzles as potters pared Herodian lamp nozzles after attaching them to the lamps' wheel-made bodies.

To my knowledge, currently no examples of Northern Darom lamps have been found outside of the Galilee. Accordingly, this undecorated type probably originated locally rather than in Judea. To make both Northern undecorated and Northern Darom lamps, Shikhin's potters carved molds into soft chalk. Many of the mold blanks were made from waste cores that craftspeople discarded after turning chalk "mugs" on a lathe; the cores were sawn down the center lengthwise to create blanks into which molds for upper and lower parts of lamps were carved.[4] Shikhin's lamp industry, therefore, was able to exploit another local industry: the manufacture of

Figure 8.6 Fragment of a large, unused knife-pared Herodian lamp found among waste from the manufacture of ceramics at Shikhin.

Source: Photo by Gabi Laron. Used with permission.

chalk mugs, which ostensibly enabled their users to maintain ritual purity (Strange and Aviam, 2017).

Not counting twelve examples from Shikhin, Anastasia Shapiro recently examined a small sample of twenty-two lamps and lamp fragments from six sites in the Galilee and one in the Golan: Yodefat (2), I'billin (6), Khirbet Wadi Ḥamam (4), Makberat B'not Ya'akov (2), Tel Rekhesh (1), Daburiyah (5), and Gamla (2) (Shapiro, 2017). She determined that, in her sample, four sites had a total of fourteen lamps made of clay from the vicinity of Shikhin. Knife-pared Herodian lamps made of this clay were found at Yodefat (one), I'billin (two), and Daburiyah (one). Northern undecorated lamps were found at I'billin (one) and Khirbet Wadi Ḥamam (one or two). Northern Darom lamps were found at I'billin (two or three) and Daburiyah (three or four).

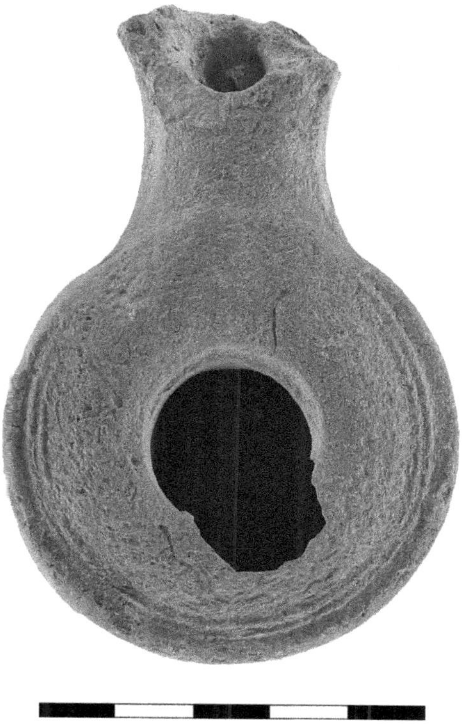

Figure 8.7 A Northern undecorated lamp.

Source: Photo by Gabi Laron. Used with permission.

It is reasonable conjecture that if her sample were larger, she would find more Galilean sites at which examples of these three types were manufactured from clay originating near Shikhin. That is work for the future.

Shapiro has also determined that a Hasmonean "pinched" lamp found in a pit beneath Shikhin's synagogue was made from local clays and that it was over-fired (Shapiro, 2017). This is an indication that lamps were made in the village between the late second century and mid-first century BCE. In combination with the evidence from I'billin and Daburiyah, the identification of the Herodian lamp at Yodefat suggests that before 70 CE, Shikhin's kilns had started producing knife-pared Herodian lamps for regional export. The manufacture of Herodian lamps could have continued after 70 CE, if the refusal of Sepphoris to join the revolt against Rome also meant that Shikhin—a village within Sepphoris's jurisdiction and a mere twenty-minute walk from the city—was also spared. The discovery of Northern undecorated and Northern Darom lamps at Galilean sites produced from clay that originated near Shikhin suggests that the industry continued to at least 135 CE, and perhaps closer to the mid-second century CE, as it is also difficult to detect the direct effects of the Bar Kokhba War in the Galilee (Khirbet Wadi Ḥamam is an exception; Leibner, 2018; Leibner and Bijovsky, 2013).

Shikhin's synagogue offers some further evidence to consider. Pottery and coins found in pits beneath its floor and pottery recovered from a section of one of its stylobates indicates that it was built no earlier than the late first century CE and maybe after 135 CE. Furthermore, it incorporated stones from an earlier public structure. The pitched roof of the latest synagogue was held aloft by Ionic columns built of drums varying in diameter between 63 and 67 centimeters.[5] That diameter allows us to estimate the height of the standing columns at between 5.67 and 6.03 meters, or between around 19 and 20 Roman feet.[6] It is possible that the building stretched over 18 meters in length.[7] The threshold in the façade accommodated a double-leafed doorway 1.58 meters wide, or a little over 5 Roman feet (Strange, 2015). Because of the coincidence with the making and distribution of molded lamps at Shikhin, it is tempting to associate the dismantling of an earlier public structure and the construction of a large synagogue with the arrival of Judean refugees, and as an expression of identity and piety that in part responded to the calamity of 70 CE. Admittedly, this coincidence does not require causation as an explanation.

Returning for a moment to the common decorations on Northern Darom lamps, and to lamps and lamp fragments found at Shikhin, it should be noted that in Judea and the Galilee, aside from decorations on the shoulder, the shape of the lamp itself, with its distinctive bow- or axe-shaped nozzle and a pair of "wings" where the nozzle meets the body (Figures 8.4 and 8.5), is probably a marker of Jewish identity. (This is less assured with the similar style of lamps found at the more cosmopolitan Beth-She'an/Scythopolis, but it may be the case there as well.) If so, then the lamp itself offers evidence of refugee migration, for it appears to emerge in the aftermath of the catastrophe of the temple's loss, and its first appearance in Judea (so far as we know), presumably followed shortly by appearances just south of the Galilee in western Decapolis (Beth-She'an) and Lower Galilee, suggests that people leaving Judea brought the lamp and the technology for making it with them.

More data are certainly required in order to reach firm conclusions. We can, however, say that without the evidence of the manufacture and distribution of Northern Darom lamps at Shikhin, the expansion of Shikhin's pottery industry in the late first century CE need not point to the arrival of Judean refugees. The manufacture of Darom-style lamps, however, is the clearest suggestion that we are seeing evidence of refugee migration, even if the population of refugees was relatively small, for it is easier to explain that in the decade or so following 70 CE, during what were likely increased hardships in Judea, Judeans moved northward into a region with a strong cultural compatibility. That Galilean Jews traveled to war-ravaged Judea and returned with a new style of lamp and the technology for making it, or that northerners introduced the lamp type in the south, are more complicated explanations than the data require.

How to test the hypothesis? First, one possibility is to compare pottery from the thirty buckets at Shikhin that contained Early Roman period pottery, knife-pared Herodian lamps, and Northern Darom lamps with pottery recovered at sites destroyed in the late 60s by Romans, such as Yodefat, Magdala, and Gamla, particularly pottery from destruction layers. That comparison may enable us to detect morphological changes in pottery that we can assign to an Early Roman 2 or Middle Roman 1 period at Shikhin and other sites: the period between 70 and 135 CE or so. Second, we can reevaluate the Early (37 BCE–70 CE) and Middle Roman (70–250 CE) strata at other sites, looking for similar evidence of population growth and new industries at that horizon. If the hypothesis about what happened at Shikhin is correct, then even if it were limited, refugee migration and settlement may have happened in similar ways at other Galilean villages. Third, we can reexamine Early Roman pottery manufacture and distribution at Kefar Ḥananya, asking if the industry's flourishing can be tied to the same period: 70 to 135 CE or later. Finally, at these sites we can look for sealed deposits from foundation trenches and beneath floors where pottery, lamp fragments, and coins might allow us to date construction to the late first or early second century CE. As at Shikhin, new construction, especially of public buildings, may corroborate other data from the site that suggest the settlement and integration of Judean refugees. The sum of evidence from many sites will permit the inference that we are seeing the phenomena associated with Cernea's Impoverishment Risks and Reconstruction model, such as joblessness (evident in the creation of Shikhin's lamp industry or its expansion of one that existed), homelessness (visible in construction of new homes in whose courtyards the levigating of clay, throwing and molding of lamps, and firing took place), and access to common property assets (such as chalk vessel waste material for the molds).

Conclusion

Literary and material evidence does not support a claim that the destruction of Jerusalem and the war in Judea displaced large numbers of refugees that Richmond would rank on the reactive end of his continuum. The movement of some Judean refugees on the proactive end of the continuum—perhaps an extended family of lamp and mold craftspeople—into the Galilee provides a plausible explanation for the expansion of Shikhin's lamp-making industry in the late first century CE. That industry produced a variation of a lamp form that apparently originated in Judea: the so-called Northern Darom lamp. A much larger population of refugee families no doubt came after 135 CE, although it should be noted that we have similar challenges in identifying material evidence of these people.

If the hypothesis presented here is correct, the site of Shikhin and its environs in Lower Galilee—the territory controlled by Sepphoris—shows how some refugees were able to integrate into various social systems, including the manufacture and distribution of goods regionally, and by extension into other systems, such as kinship, religious practice, education, and social ranking. Presumably, when various factors in Jerusalem or in the region of Judea created a social system that no longer provided for the biological, economic, and social needs of these people, they traveled to a region that offered a high degree of cultural compatibility: a host society sharing with Judea the cultural expressions of language, values, traditions, lifestyle, religion, political views, and food habits. There is no need to paint Judeans and Galileans as indistinguishable, or to brush away challenges to integration that Judeans might have faced, in order to anticipate that the cultural similarities between the new arrivals and the host society eased the transition of some. We should also anticipate that a lack of some advantages, such as skill in a trade, the possession of wealth, high social status, or a combination of these and other traits, hampered the integration of others.

Notes

1. I thank Mordechai Aviam and Uzi Leibner for this insight.
2. I am indebted to Yeshu Dray for this insight.
3. For example, the excavation has recovered a few Late Bronze period sherds along with some evidence of a decrease in population in the Persian period and a possible period of abandonment in the third century CE. Furthermore, excavations began to turn up a very few Islamic sherds, together with some Islamic lamps and lamp fragments. The current explanation for the appearance of Islamic forms is that local farmers from Sepphoris or other nearby towns left them while cultivating Shikhin's hilltop.
4. Until sometime in 2018 or 2019, one could find many such discarded cores at two Galilean chalk vessel manufacturing sites, one about a kilometer south of Reina on Highway 754 and the other within the town of Reina itself. When Yeshu Dray took me to see these sites in June 2019, the one on Highway 754 had been bulldozed, and the one within Reina proper was being covered by a modern construction dump.
5. These measurements were made in the field in 2019.
6. The estimate is based on a factor of height = 1 diameter × 9.
7. The building is not oriented north to south; rather, the southeastern exterior wall, containing a central threshold, faces around 30 degrees south of west.

Bibliography

Adler, Noam. 2004. *Oil Lamps of the Holy Land: The Adler Collection*. Jerusalem: Ruth and Stephen Adler.

Aviam, Mordechai. 2015. "Yodefat-Jotapata: A Jewish Galilean Town at the End of the Second Temple Period." Pages 109–26 in *The Archaeological Record from Cities, Towns, and Villages*. Vol. 2 of *Galilee in the Late Second Temple and Mishnaic Periods*. Edited by David A. Fiensy and James Riley Strange. Minneapolis: Fortress.

Avi-Yonah, Michael. 1962. "A List of Priestly Courses from Caesarea." *Israel Exploration Journal* 12, no. 2: 137–9.

———. 1964. "The Caesarea Inscription of the Twenty-Four Priestly Courses." Pages 46–57 in *The Teacher's Yoke: Essays in Memory of Henry Trantham*. Edited by E. Jerry Vardaman and James L. Garrett Jr. Waco: Baylor University Press.

Berlin, Andrea. 2005. "Jewish Life before the Revolt: The Archaeological Evidence." *Journal for the Study of Judaism in the Persian, Hellenistic, and Roman Period* 36, no. 4: 417–70.

———. 2014. "Household Judaism." Pages 208–15 in *Life, Culture, and Society*. Vol. 1 of *Galilee in the Late Second Temple and Mishnaic Periods*. Edited by David A. Fiensy and James Riley Strange. Minneapolis: Fortress.

Burke, Aaron A. 2011. "An Anthropological Model for the Investigation of the Archaeology of Refugees in Iron Age Judah and Its Environs." Pages 41–56 in *Interpreting Exile: Interdisciplinary Studies of Displacement and Deportation in Biblical and Modern Contexts*. Edited by Brad E. Kelle, Frank R. Ames, and Jacob L. Wright. Ancient Israel and Its Literature 10. Atlanta: Society of Biblical Literature.

———. 2018. "Refugees in the Near East and Eastern Mediterranean, Archaeology of." Pages 1–6 in *Encyclopedia of Global Archaeology*. Edited by Claire Smith. New York: Springer.

Cernea, Michael. 2000. "Risks, Safeguards, and Reconstruction: A Model for Population Displacement and Resettlement." Pages 11–55 in *Risks and Reconstruction: Experiences of Resettlers and Refugees*. Edited by Michael M. Cernea and Chris McDowell. Washington, DC: World Bank.

Chataf, Ortal, and Joe Uziel. 2020. "Jerusalem, City of David: Preliminary Report." *Hadashot Arkheologiyot: Excavations and Surveys in Israel* 132. http://hadashot-esi.org.il/report_detail_eng.aspx?id=25841&mag_id=128.

Dagen, Reinar. 1973. "An Inscription of the Twenty-Four Priestly Courses from Yemen" [Hebrew]. *Tarbiz* 2/3: 302–3.

Damati, Emmanuel. 1999. "A Greek Inscription from a Mausoleum in Tiberias" [Hebrew]. *'Atiqot* 38: 91*–92*.

De León, Jason. 2013. "Undocumented Migration, Use Wear, and the Materiality of Habitual Suffering in the Sonoran Desert." *Journal of Material Culture* 18, no. 4: 231–45.

Driessen, Jan, ed. 2018. *An Archaeology of Forced Migration: Crisis-Induced Mobility and the Collapse of the 13th c. BCE Eastern Mediterranean*. Aegis 15. Leuven: Presses Universitaires.

Eshel, Hanan. 1992. "Fragments of an Inscription of the Twenty-Four Priestly Courses from Nazareth?" [Hebrew]. *Tarbiz* 61: 159–61.

Finegan, Jack 1992 *The Life of Jesus and the Beginning of the Early Church*. Rev. ed. Princeton: Princeton University Press.

Gutfeld, Oren. 2009. "Horbat Bet Loya." *Hadashot Arkheologiyot: Excavations and Surveys in Israel* 121. http://www.hadashot-esi.org.il/report_detail_eng.aspx?id=1065&mag_id=115.

Hachlili, Rachel. 2001. *The Menorah, the Ancient Seven-Armed Candelabrum: Origin, Form and Significance*. Leiden: Brill.

Israel Antiquities Authority. [2009]. "One of the Oldest Synagogues in the World Was Exposed at Migdal (9/13)." Israel Antiquities Authority Archive. http://www.antiquities.org.il/article_eng.aspx?module_id=&sec_id=25&subj_id=240&id=1601.

Israel Antiquities Authority. [2017]. "Engravings of a Seven-Branched Menorah and a Cross Were Discovered by Hikers in an Ancient Cistern in the Judean Shephelah." Israel Antiquities Authority Archive. http://www.antiquities.org.il/Article_eng.aspx?sec_id=25&subj_id=240&id=4242.

Israel, Yael, and Uri Avida. 1988. *Oil-Lamps from Eretz Israel: The Louis and Carmen Warschaw Collection at the Israel Museum Jerusalem*. Jerusalem: The Israel Museum.

Kaufman, Josef Chaim, and Robert Deutsch. 2012. *Haneroth Halalou: Ma collection d'anciennes lampes à huile d'Eretz Israël / My Collection of Ancient Oil Lamps from the Land of Israel*. Jaffa: Archaeological Center Publications.

Klein, Samuel. 1909. *Beiträge zur Geographie und Geschichte Galiläas*. Leipzig: Haupt.

———. 1923. *Neue Beiträge zur Geographie und Geschichte Galiäas*. Vienna: Menorah.

Kunz, Egon F. 1981. "Exile and Resettlement: Refugee Theory." *The International Migration Review* 15, nos. 1–2: 42–51.

Lapp, Eric C. 2016. *Sepphoris II: The Clay Lamps from Ancient Sepphoris; Light Use and Regional Interactions*. Winona Lake, IN: Eisenbrauns.

Leibner, Uzi. 2018. *Khirbet Wadi Ḥamam: A Roman Period Synagogue in the Lower Galilee*. Qedem Reports 13. Jerusalem: Israel Exploration Society.

Leibner, Uzi, and Gabriella Bijovsky. 2013. "Two Hoards from Khirbet Wadi Ḥamam and the Scope of the Bar Kokhba Revolt." *Israel Numismatic Research* 8: 109–34, pls. 29–30.

Magen, Izchak, Y. Tzionit, and O. Sirkis. 2004. "Khirbet Badd 'Isa—Qiryat Sefer." Pages 179–241 in *The Land of Benjamin*. Edited by Izchak Magen, D. T. Ariel, G. Bijovsky, Y. Tzionit, and O. Sirkis. Jerusalem: Israel Antiquities Authority.

Mendel-Geberovich, Anat, Ortal Chalaf, and Joe Uziel. 2020. "The People Behind the Stamps: A Newly-Found Group of Bullae and a Seal from the City of David, Jerusalem." *Bulletin of the American Schools of Oriental Research* 384: 159–82.

Meyers, Eric M. 1999. "Sepphoris on the Eve of the Great Revolt (67–68 C.E.): Archaeology and Josephus." Pages 109–23 in *Galilee through the Centuries: Confluence of Cultures*. Edited by Eric M. Meyers. Winona Lake, IN: Eisenbrauns.

Miller, Stuart S. 2007. "Priests, Purities, and the Jews of Galilee." Pages 375–402 in *Religion, Ethnicity and Identity in Ancient Galilee: A Region in Transition*. Edited by Jürgen Zangenberg, Harold W. Attridge, and Dale B. Martin. Wissenschaftliche Untersuchungen zum Neuen Testament 210. Tübingen: Mohr Siebeck.

Rapuano, Yehuda. 2013. "The Pottery of Judea between the First and Second Jewish Revolts." *Strata* 31: 57–102.

Reich, Ronny. 2014. "A Depiction of a Menorah Found near the Temple Mount and the Shape of Its Base." *Zeitschrift des Deutschen Palästina-Vereins* 130, no. 1: 96–101.

Richmond, Anthony H. 1988. "Sociological Theories of International Migration: The Case of Refugees." *Current Sociology* 36, no. 2: 7–26.

———. 1993. "Reactive Migration: Sociological Perspectives on Refugee Movements." *Journal of Refugee Studies* 6, no. 1: 7–24.

Shamir, Orit. 2018. "Textiles, Threads, and Cordage from the Cave of Letters: 2000–2001 Excavations." Pages 189–220 in *Dead Sea: New Discoveries in the Cave of Letters*. Edited by Philip Reeder, Richard A. Freund, Harry M. Jol, and Carl E. Savage. New York: Lang.

Shapiro, Anastasia. 2017. "A Petrographic Study of Roman Ceramic Oil Lamps." *Strata* 35: 101–14.

Shivti'el, Yinon. 2014. "The Use of Caves as Security Measures in the Early Roman Period in the Galilee: Cliff Settlements and Shelter Caves." *Caderno de Geografia* 24, no. 41: 77–85.

———. 2017. *Cliff Shelters and Hiding Complexes in the Galilee during the Early Roman Period*. Novum Testamentum et Orbis Antiquus, Series Archaeologica 6. Göttingen: Vandenhoeck & Ruprecht.

Stepanski, Yosef. 1999. "Two Mausoleums on the Fringe of the Roman Period Cemetery of Tiberias" [Hebrew]. *'Atiqot* 38: 73*–90*. English summary: 226–7.

Strange, James F., Dennis E. Groh, and Thomas R. W. Longstaff. 1994. "Excavations at Sepphoris: The Location and Identification of Shikhin Part I." *Israel Exploration Journal* 44, nos. 3–4: 216–27.

———. 1995. "Excavations at Sepphoris: The Location and Identification of Shikhin Part II; With a Contribution by David Adan-Bayewitz, Frank Asaro, Isadore Perlman and Helen V. Michel." *Israel Exploration Journal* 45, nos. 2–3: 171–87.

Strange, James Riley. n.d. "Shikhin Lamp Kiln." The Levantine Ceramics Project. https://www.levantineceramics.org/kilns/39-shikhin-lamp-kiln.

Strange, James Riley. 2012. "Shihin, Survey." *Hadashot Arkheologiyot: Excavations and Surveys in Israel* 124. http://www.hadashot-esi.org.il/report_detail_eng.aspx?id=2195.

———. 2015. "Kefar Shikhin." Pages 88–108 in *The Archaeological Evidence from Cities, Towns, and Villages*. Vol. 2 of *Galilee in the Late Second Temple and Mishnaic Periods*. Edited by David A. Fiensy and James Riley Strange. Minneapolis: Fortress.

Strange, James Riley, and Mordechai Aviam. 2017. "Shiḥin Excavation Project: Oil Lamp Production at Ancient Shiḥin." *Strata* 35: 63–99.

Sukenik, Eliezer. 1926. "Three Ancient Jewish Inscriptions from Eretz-Israel" [Hebrew]. *Zion* 1: 16–7.

Sussman, Varda. 1982 [orig. 1972, Hebrew]. *Ornamented Jewish Oil-Lamps from the Destruction of the Second Temple through the Bar-Kokhba Revolt*. Warminster: Israel Exploration Society.

———. 2012. *Roman Period Oil Lamps in the Holy Land: Collection of the Israel Antiquities Authority*. Biblical Archaeology Review International Series 2447. Oxford: Archaeopress.

———. 2017a. *Late Roman to Late Byzantine/Early Islamic Period Lamps in the Holy Land: The Collection of the Israel Antiquities Authority*. Oxford: Archaeopress.

———. 2017b. "The Palm Brand and *Lulav* Motifs on Oil Lamps from Antiquity." *Liber Annuus* 69 (2019): 395–440.

Tsafrir, Yoram, and Boaz Zissu. 2002. "A Hiding Complex at 'Ain-'Arrub in the Hebron Hills." Pages 7–36 in *Late-Antique Petra, Nile Festival Building at Sepphoris, Deir Qal'a Monastery, Khirbet Qana Village and Pilgrim Site, 'Ain-'Arrub Hiding Complex, and Other Studies*. Vol. 3 of *The Roman and Byzantine Near East*. Edited by J. H. Humphrey. Journal of Roman Archaeology Supplementary Series 49. Portsmouth, RI: Journal of Roman Archaeology.

Vardaman, E. Jerry. 1964. "Introduction to the Caesarea Inscription of the Twenty-Four Priestly Courses." Pages 42–3 in *The Teacher's Yoke: Essays in Memory of Henry Trantham*. Edited by E. Jerry Vardaman and James L. Garrett Jr. Waco: Baylor University Press.

Wassén, Cecilia. 2019. "Stepped Pools and Stone Vessels: Rethinking Jewish Purity Practices in Palestine." *Biblical Archaeology Review* 45, nos. 4–5: 52–8.

Yadin, Yigael. 1963. *The Finds from the Bar Kokhba Period in the Cave of Letters*. Jerusalem: Israel Exploration Society.

Zissu, Boaz, and Amir Ganor. 2009. "Horvat 'Ethri—A Jewish Village from the Second Temple Period and the Bar Kokhba Revolt in the Judean Foothills." *Journal of Jewish Studies* 60, no. 1: 90–136.

Epilogue

Jürgen K. Zangenberg

Introduction

Presumably, none of us likes to pay taxes, although we—as citizens of democratic states—all understand that public tasks decided upon by the majority have to be funded by all. Taxation implies and presupposes participation in the political process. Nobody knows this better than those citizens of colonial Boston who refused to pay taxes to a king who did not want them to take a share in his power over them—and rebelled.

In antiquity, taxes had different connotations and practical implications than today. Taxes were raised by various bodies on the imperial, provincial, and local levels; and there were not a few types of taxes, including taxes on property, goods, or the pure existence of a person (*caput*). Those who made decisions over taxation policies rarely shared their authority with those who were ruled. Rulers raised and eased taxes at will, manifesting themselves as benign or harsh leaders of their subjects. In a passage likely taken from Herod's friend and advisor Nicolaus of Damascus, Josephus still applauds Herod for easing taxes after a famine had struck Judea (*A.J.* 15.365).

For those who collected taxes on behalf of the government, they were an easy means of income, while those who had to pay them saw them as a most obvious sign of being oppressed. Very often, taxpayers were not allowed to share in power and decision-making processes in the Roman Empire and its predecessor states. But differences were great between various parts of the empire. In the East, for example, people were accustomed to being taxed, though not being happy with it.

Where Roman rule was extended to territories without any comparable system, however, the often chaotic and brutal mechanism of taxation and its no less violent consequences became evident in all its aspects. Let me give an example: When Varus took over the newly occupied regions east of the Rhine to form the new province of Germania, he reorganized the indigenous legal system by introducing Roman law as the only source to settle internal disputes, and he tried to transform traditional systems of economic exchange by introducing taxes (see Tacitus, *Ann.* 1.59.4–5: jurisdiction, taxes; Dio Cassius, *Hist. rom.* 56.18.3–4: jurisdiction, taxes; Florus, *Epit.* II 30:

jurisdiction; Velleius Paterculus, *Hist.* 2.117.2–4: jurisdiction, taxes). When Augustus took over the former core territory of Herod's kingdom, he had a census organized by the Syrian financial procurator Quirinius (Josephus, *A.J.* 18.1–2; Luke 2:1–2). Such a census not only counted the population to be entered into tax registers, but also established every inhabitant's legal status and property—a clear sign that Judea would from then on be more tightly connected to Roman rule, and its inhabitants taxed as provincials.

Most of these taxes, one needs to know, had to be paid in kind since Germanic society was not yet sufficiently monetized, which means that a large part of the surplus was no longer available for internal exchange of goods and to maintain social relations, but was channeled to the new masters of the land. Right from the beginning of provincialization, Rome deeply interfered in formerly decentrally organized social and economic affairs. Strict taxation was not only a demonstration of the victors' superiority; it was also used to break the last sparks of freedom and force the last dissenters into submission. Often this approach worked through sheer power and intimidation; in other cases, such demonstrations of authority backfired. Originally, the Frisians had been loyal to Rome thanks to Drusus's lenient, apparently more or less symbolic method of taxation. However, after offering their wives and children into bondage without receiving relief, they went into open rebellion in 28 CE when a subordinate officer charged with collecting the cowhides refused them because they were too small. The Romans sent the army to restore order but were defeated, and Frisia was lost to them for good (Tacitus, *Ann.* 4.72–73).

Being taxed as such was apparently considered acceptable if the system was based on mutual benefit (such as new opportunities for indigenous leaders) and respect. If that mutual benefit and respect is lacking, however, taxation becomes a symbol of lost freedom; and the taxed must then make a choice and ultimately decide on which side they want to stand. It is interesting to see how often the leaders of such rebellions have been in Roman service before (the Cheruscans Arminius and Segestes: Tacitus, *Ann.* 1.55–60, and Velleius Paterculus, *Hist.* 2.118.2; or the Frisian Cruptorix: Tacitus, *Ann.* 4.74). Taxation, therefore, has not only economic, but also sociopsychological implications.

These examples from the extreme northwest of the Roman Empire illustrate that motivations for and sentiments against taxation were generally not that different from what we know of those at the eastern end of the Mediterranean world, which is the primary focus of this volume. Let us therefore now turn to the book itself.

Assessment

Before the book delves into the details of regional taxation and resistance, John T. Fitzgerald introduces us to broad and lively ancient discussions about the legitimacy of taxation. In his programmatic article, Fitzgerald makes clear that two superior powers were the source of all taxation in the ancient world: the gods, represented by their priestly servants ("the temple"), and the kings with their palatial entourages ("the palace"). According to ancient ideology and practice, taxpayers and tax recipients were connected in a kind of "axis of reciprocity": in return for wealth, the superior powers will protect their subjects, showing how deeply influential models of economic exchange became for defining political and religious relationships. Fitzgerald's remarks are especially interesting because they show how deeply rooted both the acceptance of taxes was in the ancient world, and how great expectations were that people would receive something in return for their loyalty as taxpayers. This "axis" could break on either side: if taxes were not "returned" by care for the subjects, the willingness to pay them would decrease. And if taxes were refused, rulers would see themselves justified to extract by force what they considered their god-given right. It is therefore crucial to keep both expectations in balance to keep the system running, even if—as Fitzgerald rightly remarks—they always remained asymmetrical.

I am not sure, however, how far Fitzgerald's distinction between "tribute" and "taxation" is indeed helpful for the situation in antiquity. No other author in this volume seems to follow him.[1] The distinction between "falling within redistribution or outside of it" might be cut too much along modern lines, although Fitzgerald does have a point if one compares how classical Athens taxed its own citizens, on the one hand, and made its allies pay tributes, on the other. What does, however, characterize all systems of taxation and tribute is that they were "asymmetrical," giving those who wielded power over resources (wealth, military, access to gods) the decisive edge over those who did not, or only wielded such power occasionally. Though Athenians and Spartans differed in political outlook and values, they both sought to maintain control over their allies by either extracting money from them or, in the case of the latter, ensuring that pro-Spartan oligarchs stayed in power. Exacting money, therefore, is only another means of forcing subordinates to offer loyalty. Depriving the dependent partner of some of his material wealth by diverting it would limit his ability to make independent decisions that might go against the will of the superior. Taxation is clearly an instrument to rule over "insiders," while tributes fulfil the same goal regarding subordinate "outsiders."

It is therefore not surprising that Greek authors such as Isocrates or, more than five hundred years later, Aelius Aristides entered into lively and controversial discussions about which taxes or tributes were just and fair, and which might come close to or need to be called outright enslavement. When is resistance against tributes justified, and when is it rightly punished as insubordination? We can imagine that similar debates would take place in other cultures when some groups experienced taxation as too heavy or unjustified. While the reasons for such opposition might differ according to varying cultural identities across different regions of the Mediterranean, the criterion of "justness" seems to be a basic requirement. Taxation based only on sheer force is dangerous; demanding and paying taxes needs a commonly accepted ideological *Überbau* ("superstructure"). If the *Überbau* is broken, resistance is at hand, often in the name of an alternative, competing *Überbau*. I think we can assume, even reconstruct, similar discourses about just taxation to be accepted, and unjust taxation that ought to be resisted also in Judea before the outbreak of the First Revolt. Both Josephus (*A.J.* 18.4) and the New Testament (Mark 12:13–17 parr.) give valuable insights into the breadth of the debates and the various arguments that often resembled contemporary discourses in Roman literature on taxation as being a form of servitude (Tacitus, *Hist.* 4.59, 74; Valerius Maximus, *Mem.* 4.3.8, on Macedon). Jewish rebels not only killed the hated tax collectors, but also plundered oppressors and their sympathizers alike, to put their possessions to new use by either transforming them physically (coins with new inscriptions made from old silver) or integrating them functionally into their own households (defaced bronze jugs). Even here, plunder is not only robbery, but also a form of "reversed tribute," demonstrating that power relations have now turned against the oppressors, while the oppressed have become free.

Agnes Choi takes the "first look on the ground" in this book, using Ptolemaic and Roman Egypt, the "bread basket of the ancient world," as a case to analyze the mechanics of assessing and collecting taxes. Like no other region of Hellenistic and Roman antiquity, Egypt has provided us with very detailed, sometimes even personal, evidence in the form of thousands of documents on papyrus and other writing materials. These documents allow us to take a uniquely detailed look into not only the system of taxation, but also its social implications. For Choi, Egypt as "bread basket" does imply transporting grain to Rome, but it starts with how the grain was collected from the producers to be shipped elsewhere. In this process, Choi sees many specific roles and responsibilities of figures from both the rural, agrarian context and the urban context. The backbone of the Egyptian system was the tax farmer, a private entrepreneur who bought leases from the government that allowed him to collect the taxes from a particular village or area and reap benefit for himself from such a transaction. Often, the tax farmer would not collect the taxes himself, but do this via governmentally supervised collectors. Typically for Egypt, the taxes were assessed annually based on the size of the property and the extent of the Nile floods. The papyri allow fascinating insights into the complexity of the recording and assessment system involving several levels of local, district, and governmental officials such as scribes and supervisors, all designed to avoid fraud and secure an equally fair share of burden for all producers. While recording took place at the spot in the rural environment, local records were collected and assessed in the district capitals and later in Alexandria, where the final decisions were taken about the amount of tax to be raised in that particular year. In Egypt, the tax was paid in kind; that is, usually in wheat, more rarely in barley, by being collected from the harvest, either at the village threshing floor or later, at the granary in the town. Here the tax farmer came, claimed the officially allotted amount of grain (= taxes), paid the cultivator for it, and took his share of the grain and sold it at a higher price elsewhere; the rest remained with the cultivator. Choi rightly emphasizes how time consuming and labor intensive this process was. Tax farming apparently was not money easily made.

Could we perhaps go a step further? In the New Testament, we do hear about village scribes, and in Josephus about tax archives. Mostly, these scribes are perceived as safeguarding tradition and setting up and copying legal and religious documents. However, with the ability to read and write, and being versed in appropriate legal formulae, were at least some of these scribes not also able to measure fields and calculate the harvest to provide the basis for taxation? What would prevent us from combining the existence of village scribes with the existence of tax offices in the residential cities of Tiberias or Sepphoris? Choi clearly shows that the existence of scribes and tax offices only makes sense if both are considered elements of a joint rural-governmental administration. Of course, the New Testament does not mention such expertise when it talks about scribes, as it is not interested in correctly representing administrative details in general. The synoptic tradition shapes the scribes very much according to the needs of later Christian congregations, thereby creating hybrid figures with a strong emphasis on the preservation of Jesus traditions and a correspondingly reduced impulse for the accurate representation of details of the pre-revolt Galilean administration, which to them was either alien or a thing of the past. If such a scribe-tax record combination is acceptable, what would prevent us from adding a third player, the tax farmer (*publicanus*), who is also frequently mentioned in the synoptic tradition, to come close to a system that Choi is describing? How comparable are the situations in ancient Egypt and Palestine?

It is therefore very helpful that the following article by David B. Hollander focuses on just that system of tax farming by bringing Roman tax collectors into closer view, their "business concept"—and their poor reputation. While formally relatively low (around 10 percent according to Keith Hopkins), Roman taxes became high and a perceived burden both economically as well as psychologically. This was due not only to the entrepreneurs who acted as intermediaries between the Roman authorities who levied taxes per province, but also to the amount that each individual ultimately had to pay. So, there was a potentially high difference between "declared" and "effective" tax rates. The former almost remains an only theoretical item, while the latter is difficult to calculate because it depends upon many local factors. Effective tax is a product not only of governmental decisions, but also of the private desire to create revenue. Apart from that, Hollander rightly reminds us of several uncertainties and emphasizes that "the level of Roman taxation might never be resolved to everyone's satisfaction" (p. 61). Regarding Palestine, it is evident that in addition to governmental taxes and fees, there also were various other tributes to be paid to religious authorities, at least if one belonged to a Jewish family (tithes, temple tax). The financial burden might, in fact, therefore have been higher in Judea than in many other parts of the empire (a topic that G. Anthony Keddie later takes up in his essay). Rightly refraining from coming up with quantitative statements about Roman taxes, Hollander nevertheless mentions three factors that need to be taken into consideration when analyzing people's responses to taxation: "The Roman tax system was routinely opaque," "Roman taxes were perversely inconsistent," and "Roman taxes were flagrantly unfair." Rejection of taxation might have been aggravated by the unequal distribution of benefits and revenues officials drew from taxation (how much was returned?) and the arbitrary distribution of privileges (for citizens or certain priests), and subsidies that had more the character of spontaneous favors than of support people could rightly claim and count on. Accountability was certainly not a strength of the Roman administration, so people could rightly feel fleeced. What responses did such unpredictability create on the side of the taxpayers? How much aggression did it arouse when people felt cheated about their taxes by someone whose sumptuous way of life was a direct result of others being exploited? In any case, the New Testament is a telling witness of how strongly tax collectors as individuals were despised by the population and how much people desired the entire system to stop (examples of repentant tax collectors). Resistance against tax collectors, however, is no in-principle rejection of taxes.

G. Anthony Keddie takes up the issue of Roman provincial censuses and analyzes their sociopolitical implications. Carrying out a census, he rightly argues, is much more than simply writing up lists of how much property somebody possesses to later take some of it away. According to Keddie, censuses *construct* and *regulate*: they draw lines between members of communities and lump others together; they define and record legal, ethnic, and social status. In short, they first create what they later charge: provincial subjects. The situation in Judea, of course, was different than the one I touched on above regarding Germania. Unlike the Cheruscans, who had, according to our ancient sources, so far enjoyed freedom and independence and had not known taxes, the Judeans had been subject to priests and kings for generations and were accustomed to giving away some of their property to God and throne. While the census symbolized the transition from freedom to subjection for the Cheruscans, what did it mean for the Judeans? What more did the transition from Herod to Augustus and his governor mean than the shift from one lord to another? Did the Romans not only change the administration and introduce new and more effective agents, but also establish new taxes (land tax in addition to traditional capitation tax)? In Egypt, the Romans apparently did; so also in Judea? Perhaps not. Much more important than a means to raise money, the census enabled the Romans to make Judea part of their empire. They added a whole new layer on top of the existing societal pyramid: Roman citizens. There might not yet have been many of them, but their sheer existence automatically relegated the previous, mostly indigenous elites to second rank. Roman citizens were exempt from taxes that others had to pay, enjoyed a much higher degree of political participation than noncitizens, and enjoyed various other public and economic privileges. Former elites could, but did not automatically, receive equal status with Roman citizens, but this required the effort of loyalty. Next to this, a census defined and recorded not only legal differences between citizens and noncitizens or pertaining to material wealth, but tax registers also often recorded the physical characteristics of every single member of a household. In the end, a tax official needed to be able to identify and count every family member to check if taxes had correctly been paid in the past and, if necessary, to correct the bill. Evading these procedures would not only make a person (i.e., usually the father of the house) liable to punishment, it would also jeopardize other civil rights; for example, making an inheritance and thereby providing for the next generation. By recording physical appearance, marital and social status, property and children, and so on, the census not only turned an occupied or annexed territory into an area of *Roman* exertion of power, it also populated this provincial area with subjects under a new elite. It might have been just this redefinition of people and their identities, of elements that still counted and other that did not, which may have made people the most aware of what they had lost: self-determination.

There are several examples in ancient literature that describe what happens when resentment turns into resistance and outright revolt. Among them, Flavius Josephus's account is certainly the most detailed and dramatic. In his article, Mordechai Aviam adds the archaeological story and describes what we know about the most important sites in the Galilee before, immediately preceding the Roman onslaught, and after it. He concludes that despite large losses of life and devastation of property, the Galilee recovered quickly. I am not so sure about this. Much, of course, depends on the quality of our evidence; that is, of properly dated, documented, and published excavation and survey results. Aviam is right to point out that most of what we have as evidence for destruction comes from Yodefat and Gamla. The picture here is indeed dramatic, well dated, and very detailed.

There are, of course, sites that do not show any evidence of destruction, like the big Decapolis or coastal cities in the periphery of the Galilee, but these did not take part in the revolt and were therefore not affected by Roman punitive actions—as was Sepphoris, which, although a predominantly Jewish city, remained loyal to the Romans, as well. From other sites that did play a role in the war, like Magdala or Tiberias, no evidence of destruction has apparently come to light and been published, though Yizhar Hirschfeld was able to excavate a small part of an early first-century CE palatial house that was covered by a destruction layer containing pottery that suggests a fire at around the time of the revolt. Unfortunately, the evidence has not been published yet. Evidence from excavations at Magdala is inconclusive (especially the dating of the various synagogue phases) since neither pottery nor stratigraphic scenarios have been published. Aviam's scenario that the synagogue was blocked during Magdala's preparation for war and remained out of use afterwards is certainly attractive, but cannot be considered proven. No destruction of 67 CE was observed in the Franciscan part of the town, nor was any documented in Capernaum. Here, too, we still lack detailed stratigraphic documentation, so the last word might not have been spoken on these sites. Aviam rightly states that there was no long fighting in Magdala because the rebels retreated out onto the water and were defeated there.

Leaving Tiberias and Magdala out of the picture, the destruction and depopulation of Yodefat and Gamla do resemble the devastating destruction that Jerusalem had to bear. With their fortifications and their function as regional centers, Yodefat and Gamla certainly attracted many refugees and rebel soldiers who hoped to put up a stand against the Romans. Apart from purging rebel nests in caves in mountainous areas, the entire destruction of all villages was not necessary. It was enough for the Romans to encircle as many rebels as possible in Yodefat and Gamla, which they successfully achieved, and then move on to Jerusalem and encircle the rest of the Galilean rebels and their Judean brothers-in-arms there. I cannot imagine that the Galilee recovered quickly. As I have said, our evidence from the Galilee does suggest massive destruction at rebel concentrations with high loss of life and wide-scale purges in the surrounding areas. The effects of this policy must have been devastating for the local population. Moreover, one needs to ask if we have enough evidence from the immediately post-67 CE period to propose any sort of direct continuity. Tel Rekhesh is indeed an interesting site, but it is so far the only one where such continuity can apparently be observed. Other sites, like Capernaum, with its large-scale excavations, do not show signs of a violent break of habitation; however, this does not mean that life continued peacefully.

Thus, in the end, the impact indeed appears dramatic only at the sites that Aviam considers exceptions. So, should we not better take Aviam's exceptions—Yodefat, Gamla, and Magdala—as evidence for the rule, not necessarily for a uniform Roman way of military action, but for the devastating effects that Vespasian's campaign had? Tel Rekhesh might then be symptomatic of the fact that the Romans did not need to destroy every single village because they had already achieved their goals through the spectacular victories at fortified bastions like Yodefat and Gamla.

For many years, the village/town identified as Khirbet Qana has proved one of the key sites in contemporaneous Galilean archaeology. C. Thomas McCollough has been involved in its excavation for many years and zooms in on that site. Such detailed work "on the micro level," as McCollough calls it, makes a lot of sense, since—despite huge progress in Galilean archaeology in general—we are still far away from broad conclusions. Often enough, if one looks on the ground, things suddenly become blurry and murky.

Khirbet Qana is one of the few sites with well-documented post-70 CE structures, and so could fill the gap that Aviam's survey article left when it comes to questions of continuity before and after the revolt. McCollough is especially interested in patterns of economic behavior and recognizes signs of significant change after 70 CE that reflect a complex response to colonization, including both accommodation and resistance. But the picture that McCollough presents can only insufficiently be expressed by the term "continuity"; it is more than that. Through the influx of "assets" (McCollough mentions both population and wealth) into the Galilee, the formerly isolated village became more connected to transregional trade and industry. Next to all "continuity," there is also a lot of "new beginning." Were there new immigrants from the south who filled the gaps that the many victims of the revolt had left? In any case, in spite of only giving in to "market dynamics," Cana engaged in selective and opportunistic behavior by combining economically feasible activities with a "nonquantifiable 'spirit' of resistance to the values and mores of the dominant power" (p. 114). The fact that villagers were able to make choices, develop a hybrid stance towards the ruling power, Rome, and find a new place between adaptation and resistance suggests that times had really changed after two revolts with bloody consequences for both sides. Apparently, more local autonomy was granted that led towards an undeclared symbiosis between Roman authorities and local Jewish dignitaries. On the basis of only archaeological evidence, we cannot know who exactly initiated and organized these changes. But McCollough gives us an important hint by mentioning a house close to the synagogue, larger than other dwellings, which might have been inhabited by a priestly, certainly local, elite family (p. 118). Did these people come from Jerusalem after the revolts or were they descendants of the pre-70 CE indigenous regional elites? We can find traces of local societal differentiation even before 70 CE not only in the larger cities like Sepphoris and Magdala, but also in more traditional local centers such as Yodefat (e.g., the "painted house"; see Aviam above). Not only in Jewish Galilee, these local elites were often the motor of innovation and inculturation. Later, they became crucial as sponsors of synagogues and local leaders behind the intellectually oriented rabbis. It is very likely that all this proceeded without any active intervention by Roman authorities, who had no intention of interfering in local affairs as long as things ran smoothly. Did this new balance between rulers and ruled have effects on taxation? Did the local elites receive privileges (like Hollander mentions), and did they feel that they should utilize their socially prominent positions not only to carry out their elite tasks of "home rule" but also to safeguard the stability of the area for Rome? I could well imagine that there was—despite all cultural barriers and religiously inspired taboos—some kind of mutual respect, common among Mediterranean elites, which made collaboration possible. As long as stability was guaranteed, these local elites were free to handle their internal affairs according to their own traditions and had all opportunity to further develop their Jewish identity, like dietary and purity laws. Refusing to participate in certain activities popular with the dominant culture was not considered an offense or a sign of insubordination. It almost seems that there were only winners in such bright times!

It is therefore fortuitous that David A. Fiensy deliberately takes a look at the "dark side" of Galilean life (to modify a popular Monty Python theme). Who sat there? Was it the notorious "social bandits" who have been haunting research for several decades? Fiensy challenges that idea and bluntly disconnects poverty from socially deviant behavior. According to him, social banditry was a common and ubiquitous phenomenon in the Roman Mediterranean, and there were many reasons for somebody to leave home and "go into the wilderness" and lead a life as a "bandit." To Fiensy, all comes down to a basic value system culminating in the dictum "if one can gain power, one should" (p. 126). Opportunities, apparently, make "bandits," and these opportunities may differ radically with respect to region and social situation. Banditry might not always be an indication of economic hardship and political instability. In that sense, I agree with Fiensy. Regarding first-century CE Galilee, one might even consider if the relative prosperity during the early first century CE might not have had a paradoxical effect on society. Economic prosperity (although unequally distributed) might have led to a growth in population, but since resources (available land and opportunities to earn money, both of which allowed one to create one's own household) were not growing at the same pace, people were marginalized and had no other choice than to organize their existence outside of society. That these groups did not cut all ties to mainstream society, that many of them sought to base their movements and way of life in religious motives and nonconformism, and that some even tried to establish a counter-society with hierarchies and power struggles does not speak against the broader picture, but is part of it. "Social bandits" are notoriously diverse. Their existence is not the product of a common ideology (though some eagerly saw themselves along such lines), and social banditry might not be an indication of a generally impoverished and socially fragile society, but its presence could reveal that the seed of social conflict and eventual collapse is already inherent even in an apparently affluent society.

In the final essay, James Riley Strange brings a group of people back onto the agenda that has not received sufficient attention: refugees who fled north from devastated Judea to the Galilee after 70 CE; in our jargon probably more accurately termed "internally displaced persons." These newcomers, Strange claims, can be contoured with the help of archaeology. Although Judeans and Galileans shared almost all aspects of material culture, a certain lamp type appeared after 70 CE in the Galilee that has a distinctly "southern" pedigree. Strange himself leads excavations at Shikhin, a rural site close to the regional center of Sepphoris where these lamps were not only sold and used, but also produced. So these (admittedly rare) southern influences are not simply a result of *transporting* the goods up north through trade, but rather that the people themselves, who liked and made these objects, had *come* up north. One may wonder, however, if such a small segment of material culture like certain (not all!) lamp types provides a sufficient basis for Strange's rather far-reaching hypothesis. In a way, however, Strange's ideas are attractive because they partly answer the question of how the Galilee was so quickly repopulated that it seems like a continuity to us (see my comments on Aviam's article), and he may also help us pin down the new, upcoming elite that McCullough discusses by a potential element of their material culture. One should not forget that new developments rarely start with a bang, but with a whisper. Only future research will show if and how the whisper grew into a fully resounding choir.

Conclusions

All things considered, this is a refreshingly diverse "down-to-earth" volume. Of course, theory (economic, social) does play a role in more or less all articles, but opinions about how to theoretically describe economy and taxation in ancient Galilee and beyond are certainly not in the foreground. Wherever they are discussed, they never diverge so much that dialogue becomes impossible because general approaches to the phenomena are incompatible. Some readers might of course deplore what they diagnose as "lack of theory." But in the end, the wealth of detail and evidence "from the ground" is necessary in order to be able to move forward towards developing a new, refined model for the ancient Galilean economy. We still know too little about everyday life, so any progress on individual sites and all aspects of material culture is very much appreciated. I personally believe that the hermeneutical helix from data to theory and back needs to move "from the bottom up." This volume offers tremendous help, many data, and challenging observations to walk the helix.

The downside of such a grassroots approach, however, is that the wealth of data and observations that each essay offers to us, often stands alone by itself. It is not that these essays are in any way "isolated." They do, however, require that the readers to do a lot of synthetical thinking by themselves. The "unity" that the Mediterranean world constituted in all its diversity might sometimes not sufficiently come to the fore among the various articles. How can I relate, for example, data from classical Athens to observations about early Roman Egypt in a way that helps me better understand post-70 CE Galilee? Who helps me, the reader, sail the murky waters between all those beautiful islands? How can I reach one island from the other without losing my way? To a certain extent, the diversification evident in this volume is a product of the way each author worked on his or her respective article. Most of the articles go back to papers held at a conference where participants were able to hear what colleagues presented, and communication ensued. These articles did not originate in isolation. But what came later? Apart from the editors, I may have been the only person in the privileged position to look at each island from above and realize the vast sea between them all. Does it mean that I have a suitable map to be able to connect them? No! Perhaps there is none—yet. Perhaps there may be one in the future? It should be a rewarding challenge for all those distinguished contributors to this book and beyond to take on the next step and to consider how such a map could look. Thanks to this book, we see many beautiful islands more clearly than before; let us see if we can bring them together and put them on a map—as hypothetical as this may be.

Note

1. Editors' note: The distinction between taxation and tribute is also utilized in the Introduction to this volume (pp. 2–3); thus, Fitzgerald is not the only writer in the volume to make this distinction. The editors note, however, that the Introduction had not yet been written when Jürgen Zangenberg wrote the Epilogue, thus preventing him from taking it into account.

Index of Primary Sources

Prepared by Agnes Choi

Index of Subjects

Prepared by Agnes Choi

For Product Safety Concerns and Information please contact our EU
representative GPSR@taylorandfrancis.com
Taylor & Francis Verlag GmbH, Kaufingerstraße 24, 80331 München, Germany

www.ingramcontent.com/pod-product-compliance
Ingram Content Group UK Ltd.
Pitfield, Milton Keynes, MK11 3LW, UK
UKHW020004200926
475702UK00015B/2473
* 9 7 8 1 0 3 2 2 6 4 2 2 6 *